DATE DUE

DE 19 01			
JY 28 09			

DEMCO 38-296

Historical Nightmares and Imaginative Violence in American Women's Writings

Recent Titles in
Contributions in Women's Studies

"Some Appointed Work to Do": Women and Vocation in the Fiction of
Elizabeth Gaskell
Robin B. Colby

Women, Politics, and the United Nations
Anne Winslow, editor

Envisioning the New Adam: Empathic Portraits of Men by American Women Writers
Patricia Ellen Martin Daly, editor

Before Equal Suffrage: Women in Partisan Politics from Colonial Times to 1920
Robert J. Dinkin

"Nobody Wants to Hear Our Truth": Homeless Women and Theories of the
Welfare State
Meredith L. Ralston

Spanish Women in the Golden Age: Images and Realities
Magdalena S. Sánchez and Alain Saint-Saëns

Russian Women in Politics and Society
Wilma Rule and Norma Noonan, editors

New Perspectives on Margaret Laurence: Poetic Narrative, Multiculturalism, and
Feminism
Greta M. K. McCormick Coger, editor

Women Shapeshifters: Transforming the Contemporary Novel
Thelma J. Shinn

Petticoats and White Feathers: Gender Conformity, Race, the Progressive Peace
Movement, and the Debate Over War, 1895–1919
Erika A. Kuhlman

With Her in Ourland: Sequel to *Herland*
Charlotte Perkins Gilman
Edited by Mary Jo Deegan and Michael R. Hill

(Un)Doing the Missionary Position: Gender Asymmetry in Contemporary Asian
American Women's Writing
Phillipa Kafka

Historical Nightmares and Imaginative Violence in American Women's Writings

Amy S. Gottfried

Contributions in Women's Studies, Number 163

GREENWOOD PRESS
Westport, Connecticut • London

Library of Congress Cataloging-in-Publication Data

Gottfried, Amy S., 1960–
    Historical nightmares and imaginative violence in American women's
writings / Amy S. Gottfried.
        p.   cm.—(Contributions in women's studies, ISSN 0147–104X ;
no. 163)
    Includes bibliographical references and index.
    ISBN 0–313–30160–3 (alk. paper)
    1. American fiction—Women authors—History and criticism.
2. Violence in literature.   3. Historical fiction, American—History
and criticism.   4. Postmodernism (Literature)—United States.
5. Literature and history—United States.   6. Women and literature—
United States.   7. Nightmares in literature.   8. Victims in
literature.   I. Title.   II. Series.
PS374.V58G68   1998
813′.5409353—DC21   97–39722

British Library Cataloguing in Publication Data is available.

Library of Congress Catalog Card Number: 97–39722
ISBN: 0–313–30160–3
ISSN: 0147–104X

First published in 1998

Greenwood Press, 88 Post Road West, Westport, CT 06881
An imprint of Greenwood Publishing Group, Inc.

Printed in the United States of America

The paper used in this book complies with the
Permanent Paper Standard issued by the National
Information Standards Organization (Z39.48–1984).

10 9 8 7 6 5 4 3 2

In memory of my parents, Ruth and Norman Gottfried,
who knew how to tell a good story,
and for Vince, who knows the importance of living one

Contents

Acknowledgments

My shaping of this book has been eased along by several people whose forbearance and willing help leave me always and happily indebted to them. In its first incarnation as doctoral thesis, this study was directed by Elizabeth Ammons, whose tough-mindedness is matched only by her generosity of time and spirit. I owe thanks also to Bette Mandl, for her abundant support and her good heart; to Trudy Christine Palmer, for her keen insight and her constant kindness; and to Jane Hosie-Bounar, for fifteen years of inestimable friendship and for her computer knowledge (not to mention her patience with my lack thereof). To my husband, Vince Kohl, who never let me forget how lucky I am to teach and write for a living, and whose love, humor, and intellectual rigor have been a godsend to me, I owe more than I can say here, or ever.

There are also quite a few people whose friendship and kitchen-table conversations helped me navigate this project in more and less tangible ways. They include Ariel Balter, Carl Beckman, Khaled Bounar, Barbara Burtness, Carole Doreski, Sara Eddy, Julie Gottfried, Kingston Heath, Deborah Horvitz, Susan Hubbard, Jill Jones and Rob Solomon, Ann Knickerbocker and Charley Tarlton, Jim Lindsay and Laurie Hussey, Thomas and Leslie Moore, Shirley Peterson and Gordon Crock, Jeanne Smith, and Karen Schneiderman. Over the years, my students at Suffolk, Tufts, and Boston Universities have been eager and challenging audiences for some of the earliest ideas in this book, and I only hope that I have put into practice at least some of what I have taught them about writing. Scholarship is not a solo journey, and for that, I am infinitely grateful.

Tell all the Truth but tell it slant—
Success in Circuit lies
Too bright for our infirm Delight
The Truth's superb surprise
                    —Emily Dickinson

Some words live in my throat
breeding like adders
others
know sun
seeking like gypsies
over my tongue
to explode through my lips
like young sparrows
bursting from shell.

Some words
bedevil me.
                    —Audre Lorde, "Coal"

Chapter 1

Private Stories Rendered Public: An Introduction

It seems a bit strange that the words of poets, rather than fiction writers, should provide the epigraphs for a study of fiction about violent revelations, an irony perhaps intensified by the identity of the first poet, a nineteenth-century American woman noted for her privacy. Yet Emily Dickinson's "Tell all the Truth but tell it slant" does offer an apt jumping-off point for a discussion of contemporary American women authors' narrative strategies. Questioning the parameters of privacy for both teller and listener, a significant number of novels written within the past twenty years explore how ignored or suppressed moments of violence catalyze the reclamation of national and personal histories. Additionally, because these narratives are informed by a postmodern impulse, they are also marked by a disruption of received histories and ways of knowing the world. Audre Lorde's "Coal" speaks to the rhetorical and epistemological violence necessarily inherent in such disruption and to the urgency of that reclamation.

Before I can explain the particularities of Dickinson and Lorde's connections to this book, I should clarify a few of its dimensions and limits. What began as a study focusing on contemporary American writing has gradually become a study of challenges to received narrative structures, mainly in terms of gender, nationality, and race. While the specific books I discuss here are all written by U. S. authors, I have become more interested in seeing how these works offer variations on and revisions of what Rosemary

Hennessy has called "the master narratives of western knowledge" (1). What intrigues me is the recurring, and shape-shifting, trope of violence in all these narratives. An equally important consideration is the authors' sex: what might it mean for a woman, traditionally a victim of violence in Western culture, to wield and in essence re-create violence in her own work? Such a creative enterprise is obviously risky, and not simply because it must in some part rely on the very master narrative of violence it seeks to revise or even transcend. Pitfalls include the treacherous lure of violence itself, as well as the potential lapse back into now-over familiar, perhaps even tedious, re-capitulations of victimization and resentment, and thus re-inscriptions of powerlessness. Indeed, the circulation of guilt, anger, and blame (or, in at least one case, the absence of such a circulation) is integral to each of the narrative structures I am examining: Gayl Jones's *Corregidora* (1975), Marilynne Robinson's *Housekeeping* (1980), Toni Morrison's *Beloved* (1987), Cynthia Ozick's *The Shawl* (1989), and Leslie Marmon Silko's *Almanac of the Dead* (1991). Although these are all contemporary novels, their various uses of and their need for violence in their narratives may be more understandable when we remember the initial general response to the literary naturalists early in this century, who were accused of "thrusting into sight everywhere the foulnesses that are better ignored" (*Literary History of the United States* 825; qtd. in Jones, *Liberating* 185).

In arguing that women writers have a particularized relationship to violence, I do not want to claim that only women may write about violence and brutality in a certain way. Fictional narrative is, above all other things, a leap of imaginative faith that, when successful, allows the writer to think and move in a created world that transcends stereotypically imposed limitations of gender (as well as of class, race, and sexual orientation).[1] No one group can or should corner the imaginative market. Having said this, I still want to emphasize that there is a genre of contemporary narrative written by women whose use of violence may be read in a certain way. My emphasis here and throughout, as I hope this book makes clear, is on a different relationship to received narratives and histories that, apart from the past few decades, have been told predominantly by men.[2] My aim in this study is not to explore differences between the ways in which women and men "write" violence. Neither is it to stake a claim for women's ability to write violence, despite the provocative comments of editors like Rust Hills, who in his 1980 *Writing in General and the Short Story in Particular* contrasted the writing of men (adventure, sports, crime, and fantasy) with that of "ladies" ("soupy, romantic") (1).[3] Surely, as Susan Hubbard has written, "the developed imagination transcends gender" (5). My purpose in deliberately isolating the works of contemporary women is to illuminate the ways in which their relationship to violence in reclaimed and retold histories differs from that of men. Women have been writing about violence in the United States since the publication of this country's first popular work, Mary Rowlandson's 1682 *The Soveraignty and Goodness of God*, which I discuss in the next chapter.

A melding of adventure tale and Puritan exemplary biography, Rowlandson's narrative raises several issues pertinent to a discussion of contemporary literature's wielding of violence: the creation of a national narrative, particularly regarding people's relationship to their landscape; the ideologies and myths necessary for the forging of a national identity; and the conflicts inherent in a narrative that speaks of motherhood, victimization, and survival.

Perhaps because they are all American, the works examined in this book reflect a distinctive relationship between the demands of memory and history.[4] As Toni Morrison has said about the United States, "We live in a land where the past is always erased and America is the innocent future in which immigrants can come and start over, where the slate is clean. The past is absent or it's romanticized. This culture doesn't encourage dwelling on, let alone coming to terms with, the truth about the past" (qtd. in Gilroy 222).

The claims that national identity makes on narrative are especially noteworthy in a national literature, which, as Jonathan White observes, "is the largest and historically the longest post-colonial literature" (19). While my interest in these novels leads me in a somewhat different direction from that of postcolonialism, I do not mean to deny the tensions between a people's attempt to decolonize and a writer's attempt to construct a suppressed or ignored history.

Fraught with issues of breaking old silences, making accusations, and taking blame, all of these novels appear during a crisis in "western knowledge across a broad range of disciplines as the basic assumptions of the social sciences and humanities have been called into question" (R. Hennessy 1).[5] In documenting this crisis, each work explores a piece of America's past using a refractional perspective; that is, to go back to Dickinson, each tells a story but tells it slant. Each gives voice to narrators, direct and indirect, whose perspective differs from those espoused in traditional master narratives: a Native American woman who capitalizes on her psychic abilities and exotic looks to fund a revolution, a runaway slave woman who murders her baby,[6] or a dreamy, seemingly enervated young girl who turns drifter for the rest of her life. Simultaneously, these "old" stories about slavery, mother love, domesticity, and family are woven into narrative structures that circumvent traditional forms of temporality, chronology, and narrative authority. Morrison's *Beloved*, for example, breaks up its horrific history into segments with abrupt shifts in time and space and, at one point, a jarring disruption of conventional syntax. Silko's *Almanac of the Dead* too violates convention-alities of form, incorporating the author's invented fragments of ancient almanac writings and prophecies into its skein of multiple narrative threads. Common to all these novels is the question of authority as it meshes with history; as Hayden White has noted, "the truth claims of the narrative" as well as "the very right to narrate [hinge] upon a certain relationship to authority per se" (18). And the act of narrative choice—which series of events to narrate, from which perspective to tell them—is often marked by the tension that Audre Lorde's "Coal" sees between her hidden adders and her young sparrows who explode into the light: the desire to keep secrets contending with the nearly physical urge to speak out.

Not coincidentally, a rising number of published "new critical voices" accompany this increasing focus on the retrieval of national and personal histories—histories whose status is no longer unchanged or fixed.[7] Intended primarily as a set of readings, this book focuses on figures who, like the speaker in Lorde's "Coal," are so bedeviled by their own histories, if not by words, that they can no longer remain silent victims: four generations of black women with a long history of enslavement and sexual abuse; a white, socially outcast daughter of a suicidal mother; a group of ex-slaves; a Polish immigrant and Holocaust survivor; and a series of displaced Native American, Mexican, and Mexican-Indian people.   Concurrent with the overwhelming urge to speak, however, is also the awareness that certain horrors can never truly be discursively represented, like *The Shawl*'s scene of infanticide.   In that sense, they correspond to James Phelan's notion of "the stubborn": unlike "the difficult," which is "recalcitrance that yields to our explanatory efforts," the stubborn is "recalcitrance that will not yield" (714). Phelan advises that readers (and in this case, perhaps novelists as well) should focus on not "explicating" the stubborn but rather "explaining the purpose of its recalcitrance" (715).   Such a shift, Shlomith Rimmon-Kenan observes, demands that we recognize "the impossibility of mastering such an emotionally wrenching experience" (119).

Of course, women's history is not defined solely by the conditions of victimization, voicelessness, and passivity, as Joan Kelly's *Women, History and Theory* and Hazel Carby's *Reconstructing Womanhood* argue, Kelly in her analysis of feminist discourse written four centuries before the French Revolution and Carby in her documentation of the political, cultural, and intellectual achievements of nineteenth- and twentieth-century black American women. Additionally, Elizabeth Fox-Genovese (*Feminism Without Illusions*) provides a cogent discussion of early European and American feminist writings.   Distinguishing much of the writing studied by these scholars is a long tradition of literacy; as Fox-Genovese writes, "for centuries—probably since women first began to write at all—at least some literate women had been writing in defense of their sex" (*Feminism* 132). In contrast, the narratives that interest me most highlight the struggles of disenfranchised, illiterate, or outcast figures, all of whom have been denied a place in literary history.[8] Through their female authorship, the works examined here have an often uneasy alliance with the by now familiar scholarly discussions of history as something either "real" or constructed, in large part because traditional historical narratives claim access to the "real" and thus, "interpretive power in a world of discourse" that ultimately privileges the male subject "as universal source of meaning" (Anderson 131). These novels thus illuminate a convergence of history and narrative that is affected precisely by gender.

As these narratives position themselves as (re)shapers of history, the abusive pasts they document serve as incentives for strategies of empowerment and survival. Not content with a mere illustration of women's subjection to tyranny, contemporary women's literature often recognizes the violence within women, using it to catalyze the creation of their authorial voices and recognizing its potential for changing women's lives. Thus these narratives also recognize a "useful" violence, one that overturns old histories and offers startlingly new models for remembering and telling those histories.

In thinking about violence within these works, I distinguish two kinds: the fragments of remembered psychic and physical violence that provide the necessary spark for these histories' emergence and, perhaps more important, the imaginative violence that concerns itself with the need to reenvision, reshape, and revise the history retrieved by each novel. The presence of violence is not simply double-edged in these narratives but is also specifically linked to the fact that they are woman-authored. Their disruptive elements— in terms of syntax, plot, and narrative point of view—correspond to a French feminist theorizing of what Alice Jardine has called the "feminine spaces" within a text: those spaces that elude knowledge and traditional forms of logic. If the unquestioned authority bound up with master narratives has been masculine, Jardine observes, then a narrative attempting to explore and overturn that authority might contain textual places "over which the narrative has lost control," places that French feminists like Jardine code "as feminine, as woman" (25). There is a recurring tension between histories received and those re-imagined, between "the resistance and transformation implied by the action of 're-imagining' and a 'history' which has both determined the moment and has already been imagined" (Anderson 135). In many contemporary women's novels, there appears at some point a contradiction, a paradox, and/or a rhetorical element of narrative gaps, or slippages, often appearing when the narrative seems to edge outside traditional forms of writing and meaning.[9] As historian Linda Gordon has navigated the murky crosscurrents between history and fiction, she has marked this sense of imbalance, which for her is "a condition of being constantly pulled, usually off balance, sometimes teetering wildly, almost always tense" (22). Tension often leads to a more violent positioning, as Linda Anderson notes: "In order to try to make intelligible what history and the social order represses it is necessary to rock their very foundations" (140). My reading of this moment of imbalance, however, differs from Jardine's (and many other French feminists) precisely at the point of meaning and intent.

Jardine interprets these spaces as being outside definition and representation entirely, thus positing them as transhistorical and beyond the social construction of women's differences. By "feminine," she means a kind of disruptive process rather than a specific biological or social state of being (Jardine 41–42). Yet to separate such narrative disruptions from the social and historical forces that have catalyzed them is, I believe, pernicious because it seems to deny the existence of social and racial hierarchies, particularly in light of the recurring trope of violence in contemporary women's writing.[10]

Changing not only one particular narrative but the master narratives that depend on the smothering of other stories, this violence attests to the seething frustrations of the long suppressed. Rosemary Hennessy's excellent study of materialist feminism provides an important grounding for the unsettling force of feminine spaces. Materialist feminism examines violence against women in all forms, as well as the "persistent worldwide devaluation of femininity and women's work, and the intensified controls over women's sexuality and reproductive capacities" (R. Hennessy xi). Rather than existing purely outside history, the feminine spaces of these narratives indicate for me the need for a conceptual violence to change the currently accepted dichotomy of female victim and male assailant. The complex merging of violence that is conceptual and violence that is actually remembered and retold is evident in Barbara Omolade's description of the miscegenating slave owner who "would never tell how he built a society with the aid of dark-skinned women, while telling the world he did it alone. . . . History would become all that men did during the day, but nothing of what they did during the night" (374–75). My readings of the selected women's novels in this study thus center on what women as well as men did but did not disclose—on the gaps of narrative discourse and the historical circumstances of the women who voice that discourse.

As Mary Poovey notes, materialist feminism recognizes that "woman" has

a position within a dominant, binary symbolic order and that that position is arbitrarily unified. On the other hand, we need to remember that there are concrete historical women whose differences reveal the inadequacy of this unified category in the present and the past. The multiple positions real women occupy—the positions dictated by race, . . . class, . . . or sexual preference—should alert us to the inadequacy of binary logic and unitary selves. (60)

Taking social and economic histories into consideration, many of my readings are informed by an exploration of binary thinking, which "rests on the delineation of difference as the foundation of all knowledge and therefore promotes hierarchy [in terms of feminist thought], notably the hierarchy that places men over women" (Fox-Genovese, *Feminism* 4).

In doing violence to master narratives, this variety of feminist writing works to change traditional Western perceptions of the world, which are framed by binary oppositions pitting nature, woman, and madness against culture, man, and reason.[11] In order to wrench free of this binary logic (if such a separation is ever really possible, and I am not at all sure it is), or at least to acknowledge and begin to work against it, a narrative must require its readers to reexamine their own perceptions of truth. In the novels discussed in this book, that reexamination moves towards eliminating the dichotomy of victimized women and victimizing men.

In interrogating and moving away from Western logic and tradition, many contemporary women's novels create new forms of the sacred, including a diverse group of possibilities for earthly redemption or personal fulfillment. In the books I discuss, "ordinary" existence is punctuated by transcendent moments in which the commonplace landscape of "real" violence is heightened by supernatural phenomena: the dead reappear or speak, the past is brought back, the unalterable is made open to influence. The narratives offer their characters a chance to redeem their pasts or their dead, sometimes violently. In fact, the option to change and be changed by this new form of redemption—to create a new historical self through transforming one's past—inverts the traditional American (i.e., the United States) quest towards re-creation through abandoning that past.

The intersections of narrative form, history, and identity are familiar enough to any reader of contemporary literature and criticism. So are the pitfalls of identity politics, particularly in Western feminism, which until recently has concerned itself with an "implicitly white subject" (R. Hennessy 136 n.41).[12] While scholars and writers recognize the distinctions of race, ethnicity, sexuality, and class, many are concerned with the increasing sense of fragmentation that results from such a strong focus on identity.[13] Despite such risks, however, it is precisely where identity intersects with history that an inclusive, broader vision of American literature emerges.

Much of contemporary women's writing grapples with the re-creation of an identity other than that imposed by certain master narratives. Narratives that pivot on identity are, in fact, solidly positioned within the tradition of American literature even as they transform it, since current American literature still must acknowledge as central the motif of self-creation. Certainly some of the most vital contemporary literary criticism explores just this tradition. Henry Louis Gates, Jr., for example, discusses the African American "impulse to write the race fully into the human community" (*Signifying Monkey* 171; see also 128–69). Similarly, Hortense Spillers notes "the palpable and continuing urgency of black women writing themselves into history" (*Conjuring* 249). In American literature, particularly that which reclaims a stifled history, it is far too soon to leave the question of identity behind. A grouping of American novels written by or dealing with Native Americans, Africans and African Americans, European gentiles, and Jewish immigrants pushes out the boundaries of American literature as well as American history.[14]

Granted, a pluralist response to historic positivism—that is, an unquestioning acceptance of received history—"would merely expand existing historical categories to include women" (R. Hennessy 113).[15] Such an easy, unexamined expansion, however, is precisely what is repudiated by the women's writings I have chosen to discuss here. My choices are not exhaustive, nor are they as wide ranging in terms of race and ethnicity as they might be. Again, however, I must emphasize that the connective thread joining all of them is not a sampling of contemporary American writings but rather a recurring trope of violence in the reclamation of women's national and personal histories. The predominance of that violence (or, in the instance of Robinson's *Housekeeping*, its deliberate, pivotal suppression) links these narratives and urgently infuses their reclamations of history.

Precisely what is to be remembered, and how it is to be told, in however many forms, is subject to the erratic shifts of human memory.   Arthur Schlesinger, Jr., has made a recent connection between national and individual histories along similar lines: "History is to the nation rather as memory is to the individual.   When an individual deprived of memory becomes disoriented and lost . . . so a nation denied a conception of its past will be disabled in dealing with its present" (qtd. in Michaels 2–3). The very high stakes concerning narrative strategies used to recover history, to remember or recover a memory, occupy much of my discussion, particularly when such histories and memories are either inherently violent, or have been violently repressed, or require a kind of epistemological violence to be recovered.   Schlesinger notes that through its role in "defining national identity, history becomes a means of shaping history" (qtd. in Michaels 3), but these narratives explore not simply national identity; they also tell stories about home, about genealogy, about sexuality, about family.   And until relatively recently, such stories, particularly concerning women, have been deemed minor.

The position that these narratives have had in relation to authoritative master narratives necessitates an ongoing, shifting dialectic between the two. In what ways do Toni Morrison and Leslie Marmon Silko, for example, appropriate, or subvert, or reevaluate those master narratives? Further, how are the alternative narrative strategies explored in this book relevant to the racial and ethnic grouping of these particular authors? While such groupings are by now common in literary criticism, I think it wise to speak briefly about the second issue. When hierarchical thinking extends to the categories of "ethnic" and "mainstream" literature, it creates a false dialectic between "American" and "ethnic" writings.[16] At the same time, one might just as easily substitute "master" for "American," and "other" for "ethnic"; despite William Boelhower's statement that "being American and being ethnic American are part of a single cultural framework" (10), they are not identical parts of that framework. Oscar Handlin's famous realization that immigrants *are* American history is not quite as simple as it first appears, especially when considering, first, the myriad stories immigrant groups have contributed to the United States and, second, the horribly ironic experiences of the Native Americans, whose own migrations began in earnest when the first immigrants arrived on the continent. So Werner Sollors's observation that "ethnic writing is American writing" ("Foreword," Boelhower 3), while valid, benefits from a concurrent recognition of the complex power relations and differentials existing for writers of color.[17] Both Sollors and Bonnie Winsbro observe that since its nineteenth-century introduction into the English language, *ethnic* has "strongly emphasize[d] otherness, or difference from the dominant culture" (Winsbro 13), and that even today, the word indicates a "nonstandard . . . or not fully American" identity" (Sollors 25). In addition, the complicated relationships between ethnicity and race, particularly when involving the delineation of differences between groups of people, are necessary to include in any discussion of ethnic narratives. Although the works examined in this book are not conceptualized as ethnic literature per se, in my readings of them I recognize that those relations are differently weighted, but always important, for women writers of all races.

A variation on Mikhail Bakhtin's notion of heteroglossia provides a useful way to conceptualize the narratives of Morrison, Jones, Ozick, Robinson, and Silko, as well as the traditions they recognize and those they work against, as "American literature." Heteroglossia refers to the "social diversity of speech types" determined by "social stratification," including, I would add, race and gender (Bakhtin 263, 290).[18] While Bakhtin separates speech types according to their ideologies, belief systems, generations, and even families, he adds that these languages may be juxtaposed because they all

are specific points of view on the world, forms for conceptualizing the world in words, specific world views, each characterized by its own objects, meanings and values. As such they . . . mutually supplement one another, contradict one another and . . . interrelat[e] dialogically. As such they encounter one another and co-exist in the consciousness of real people—first and foremost, in the creative consciousness of people who write novels. (291–92)

If we see the specific conglomerations of history and tradition in the works I consider as a version of heteroglossia, we can put them into dialogue with one another—a dialogue through which they can make sense of the brutal histories they resurrect and revise. Relating contemporary American stories of motherhood, of voicelessness, of power and survival, these novels also speak to each other about the histories that have shaped them. The material realities of a runaway slave woman desperate to save her child have much to say to those of a Jewish mother in a concentration camp. So, too, do the injunctions to remember both survival and loss, whether they are directed towards a black adult incest survivor or a white adolescent girl.

Structuring my discussion of these narratives is a question: How can people reclaim their violent histories and still survive, even with joy? Such a question echoes in the space between *Beloved*'s grim dedication—"Sixty Million and more"—and *Corregidora*'s insistent, bewildered, "How can it be?" Because the works I examine raise the issue of ethical behavior in the teeth of the survival imperative, I see them as endowed with a peculiar moral sensibility. Neither prescriptive nor proscriptive, it acknowledges the tangible and confusing effects of ideology and history and, while making few judgments on its characters, examines the possibilities for grace in the aftermath of brutal oppression. Such possibilities engender three overarching themes in all these narratives.

First, each work emphasizes the need for fluidity in the reclamation of its violent historical and personal pasts.[19] Like a living language, these histories are open to change and revision through their experimental narrative forms. Second, this fiction envisions a future that encompasses a recognition of the past, thus exploring a balance between the claims of history and the need for moving forward. Finally, these works address the reader's often reluctant role as witness; because they uncover such painful historic moments, these narratives must grapple with their audience's unwillingness to learn and to remember. Strategies for drawing in readers include the use of circular narratives that not only require our participation in unraveling a tale but also reveal a brutal history in fragments rather than all at once. Another strategy is the association of lyrical language or beautiful images with particularly horrific scenes (the murder of a baby, the suicide of a mother), as if to transform their violence and victimization. It is important to remember, however, that no work tries to deny the violence that is its linchpin.

From Mary Rowlandson's description of the Narragansetts' 1675 attack on her settlement, to Willa Cather and Charlotte Perkins Gilman's linking of violence and geographical or domestic spaces, my exploration of American women's writing in the following chapter reveals a continuum of vehement encounters in the forging of United States identities and the navigation of American landscapes. Rowlandson's unintentional disclosure of the inevitable conflicts arising from the forcible settling of the North American continent coexists with her conscious depiction of the brutalities she suffered as a white woman captive and, perhaps less consciously, her grappling with Puritanical notions of Divine wrath. The latter concern surfaces more openly in Anne Bradstreet's poetry, wherein the geographical distance is measured not between Indian and white territories but between physical and spiritual planes. While the slave narratives of Harriet Wilson (*Our Nig*) and Harriet Jacobs (*Incidents in the Life of a Slave Girl*), as well as Harriet Beecher Stowe's *Uncle Tom's Cabin*, also navigate between safe and unsafe spaces, their main interest is a deliberate manipulation of violence for the political cause of abolitionism. Gilman's story "The Yellow Wallpaper" connects the politics of domesticity with her narrator's physical and figural imprisonment within a maddeningly suffocating system of domination and intellectual repression, while Cather's *O Pioneers!* and *My Ántonia* are more occupied with the submersion of the individual into the vast territory of the nineteenth-century American West.

No other contemporary work I examine here has attracted such an outpouring of critical and public attention since its publication as Toni Morrison's *Beloved*. The issues of narrative responsibility, of the submersion and the retrieval of racial, historical, and individual memories, and of the need for a listener all reverberate throughout Morrison's novel. Because these are paramount concerns in my study, *Beloved* occupies the first of my contemporary discussions, wherein I investigate Morrison's revision of immigration and assimilation histories in the context of the Middle Passage and black life in nineteenth-century America. *Beloved*'s variation on what Mikhail Bakhtin calls a "chronotope"—a merging of the spatial and the temporal in literature—creates what is one of the most demanding and vital renderings of the Middle Passage in the English language. Wrought throughout *Beloved*'s motif of home founding is the rehabilitation of a long-suppressed history of displacement and slavery—a recovery that Morrison hangs upon a graphic physical and psychological reenactment of the Middle Passage. In doing so, she calls into question the tenuous balance between the equal imperatives of memory and forgetting for the survival of the book's free African American community.

Perhaps the term "free African American community" needs some qualification, particularly in connection with the often enslaving demands of remembrance.[20] Certainly it is problematized in Gayl Jones's *Corregidora*, which recasts those painful demands along the lines of the commodification of black female sexuality through slavery and prostitution. With *Corregidora* as my focus, I explore current feminist theories regarding African American women's empowerment, political self-definition, and the politicization, for good or ill, of "the woman's" body. The work of Hazel Carby, Elizabeth Spelman, Hélène Cixous, Patricia Hill Collins, and Gayatri Spivak provides a varied forum for considering the overriding connections between a woman's body as a site of violence and violation and as a source of life. Such connections are central to *Corregidora*, particularly since the female body is not only the victim but also the perpetrator of violence.[21] As with *Beloved*, issues of space and maternity are pertinent: Jones's book depicts the mother's body as both a public and a private space and examines the ways in which women's bodies are politically self-objectified, as well as objectified by others. Equally important in Jones's narrative are the strategies for handing down a family history, even when that history necessitates a painful reiteration of sexual abuse and enslavement. In venturing into the disturbing textual sites where desire and abuse converge and intertwine, this chapter also questions the influence of political ideology on the juxtaposed roles of truth teller and blues singer.

The subtler tones of a violence suppressed in Marilynne Robinson's *Housekeeping* inform two principal issues in my discussion: the challenge to nineteenth-century American binary oppositional thinking regarding human culture versus nature, and the implications of submerged violence in a specifically white novel, set in the 1940s and 1950s. Working from a perspective that acknowledges (and perhaps seeks out) instances of white privilege in this text, this chapter connects Robinson's encompassing, leveled-out treatment of loss and decay with a shedding of that privilege. As do *Corregidora* and *Beloved*, *Housekeeping* pushes at the boundaries separating people on the basis of class (specifically, the lines drawn between transience and "civilization"), even as it depicts white, middle-class female characters almost exclusively. This exclusion persuaded me to discuss *Housekeeping* immediately after *Corregidora*, which primarily depicts black, working-class women. The juxtaposition of these two chapters recognizes that a text cannot be all things to all people. Rather than requiring each work to check off a requisite number of "ethnic groups" from an arbitrarily devised column, I am more interested in the cumulative accomplishments of these writings—how they work together, at times to (re)constitute and at others, to change, the face of what Paul Ricoeur has called "the history of the defeated and the lost" (62). In short, I am interested in how they function within a system of heteroglossia to question, if not wholly refute, that notion that these stories *are* of the defeated and lost. While I agree with Ricoeur's observation that "the whole history of suffering cries out for vengeance and calls for narrative," I might add that it is through narrative, and particularly violent narrative, that a kind of vengeance is enacted (62).

Issues of violence and remembrance structure much of Cynthia Ozick's *The Shawl*, which, taking off from the work of Wilson, Jacobs, and Stowe, explores how political and theoretical concerns direct the uses of both "real" and "fictional" violence in the creation of art. Ozick's work is informed by what she calls "liturgical literature," whose primary interest is the Jewish community.   While open to artistic experimentation, liturgical literature insists that all creative techniques stem from Judaic tradition and history. Recognizing this historical imperative, *The Shawl* bears witness to the Holocaust by deliberately combining narrative fluidity with historic elements in four ways. First, its experimental form defies classification in order to circumvent the potentially desensitized category of "Holocaust literature," and thus freshly engages the Holocaust. Second, Ozick takes a stunning risk in her lyrical, transcendent, and thus problematic depiction of infanticide. Third, the returned (and protean) figure of a murdered baby meets Ozick's theological requirement of a communal audience through the medium of writing. Finally, that changeability radiates from one character out into *The Shawl*'s entire narrative, permeating the novel with an ongoing theme of metamorphosis as strategy for survival on an "Auschwitz planet" (Berger 194). Rather than attempting to resolve the struggle between brutality and beauty, Ozick makes her art out of the struggle itself.

Finally, I examine the strategies behind Leslie Marmon Silko's remarkably high rate of episodic violence in *Almanac of the Dead*, which illustrates the consequences of divorcing art from history, community, and a connection to the earth. Also, Silko dispels the myth of the "vanishing Indians" by recognizing their own capacity for ferocity and resiliency and, perhaps most important, for a tough-minded humor that works in and out of the novel's meshing of violence and comedy. Vital to this connection are the ways in which Silko distinguishes between violence tempered by humor and redeemed by the imperative of survival, and violence committed out of sheer bloodthirstiness. Through her perplexing linkage of brutality and wit, Silko defies the expectations of a dominant culture's attempts to appropriate Native American cultures without trying to understand them, to "sag back into the usual habits of sense-making, heaving melancholy sighs and thinking knowing thoughts" (Kincaid 24).

Throughout this study I am interested in searching beyond the typical (or stereotypical) representations of women and violence, but without denying their credibility. I have been struck not only by the inevitability of human brutality in these texts but also by my own hesitation to pass judgment and by an awareness of my desire to justify the violent writerly responses to that brutality.

Through their treatment of violence, these books raise matters of responsibility, repercussion, and redemption on personal, communal, and national levels, but each narrative ends on a note of ambiguity. While that ambiguity does not insist that it is enough simply to initiate an exploration, a paraphrase of William Boelhower proves apt: what suitably defines the question is often not the answer but the question itself (20). In telling an old story slant, these women's novels do not accept the past as "the version which we recognize and accept to be real because its 'realism' seems familiar" (Anderson 132). In working against the kinds of narratives that excluded their voices, these authors are equally concerned with undermining the belief that there is only one way to connect past histories and present lives. The recognition of so many possible narrative permutations and endings is not new to current literary criticism and theory. Still, the very theories that have opened publishing doors for so many authors and critics in the past two decades are often the most dangerous; as Linda Anderson notes, contemporary women's writing must acknowledge the very real danger that "post-structuralist theory can . . . [make] history disappear even before [women] have had a chance to write [them]selves into it" (134). It is a precarious endeavor, questioning the very stuff of history at the same time one is writing oneself into it: ambiguity might be the most useful, and most likely, path. Questions emerge through form as well in these narratives, which are, in the main, not "realist" novels. When I approach the ferocious magnitude of unspeakable violence, cruelty, and sheer loss dramatized in the novels here, the mutuality of our created world's in turn creating us becomes for me more frightening than merely interesting. Alongside all the good that humans have brought into being, we must also acknowledge a bloody common-wealth.[22] The increasingly urgent business of recognizing that handiwork pushes us apart as often as it brings us together, and those fluctuating tensions find voice in the uncertainties of each novel's close. It is my hope that this study will be one of many ways in which to read with, rather than through or over, those uncertainties.

NOTES

1. I am grateful to Susan Hubbard for her useful study of gender-based differences in written communication in an unpublished paper, "Sexing the Writer: Gender Stereotypes in the Writing Workshop." Valuable critical discussions of such differences include Jessie Bernard's *The Sex Game: Communication Between the Sexes* (1968), Robin Lakoff's *Language and Woman's Place* (1975), Sally McConnell-Ginet, Ruth Borker, and Nelly Furman's *Women and Language in Literature and Society* (1980), and Dale Spender's *The Writing or the Sex?* (1989).

2. This observation has long been made about women's experience and male writers; Elaine Showalter has noted that readers "encounter the myths of female sexuality as seen by Hardy and Lawrence, and the wonders of childbirth as seen by Sterne and Hemingway" (319).

3. Hubbard quotes one composition teacher who claims that certain kinds of "casual male brutality" depicted in male students' writing are "unimaginable" in the work of female students (4).

4. See also Michaels, especially 1–3.

5. See also R. Hennessy xi, xv, 8, 11; and G. Jones, *Liberating Voices* 178. Similarly, Alice Jardine defines modernity as an "epistemological crisis specific to the postwar period" (23). (As I discuss in my third chapter, this crisis has extended to the disruption of mainstream feminism.) Although feminist treatments of this crisis are too numerous to cite exhaustively, other scholars who discuss the issue include Carby (*Reconstructing Womanhood*), Jaggar and Bordo, Harding, Spelman, and M. O'Brien.

6. As Sally Keenan notes, Sethe's "unspeakable" act of infanticide is shocking enough—even for a somewhat jaded late-twentieth-century audience—to create for her an outlaw status that is quite different from that of the heroic outlaws highlighted in long-established slave narratives such as *Narrative of the Life of Frederick Douglass, an American Slave* (1845) and Harriet Jacobs's *Incidents in the Life of a Slave Girl* (1861). See Keenan 70.

7. A small sampling of recent anthologies exemplifies the current literary and academic focus on what is often called "ethnic" or "minority" writing. These include Edith Blicksilver's *The Ethnic American Woman: Problems, Protests, Lifestyle* (Dubuque: Kendall-Hunt, 1978); Dexter Fisher's *The Third Woman: Minority Women Writers of the United States* (Boston: Houghton Mifflin, 1980); Rayna Green's *That's What She Said: Contemporary Poetry and Fiction by Native American Women* (Bloomington: Indiana UP, 1984); Joseph Bruchac's *Breaking Silence: An Anthology of Contemporary Asian American Poets* (New York: Greenfield Review, 1983); Evelyn Beck's *Nice Jewish Girls: A Lesbian Anthology* (Boston: Beacon, 1989); and Gloria Anzaldúa and Cherríe Moraga's *This Bridge Called My Back: Writings of Radical Women of Color* (New York: Kitchen Table P, 1983). Despite its continued use, I find the term *minority literature* outdated, especially as demographics shift and more attention is paid to the ethnicity of all racial groups.

8. The immigrant protagonist of Ozick's *The Shawl* is the only exception of sorts; her Polish is flawlessly lyrical, but her English is "crude" (Ozick 14).

9. *Corregidora, Housekeeping*, and *The Shawl* contain moments of disturbing contradiction and paradox in their respective depictions of desire and abuse, death and resurrection, and infanticide. Similarly, *Beloved*'s now-famous "Middle Passage" section is wrenched outside the boundaries of grammatical syntax and punctuation to the realm of what might be called "pre-language."

10. See also Booth 10.

11. Discussions of binary thinking are by now commonplace. Important treatments of this concept may be found in Hélène Cixous's "Laugh of the Medusa," as well as Luce Irigaray's *Speculum de l'autre femme*, and *Ce sexe qui n'en est pas un*; Toril Moi's *Sexual/Textual Politics* provides an excellent overview, and Mary Poovey's "Feminism and Deconstruction" discusses binary oppositions in terms of materialist feminism.

12. See also Ammons (*Conflicting Stories*), Carby ("White Women Listen!"), Frankenberg, The Combahee River Collective, McDowell, Moraga, Sandoval, Sivanandan, and V. Smith ("Split Affinities").

13. For example, both Elizabeth Weed and Jenny Bourne argue that identity politics ask, "Who am I?" rather than, "What is to be done?" See also R. Hennessy 136.

14. Obviously, this "canon-exploding" grouping is no longer new. Similar contemporary studies include Meese's *Crossing the Double-Cross* and *(Ex)tensions: Re-figuring Feminist Criticism*, Greene and Kahn's *Making a Difference*, Spillers's *Comparative American Identities*, and any number of dissertations on current American literature. As Marlene Lindemann writes, contemporary women's fiction can be the "unique and exciting ground upon which we are enabled and in fact compelled to 'cross any line' of race or class" (106).

15. Joan Scott's *Gender and the Politics of History* works against such an expansion in its exploration of how "the categories a history invokes or takes for granted participate in the production of knowledge for the present" (R. Hennessy 113). See also, for example, Carby's *Reconstructing Womanhood*. Fox-Genovese, however, finds fault with Scott's proposed substitution of "an analysis of language for an analysis of social and gender relations—of politics and class" (*Feminism* 157; in addition, see 145–57). The works Fox-Genovese cites are "Deconstructing Equality-Versus-Difference: Or, the Uses of Poststructuralist Theory for Feminism," and Scott's review of Gertrude Himmelfarb's *The New History and the Old*.

16. This is not to deny the importance of works like Bonnie TuSmith's recent study of contemporary ethnic American literatures, which focuses deliberately on "writers who have made the conscious choice of drawing from their ethnic backgrounds" (29).

17. Similarly, Boelhower warns "advocates of the multi-ethnic paradigm" against repeating the "essentialist errors of their monocultural predecessors in attempting to trace out a blueprint of clear and distinct and ultimately reified ethnic categories" (20).

18. See also Henderson, "Speaking in Tongues" 139 n.6.

19. This fluidity is embodied in images of water (in *Beloved* and *Housekeeping*), air (in *The Shawl*), the blues (in *Corregidora*), and shifting notions of time and space (in *Almanac of the Dead*).

20. As Sally Keenan asks about *Beloved*, "what sense of the past or future could the ex-slave mother pass on to her daughter which would not reenslave her within the logic of their history?" (54).

21. Naturally this is also the case in *Beloved*, although my discussion of that text is directed elsewhere.

22. This realization too is peculiarly American, when one considers the brotherhood of evil that so concerned Hawthorne.

Chapter 2

American Spaces, American Violence: A Historical Prologue

Truism: no fiction emerges, whole bodied and full souled, from a vacuum. Anyone who has labored and watched over any piece of writing understands this. Influences on an author's work, both conscious and unconscious, can be traceable over an extended period of time, even centuries. When thinking about writers in terms of their race, ethnicity, or gender, however, one is in danger of seeing the literary traditions they recognize as, in the words of Henry Louis Gates, Jr., "some mystical collective unconscious determined by the biology of race or gender." Gates adds that literary traditions emerge

because writers read other writers and *ground* their representations of experience in models of language provided largely by other writers to whom they feel akin. It is through this mode of literary revision, amply evidenced in the *texts* themselves—in formal echoes, recast metaphors, even in parody—that a "tradition" emerges and defines itself. . . . sexuality, race, and gender are both the condition and the basis of *tradition*—but tradition as found in discrete acts of language use. (Foreword: "In Her Own Write" xviii)

In her discussion of Toni Morrison and the sentimental novel, Nancy Armstrong observes that Morrison articulates our contemporary "moment of multiculturalism" (embodied in *Beloved*'s representation of a changing family that adapts to a new country) by "clearing an intellectual-historical pathway for us back to the writing of colonial women" (19). It is such a path that I examine in this chapter.

American writing in all its spectrums has been indebted to certain ideas, initially through their presence and, in more recent years, through their tangible, deliberate absence: a persistent navigation of boundaries between wilderness and settlements, an ongoing series of cultural clashes (initially between Indians and European or British whites), the potential and real angers of a God whose followers fail to measure up spiritually, and—often in direct conflict with the previous themes—a continual quest for freedom. These concerns have spread out of and sometimes grown over the fault line of violence that runs beneath the forging of an American identity. From its earliest forms to its most current, United States literature has evoked violence in its historical creations and re-creations. The very first issues in our historical narratives are those of violence, centered on settlement and invasion: Britons and Europeans coming to terms with what they define as a formidable landscape, and Native Americans confronting the brutalities of having their homeland redefined as a savage wilderness fit only for domination.

I do not intend to offer an exhaustive historical survey of narrative strategies employing violence in American women's writing from its inception to the present, as the focus of this study is late twentieth-century narrative. Still, a discussion of the literary historical precedents, consciously chosen by writers and coincidentally discovered by readers, for the later narratives examined here will help create a better-informed context for contemporary writings by American women. In this discussion, which moves from the late 1600s to the early years of this century, the question for me is not so much, "Who are the literary foremothers here?" but rather, "Where are the literary echoes?" I use the word *literary* deliberately, since the writerly echoes I am seeking must, by definition, entail an admittedly incomplete examination of American canonical narrative, by excluding oral narrative forms, such as Winnebago, Iroquois, and Zuni Emergence and Origin tales, that existed long before the first written work I discuss in this chapter, Mary Rowlandson's captivity narrative. Yet it is Rowlandson's narrative that offers a particularly apt jumping-off point for this investigation.

When I first began thinking about this subject, two writers came immediately to mind: Toni Morrison and Flannery O'Connor. Biblical influences, absorption in the finding of true grace, moments of astonishing violence, a steady (if somewhat unusual) emphasis on the existence of a spiritual plane: these qualities are prominent in the work of both authors. Yet Flannery O'Connor is not the literary foremother of Toni Morrison, any more than Mary Rowlandson is the literary foremother of Flannery O'Connor. I soon realized that the connections I was searching for were not dependent on authors but instead were textually based. They were a series of pivotal moments of violence that have helped form a set of guidelines by which we may examine constructions of national, racial, ethnic, and gendered identities.

The recurrence of a fiercely purifying scourge in O'Connor's and Morrison's work is not indebted to, but must be acknowledged concomitantly with, that of Rowlandson. The critical pitfalls of tracing influence from an early white Puritan settler on a contemporary African American author are great, and I do not mean to argue that the connection is anywhere near that straightforward. Rather, I see American women's writing as a kind of continuum. The issues at stake in Rowlandson's narrative have much to do with the forcible settling of the North American continent, indeed with the very landscape itself, and the echoes of those issues still reverberate in today's narratives, clearly, if not resoundingly.

Such resonances occur more subtly in Anne Bradstreet's religious poetry. They make up a convoluted pattern that emphasizes more strongly what Rowlandson deals with only partially: the kind of violence measured by loss and Divine destruction rather than by human agency.[1] The latter takes on greater prominence in the nineteenth century, particularly in women's novels invoking African American slave narrative traditions. Harriet Wilson's *Our Nig* (1859) and Harriet Jacobs's *Incidents in the Life of a Slave Girl* (1861) spiral, tornado-like, from the violence that underlies the urgent call for change, as well as the extraordinary instinct for survival, that defines both of these works. Similarly, although Harriet Beecher Stowe's *Uncle Tom's Cabin* (1852) is a white-authored fictional work, I group it with these slave narratives because all three are also determinedly political, intended to create sympathy for the abolitionists' cause.[2] This intention gives them a significant role in my investigation, for they are the first full-length women's narratives that *deliberately* wield instances of overt violence for ideological motives. What they do with that brutality speaks to the texts that I discuss in later chapters.

Finally, Charlotte Perkins Gilman's "The Yellow Wallpaper" (1892) ushered in the twentieth century with a story whose theme of violent repression takes ominous shape in the very patterns on the wall; in this reading, one does not hear echoes but instead sees what is inscribed on the landscape of a woman's postnatal confinement (or, depending on how one reads the tale, outright imprisonment). Although the repression and brutality of Gilman's tale are muffled, they are clearly recognizable. Such is not the case in the work of Willa Cather, which has generated responses primarily to her extraordinary evocations of the American West, her explorations of the immigrants' experiences, and her refusal to adhere to her contemporaries' constraining definitions of gender.[3] Yet her novels *O Pioneers!* (1913) and *My Ántonia* (1918) both enclose—indeed, at times seem to carpet over— shocking moments of violence when ideologies and values collide. The positioning of these brutal instants within a specific geographical space offers a way to juxtapose them with Gilman's depiction of a fiercely stifling internal, domestic sphere. Here, my overview ends, although it certainly could encompass a far greater number of authors and titles: the Eastern European immigrant Anzia Yezierska, whose anger erupts continually through the seams of her autobiographical and fictional narratives, including the short story collection *Hungry Hearts* and the novels *Bread Givers* and *Arrogant Beggar*; Zora Neale Hurston, whose *Their Eyes Were Watching God* spins its heroine's charismatic voice out of her face-to-face confrontation with repression and murderous rage; Shirley Jackson's much-anthologized short story "The Lottery," with its cold-eyed exposure of blind faith in atavistic ritual and the human need for a scapegoat;   Nella Larsen's *Quicksand* and *Passing*, which close, respectively, with one woman's total deterioration after a merciless series of childbirths and another's violent response to the threatened exposure of her vital secret; Flannery O'Connor's uncompromising vision of a divine grace so fierce that it virtually burns away the flesh. And there are more recent writers who are part of this continuum, including Adrienne Rich, Sandra Cisneros, and Maxine Hong Kingston. The list from Rowlandson to Cather is by no means exhaustive, even within my limited context, but it is Cather I choose to close with, for reasons of chronology, theme, and stature.

First, the publication of *My Ántonia*, coming as it does at the end of World War I, coincides with the closing of a certain stage in the formation of an American identity. The United States' entry into the war, however belated (this is thematically pivotal to Cather's only war novel, the Pulitzer Prize-winning *One of Ours*, published in 1922), helped create a national identity in relationship to large European powers. While the Mexican War (1845–1847) and the Spanish-American War (1898) were also wars on foreign soil, they did not provide the grand scale of World War I, entered by the United States in 1917. With the closing of this war, Europe's "place in the world economy was impaired beyond recovery . . . [while] America and Japan had been making colossal strides" (Garraty and Gay 992). As important as a consideration of national status, however, is one of the effects of this war on the returning soldiers; as Paul Fussell notes in his study, *The Great War and Modern Memory*, no more could people put their faith in an innocent worldview. (Considering the United States' early relations with Native Americans, Africans, and African Americans, however, that worldview was always false). World War I forced on this country the public recognition of mass brutalities, the horrifying potential "for violence even in their own selves, that nothing in the genteel, repressed world of before 1914 had prepared them for" (Garraty and Gay 992). For a closing moment in this examination of literary forerunners to contemporary explorations of personal and national histories of violence, then, 1918 seems a fitting choice.

Second, the narrative themes and structures from Rowlandson to Cather offer logical and fitting precursors to the discussions I take up in my later chapters: Rowlandson's captivity narrative foregrounds the territorial struggles and the racial, "other-to-other" conflicts that compose so much of Silko's *Almanac of the Dead*, as well as Morrison's *Beloved* and Jones's *Corregidora*. Additionally, both Rowlandson and, more explicitly, Bradstreet grapple with issues of Divine violence and loss, the same issues recurring in

Robinson's *Housekeeping* and, in a different way, Ozick's *The Shawl*. The slave narratives of Stowe, Wilson, and Jacobs not only treat the United States' history of slaveholding but deliberately connect the themes of violence with those of politics, an endeavor that Jones re-examines from a different perspective.   Finally, Cather and Gilman's yoking together the concerns of violence and space reappears in Robinson's disruptive notions of homemaking, as well as Silko and Morrison's respective explorations of how various peoples try to make themselves "at home" in a particular landscape. To put it another way, these works, to my understanding, offer the fullest representations of the themes I take up in my contemporary explorations. Although there are certainly other works that project those themes, to explore them all here would yield only diminishing returns.

Additionally, I address here the strong canonical ties of my chosen precedents, particularly important in a study that acknowledges varying suppressions and repressions of literary voices and histories. In large part, these works appear in this chapter precisely because of their canonicity; one cannot discuss the revisionary mission of alternative voices and narratives without initially defining exactly what they are revising or (in some cases) what works they simultaneously acknowledge and rework. Although the narratives mentioned are for the most part recognized within the American literary canon, they are still not precisely "master narratives." Indeed, some of them are only recent admissions to the more "authorized" levels of American writing (for example, Gilman, Stowe, Wilson, and Jacobs have all been "reclaimed" within the past few decades), and others, like Toni Morrison, have undergone that peculiarly contemporary experience of being canonized as alternative voices *within* the preexisting canon; they are seen as filling certain gaps. It is this double-edged positioning, in fact, that makes the earlier works I have selected particularly apt forerunners for the later narratives emphasized in my study.

What I seek to establish in this chapter is a contextualization for my later discussions, a continuance of pivotal moments of violence that speak to each other across varieties of narrative form and genre, across years, across constructions of race, national identity, economic and class strata. Violence recurs not only in strictly representational terms (physical or psychic violence wrought by an agent on a victim), but also as a trope, as a means of exploring new narrative forms and new plots. Thus do I see all these works, and all these authors, as laying the groundwork for those postmodern American women's narratives that investigate the myriad eruptions and uses of violence in both personal and national realms.

The ruptures in sensemaking that help define these narratives stem from the hegemonic assumptions of the Enlightenment. In violently repressing certain stories, these assumptions forced them outside recorded narrative and, in so doing, helped to design the role of violence in the United States' national narrative. In her 1984 study, *The Land Before Her: Fantasy and Experience of the American Frontiers, 1630–1860,* Annette Kolodny writes that in the Puritans' "preconceived cultural script, the central focus . . . was always the spiritual drama of affliction and redemption" (28). Yet even as violence serves a redemptive purpose in many of these narrative forms,[4] it also enforces the brutal repressions of those earlier stories, specifically in terms of Puritanical ideology: witness the Puritan sanction against women's speaking publicly.[5] For all these reasons, the foundations of violence in early United States culture merit exploration here. Certainly the phenomenon of violence-as-trope is ongoing, yet not essentially linear and forward moving in its contributions to the construction of national identities and narrative forms. What *are* the American women's stories of and about violence? How do the stories coming out today emerge out of, work against, speak alongside their predecessors?

SYMBOLS AND SURVIVAL

When Narragansett Indians attacked the settlement of Lancaster, Massachusetts, in February 1675, they abducted Mary White Rowlandson (*circa* 1636–1710) and her infant daughter and also indirectly catalyzed the writing of the first, most popular, and archetypal American captivity narrative, published in 1682 as *The Soveraignty and Goodness of God, together with the Faithfulness of His Promises Displayed; Being a Narrative of the Captivity and Restoration of Mrs. Mary Rowlandson.* This (abridged) title itself indicates the often paradoxical role violence plays in American women's narratives, for it suggests the extent of the self-censoring within Rowlandson's narrative and the suppression of its violence, especially in terms of her Puritanical determination to profit spiritually from her misfortunes.[6] As I will soon discuss, Rowlandson is not able to censor completely her less-than-entirely submissive responses to her particular trial. It is not surprising that Susan Howe's appellation of Rowlandson as "the mother of" all American writers precedes a description of her captivity narrative as "alive with rage and contradiction. She is a prophet" (167), or that Annette Kolodny observes that "the single narrative form indigenous to the New World is the victim's recounting of unwilling captivity . . . the history of this genre begins with a Puritan woman's story. . . . [This provided] a mode of symbolic action crucial to defining the otherwise dangerous or unacknowledged meaning of women's experience of the dark and enclosing forests around them" (*Land Before* 6).[7] What does Rowlandson do with the violence she records? Where is it allowed to appear in her narrative, and where is it either muffled, described so tersely or succinctly as to lose its force, or somehow defanged by biblical authority?

The framework created around her ordeal is preconditioned by Rowlandson's cultural filters. As such, it is as significant to readers and scholars of American culture and narrative as the ordeal; as Howe aptly notes, "The trick of her text is its mix" (127). Such a mix reminds us that any notions of history depend largely not only on what is told but how it is told and retold. And Rowlandson's way of telling her experience brings to the foreground two types of violence embedded within this early defining of a white American identity: the brutalities she witnessed and endured as a captive of the Narragansetts and the violence of her Puritanical self-censoring. Rowlandson undercuts not only the horrors of her captivity but also the control of her own story by continually referring back to biblical authority whenever she comes too close to speaking of a "crime story in a large and violent place" (Howe 125).[8] Such undercutting was determined by social necessity for Rowlandson. After all, the risks of her narrative were several. Aside from the aforementioned Puritan taboos against women's public speaking (and, by extension, writing and publishing), the particularities of Rowlandson's captivity were themselves dangerous. She had walked, from her community's perspective, "with Satan" (Metacomet/Philip, the Narragansett chief and namesake of King Philip's War), and such an association might have rendered her "suspect; vulnerable to ambivalent charges ranging from pride (she had set a high price on her own head) to sexual promiscuity, even to sorcery" (Howe 123). As Howe then notes, however, this danger might have inspired Rowlandson's writing the narrative; by couching her narrative in such deeply religious terms, she proves to her community that "she was a woman who feared God and eschewed evil" (123). Too, her narrative can be read as a written "proof" of her "election" in terms of New England Protestantism, whose religious demands "required a public recital of one's conversion" (Zafar 20; see also E. Morgan 58–62). In his recent study of Rowlandson, *American Puritanism and the Defense of Mourning*, Mitchell Breitweiser, however, sees on occasion a nonconformity rather than a constraint in Rowlandson's use of biblical allusion, particularly when she identifies with Lot's wife, who turns back to mourn the destruction of her home (95–96; Rowlandson 36). Like Breitweiser, I see reflected in Rowlandson's narrative a simultaneous acknowledgment and undermining of biblical authority. Her telling and her suppression of violence, and the way the latter emerges through the seams of her narrative, is particularly evident in her handling of the violence of Puritan typology, including an acknowledgment of a paradoxical God who so quickly, and so ferociously, converts "living subjectivity [Lot's wife] into emblem. Destruction is exegesis" (Breitweiser 96). After witnessing the killing of several relatives and friends in the initial attack, after watching her child die in her lap, and after relating a fellow captive's particularly grisly murder, Rowlandson "cannot but take notice of the strange Providence of God in preserving" her enemies, the agents of her Divine punishment.[9] Despite (or perhaps because of) Rowlandson's conflicted portrait of a volatile God, it was important that she establish herself as a devout Puritan. She needed to present herself not as changed by her experiences with Metacomet and the Narragansetts but rather, as exactly the opposite; it was imperative that she appear reinforced and solidified in her Puritanical, Anglo-American certainties. That her narrative so often questions and undercuts those certainties only serves to point out their importance to Rowlandson and her community.

Within her written testimony, therefore, divine authority must override too overt an acknowledgment of Rowlandson's precarious position among the Indians, for such an admission might lead to a questioning of the very foundations of white America's ownership of the land: the differences between the settlers and the (un)settled—the Native Americans themselves. For the Puritans, religious faith underscored the necessary violence to human survival: Indians, as "wilderness" creatures whose own spiritual beliefs appeared simply to be a defiance of Christianity, were inevitably linked with the devil, and they gradually became rationalized as targets of settlers' violence.[10] The distinctions between the violence of the "savages" and that of the Puritans had to be rigidly maintained, despite a pointed similarity in the experiences of both peoples. "[T]he fright of incomprehensible reversal and the destruction of the world" that Mary Rowlandson documents in her narrative "had been a constant of Indian experience for some time, and . . . it had provoked the war that introduced those factors to [Rowlandson]" (Breitweiser 166–67).[11]   This violent undercurrent, strengthened by the Puritans' sense of themselves as God's chosen people, creates the fault line separating white from Indian, and thus not only originates a white, national identity for Americans but also serves to create a new national identity for all Indians (who did, and do not, outside of their dealings with white Americans, share a collective group identity).

Tied into this brutal distinction between Indians and Puritans is the violence of survival, an urgency that has the potential to annul many of the differences between "civilized" and "savage."   Yet even as Rowlandson details the less-than-appetizing means by which she survives her captivity, she turns back to the Bible as though seeking to nullify the sometimes brutally graphic impact of her actions and words. When she jerks a piece of horse's hoof out of an English child's hand because the child is sucking rather than chewing it (which is, as any parent knows, how very young children eat anything large or hard), she concludes, "savory it was to my taste," and shifts the focus entirely to aligning herself with the blameless and much-persecuted Job, as she observes, "The things that my soul refuseth to touch, are as my sorrowful meat" (80). Here, biblical authority serves to mitigate the violence that is often necessary to life itself: eat or be eaten, kill or be killed. Such denial of this violence may be read as serving the ends of the warring Puritans, whose "civilized" differences from the Native Americans had to be maintained, in part to justify the Puritans' efforts to wipe them out.

Yet the denial is not monolithic. Christopher Castiglia and Mitchell Breitweiser, among others, note the tension between Rowlandson's rigidly emphasized devoutness and her "shifting allegiances" while she lives among the Indians (Breitweiser 48).[12] Over the course of her narrative, she moves from attributing all mercies to God and all trials to the Indians (as she does in the third and fifth Removes, for example, acknowledging only the hand of

Providence when a captor gives her a Bible, and another allows her to visit with her abducted son), to speaking of "common mercies" (92), and even conceding that (with God's help) the *Indians* have been kind to her, as in the nineteenth remove, when Philip himself helps her out of a swamp, gives her water to wash with and a looking glass (82), and feeds her as well. In a very real sense, then, Rowlandson's intermittent challenge to the Indians' adherence to Puritan type can be read as epistemologically violent, and risky for a woman who must convince her community that she is unchanged even after walking "with Satan."   As Susan Howe notes, "Her view of King Philip's War and her picture of Metacomet himself is a contradiction of orthodox Puritan history" (127).

Castiglia sees in Rowlandson's ambiguous account a challenge to Puritan oppositions made between a wilderness marked by Indian savagery and a white civilization informed by reason and charity, while Breitweiser observes that such actions release not only the Indians but also the Puritans themselves "from typology" and the inflexible requirements of moral righteousness (148). But I think this shift in Rowlandson's perceptions of her captors also illuminates just why the identity stakes were so high for the Puritans.   Differences between themselves and the "savages" they were battling had to be maintained in order to justify spiritually the settlers' ongoing frontier expansions.[13] Rowlandson's biblically informed censoring bespeaks not only the cultural imperatives of her time but also the inner conflicts that have in so large a part defined the origins of white America. The opposing forces of idealism, spirituality, and rampant exploitation and invasion erupt from the narrative's fissures, especially when Rowlandson unknowingly reveals the battling over resources that so largely catalyzed King Philip's War.[14] For example, in her now-famous twentieth remove, in which she marvels at how God's "strange Providence" contributes to the English army's ineptitude, Rowlandson grudgingly admires the Indians' resource-fulness:

It was thought, if their corn were cut down, they would starve and die with hunger; and all that could be found was destroyed and they driven from that little they had in store. . . . Though many times they would eat that, that a hog or a dog would hardly touch; yet by that God strengthened them to be a scourge to his people. (104)

Such untouchable foods included old bones that were scalded to rid them of worms and maggots, boiled for broth, and then ground down for a paste. That the tribes had to go to such measures in order to be "strengthened" emphasizes the fierce grappling for territory between the whites and the Indians; also foreshadowed here are the meager allotments of land parceled out to Native Americans during the following centuries.

Enclosed within her larger narrative, Rowlandson's dealings with violence emerge more openly and more deliberately when she depicts her personal struggle to survive.   In fact, in the seventh and eighth removes, Rowlandson's attention seems more taken up with her own physical survival than with biblical justifications: the former has no scriptural allusions whatsoever and involves the scene wherein, desperately hungry, she accepts a half-raw piece of horse liver from her captors and, describing it as "savory," devours it "with the blood about my mouth" (39).   Her only spiritual justification might be seen in her concluding comment that "to the hungry soul every bitter thing was sweet" (39)—the type of observation she makes several times when documenting what she receives from the hands of her captors: a pancake fried in bear's grease ("I never tasted pleasanter meat"), a piece of boiled bear meat ("how pleasant it was to me"), a broiled horse's gut (78), an unborn fawn whose bones were as tender as flesh,[15] and boiled horse's hoof—"savory it was to my taste" (44, 50, 78, 71, 80).   Sometimes these are contextualized with biblical allusions (78, 80), and sometimes not (44, 50), yet overall, Rowlandson's references to her diet with the Indians are marked by her growing realization that what is "savory to me that one would think was enough to turn the stomach of a brute creature" (50).   That is, in terms of the urge to live, she subconsciously finds that she and her captors may not be quite so different after all.

Similarly, the narrative's preface by Per Amicum (commonly believed to be Increase Mather) also reveals a momentary slippage from the view of Indians as a monolithic demonic force and makes an implicit link, albeit a brief one, between them and their Puritan captives.   On the same page, Per Amicum alludes both to the "*causeless* enmity of these barbarians" and to their "malicious *and revengeful* spirit" (emphasis mine),[16] a note Rowlandson echoes in her description of the Indians who "came upon our town, like bears bereft of their whelps" (102).   While Rowlandson notes no specific instance of Puritan *or* Indian vengeance for the loss of their children, she does document such losses, from her own to her sister's to that of the Indian "squaw" whose wigwam she shares.   Groundless violence shifts, however momentarily and subtly, to the vengeance of creatures whose cubs have been taken, forging an identification between captor and captive that transcends Puritan typology in a move of "symmetrical violence" as "the vengeful grief of one causes the grief of another" (Breitweiser 166).   There is, perhaps, no more apt summary for a powerful cause of war.

Two kinds of violence are at work (and in some sense, at war) in Rowlandson's captivity narrative: her actual represented experience and the violence of Puritan typology itself.   Towards the very end of her narrative, even amid her assurances that she is able to count her blessings, Rowlandson identifies herself as a woman forever changed by her violent experience. Her earlier fears that God has not tested her enough, that she might have her "portion in this life" (121) rather than in the next, point to one of the greatest differences between the Puritans' world and ours: the victim's role. Because victimization for them was a form of testing, of God's attention and even God's love, victimization in Rowlandson's time was more blessing than curse.   One need only think of the vehement attitude of a figure like Sethe in Toni Morrison's *Beloved*, whose powerful refusal of victimhood for herself and her children found expression in murder, to visualize the vast distance between Puritan and contemporary responses to such "blessings." As for a woman like Mary Rowlandson, her concern that she might be denied her portion of affliction here on earth overrides any complaints about God's treatment of her.   Still, this rough mark of God's love also leaves her troubled; formerly able to sleep through the night, now she often lies awake and in tears: "O the wonderful power of God that mine eyes have seen, affording matter enough for my thoughts to run in, that when others are sleeping mine eyes are weeping" (120). Grateful for God's saving hand, she is equally aware that a peaceful life can turn "otherwise": "One hour I have been in health and wealth . . . the next hour in sickness, and wounds, and death" (120).

As one who has witnessed her world upended, by either the Narragansetts or by God (or by the Narragansetts in the divine ordinance *of* God), Rowlandson has a strong affinity with another victim in the hands of a seemingly arbitrary God: Job, that biblical figure to whom she so frequently alludes. When Rowlandson asserts that she has "seen the extreme vanity of this world," she might just as well assert that she has seen the extremes to which divine admonishment can go: her child's agonized death, the haunting images of her dying friends and family, her own experiences traveling through bitterly cold rivers and swamps. She has survived the brutalities of her captors, but also the brutalities of the God who (according to the notions of Puritan typology) has set those captors to working for purposes of spiritual correction.[17] That correction, and the ideology that recognizes it as such, gives rise to a second consideration of violence in Rowlandson's narrative: the replaying of her personal terrors and brutalities in the context of Puritan typology, whose very rigidity lends itself to a form of epistemological violence, wherein whatever does not confirm a spiritually exemplary model is cut off and discarded as insignificant (see Breitweiser 24, 50; see also Bercovitch, *Puritan Origins of the American Self*). There is perhaps no better example of this brutal reasoning than the story of Goodwife Joslin, who is murdered twice—first by her Indian captors and again by the ideological demands of Rowlandson's narrative.

Pregnant (perhaps one week from delivery) and the mother of a two-year-old child, Goodwife Joslin is justifiably apprehensive when Rowlandson meets with her; in the very next line following her introduction of this captive, Rowlandson tells of their reading Psalm 27 together: "Wait on the Lord, be of good courage, and he shall strengthen thine heart, wait I say on the Lord." As both Teresa A. Toulouse and Breitweiser observe, this psalm throws into strong relief Joslin's gruesome fate; she does not wait but instead begs her captors to free her until, exasperated with her supplications, they burn her and her two-year-old alive (27).[18] While Toulouse makes an interesting argument that Rowlandson tells this tale to strengthen her own adherence to Puritanical faith and piety—she does *not* lose faith and *does* wait, after all—it seems to me there is an equally important additional message in this tale. The dangers of speaking, of refusing to accept one's fate silently, are horribly illustrated, as are the brutal rules that turn maternity into a dangerous weakness, even a flaw. After all, Joslin probably wishes to be home because she believes she stands a better chance of surviving childbirth there.   Indirectly, she is murdered because she is a mother. (The violent clash of motherhood and history implied here echoes in *Beloved*, Gayl Jones's *Corregidora*, and Cynthia Ozick's *The Shawl*, wherein motherhood provides the means for an unwitting bequest of slavery and sexual abuse, in the first two cases, and genocide, latterly.)   As if to underscore her guilty maternity, her child is burned with her, as is the unborn child within her. But this is only her "first" murder, the one entailing the dangers of maternity, and of speech. Her "second" murder occurs at the hands of Rowlandson's Puritan typology, wherein Joslin is turned into a fiery emblem. Granted, her martyrdom is depicted—"she did not shed one tear, but prayed all the while"—before Rowlandson's journey continues, but it is a notably brief laudatory moment (29).   Bereft of even one biblical allusion beyond the one hinting at her failure to "wait on the Lord," Joslin is finally sacrificed to Rowlandson's need to present her narrative in the proper religious light. In retelling her own history, and in asking to be readmitted to her community after her potentially damning experiences with the "diabolical" enemy, Rowlandson must show herself compliant and uncomplaining with respect to the harsh, even violent demands of the Puritan God. The unfortunate Joslin has passed God's test but then quickly becomes a casualty to Rowlandson's imperative.

Violence is inherent in Puritan typology itself, which Breitweiser defines as a series of "assaults on other ways of thinking, tools of negating the autonomy of other paradigms and practices" to change them into examples (25). The vehemence of Puritan certainty can be as frightening and brutal as our contemporary notion of a random, chaotic universe.   For example, when describing her devouring the boiled horse's hoof, Rowlandson is able to put her hand on an exactly apt (as opposed to metaphorical) biblical verse: Job's "The things my soul refuseth to touch, are as my sorrowful meat." Breitweiser sees in this allusion the observation that "*that hoof was meant to be*"; Rowlandson now "inhabits an area of constant message, where meaning is never subject to the buffering calm of conjecture of speculation" (81).   Thus, her chaotic abduction, the wild and horrific inversion of her world, becomes not chaos but a smashing of the diurnal banalities in order that the meaning beneath those banalities be brought forth. A peculiar thriftiness informs Puritanical approaches to violence; use must and will be made of the brutalities Rowlandson endures, just as King Philip's War itself becomes a vivid, scourging example of God's displeasure.[19]   Such an experience, such a life, is by necessity violent; the ways of knowing the world must be brutal in this kind of epistemology.

Perhaps this is why Rowlandson's descriptions of physical violence are so terse, even seemingly cold-blooded, as Breitweiser attests. Her prose takes on a muted destructive force of its own, as her "project of self-tutelage in brutality takes the form of repetitive intonation: 'All was gone, my husband gone . . . my children gone, my friends and relations gone, our house and home and all our comforts . . . all was gone (except my life) and I knew not but the next moment that might go too'" (12; Breitweiser 115). In copying the Indians' own brutal control of her fate, Breitweiser argues, Rowlandson herself seeks to "recompose a feeling of control" (115). A coldness emerges in her later abilities to distance herself from suffering children, both Indian (a dead papoose means only more room in the wigwam, while another, stretched out, with his "eyes, nose, and mouth full of dirt, and yet alive, and groaning" does not elicit the same sympathy and care as does a wounded English youth nearby) and English (from whom she takes the boiled horse hoof). Indeed, in the very first paragraph's relation of nine consecutive murders, for example, the tone is neither graphic nor lingering; a scant "knockt on the head" suffices for most killings, although the description of someone naked and "chopt in the head with a hatchet," yet still "crawling up and down," is certainly gruesome and explicit enough (9).

What is at stake in Rowlandson's captivity narrative is a violently contested quarrel over ownership: of sustenance, of country/motherland, of person, of liberty, of means of worship (at one point, a Narragansett tears Rowlandson's Bible from her hands; meanwhile, the Puritans have levied several restrictions on the Indians' rituals and religious ceremonies). The brutality she endures along the lines of this cultural quarrel becomes deeply personal; she sees two of her children taken, a third fatally wounded, one sister abducted, and another sister, nephew, and brother-in-law murdered. As Susan Howe writes, they are "abducted from the structure of experience. . . . [Rowlandson's] little girl was broken in a rift of history" (96). Like all captives, Rowlandson and her child are treated as bargaining chips, but not only from the perspective of their captors. The exigencies of Puritan typology also forced them into a role, as evidenced by Increase Mather's desire to control the manner in which King Philip's War was interpreted: not as sheer horror or (less obviously to the Puritans) the Indians' inevitable response to the disruption of their entire existence, but instead as a jeremiad-confirming act of punishment by the Puritan's God (see Breitweiser 6–7). For Mather, Rowlandson and her dead child are not made victims but rather become emblems of punishment, reminders to her audience to do better. That Rowlandson works with and against this emblematic theme has already been discussed here. But I find another context for her narrative: her depiction of a violation of place and of home—her repeated sense of being sundered violently from home and, while not explicit in her narrative, by contrast the idea of finding one's own home violently invaded, as the Indians did. Almost immediately, Rowlandson sees her home as transformed by her captors into a "lively resemblance of hell" (11); a few pages later, she mourns being forced to turn away from the town and go "into the vast and desolate wilderness, I know not wither" (13–14); and, most poignant, she relates the burial of her child by the Indians: "there I left that child in the wilderness" (21). In its focus on the meaning of place and home, particularly in its ongoing series of removes from one place to another, Rowlandson's narrative speaks to the greater part of American women's writing.[20] She is not "at home" throughout her narrative, because the landscape is hostile and unfamiliar. Her frequent supplications at various wigwams—sometimes resulting in kindness, food, and shelter; sometimes not—reveal her seeking even among these strangers some semblance of a home, however temporary and strange to her. As Annette Kolodny aptly notes, Rowlandson's knitting skills allow her to barter and thus survive with her captors, and her Bible offers her spiritual nourishment, but the American landscape is "the only terrain she can never negotiate on her own" (*Land Before* 18).

When Rowlandson discovers her kinship of survival with her captors, however grudgingly and even unwittingly, she also observes that this people's survival is intricately connected with the landscape; unlike the often-clumsy English army, they are familiar with and able to navigate a region of swamps, freezing rivers, and thickly wooded forests. Rowlandson illustrates that the early American continent "wasn't a wilderness to Native Americans" (Howe 161). Indeed, as Kolodny notes in *The Land Before Her*, *The Soveraignty and Goodness of God* can be read as a seminal document of a woman's journeying through what was to her a wilderness. While later male-authored narratives of survival beyond the settlements (such as those of Daniel Boone and Francis Scott) perpetuated a fantasy of Paradise lying just beyond the westward boundaries of white civilization, white women looked at the darkening edges of the woods and the flat, unending light of the plains and saw only a land without mercy.

Albeit in a decidedly different fashion, all the contemporary works examined in this study echo Rowlandson's overall concern: how to make sense—indeed, the question of whether one *can* make sense—spiritually and otherwise, of the devastating losses and brutality inherent in one's world. The later works replace Rowlandson's strained Puritanical certainty in God's providence with questions, doubt, and alternative religious forms (as evidenced in *Beloved*'s embracing of both Judeo-Christian and West African motifs). Differences aside, these narratives all imply that violence cannot always fit into a framework of justification.

FLIMSY HOME, FRAGILE BODY

Anne Bradstreet (*circa* 1612–1672), who died a few years before Mary Rowlandson's captivity, was, like Rowlandson, a "first": one wrote this country's first popular captivity narrative, while the other was America's first poet.[21] A second similarity has to do with each writer's focus on spiritual and fleshly trials. An important difference between the two is that Bradstreet's work has a more subdued undertone of violence, bounded by parameters of constraint and restraint rather than historical exigencies like war and abduction. With moments defined by varying degrees of violence, however, both women are deeply—perhaps primarily—concerned with the themes of loss and destruction at the hands of the Puritans' God. The sense of violence most closely linked with Rowlandson's narrative experience occurs in divine trials of the spirit and the flesh, precisely the trials that inspired Bradstreet's now-famous explorations of difficult submissions to God's will.[22]   Two works in particular perhaps best illustrate this test of spiritual conviction along the lines of Rowlandson's experience: "Upon the Burning of Our House" and "On My dear Grand-child Simon Bradstreet." [23]

The first poem begins with the speaker's being violently jolted awake with "thund'ring noise" and "piteous shrieks"; [24] Rowlandson, in her turn, is woken with gunfire and several houses burning, "the smoke ascending to heaven" (3).   Within a Puritan context, the danger and destructiveness of an Indian attack and a house fire serve to remind the audience of Divine wrathful priorities. The gutting of an earthly shelter betrays its flimsiness in the grand scheme of things.   Not for nothing does the smoke of Rowlandson's neighboring houses rise to heaven, since that is the hopeful destination of those being murdered right and left. Bradstreet too links apocalyptic vision with a subtle allusion to the afterlife, yet in her poem, the path from one to the other is longer. First must come the poet's grappling with her violent loss. In keeping with Puritan typology, personal loss bespeaks devastation on a greater scale; as Jeffrey Hammond's recent study, *Sinful Self, Saintly Self: The Puritan Experience of Poetry*, observes, "the sudden outbreak of fire parallels such depictions of the Second Coming as the opening stanzas of [Michael Wigglesworth's 1662] *Day of Doom*" (137).[25]   To parallel a jeremiad, however, is not to replicate it, as Rosamond Rosenmeier notes. Unlike most Puritan writers, Bradstreet focuses on earthly afflictions rather than the torments "of hell and damnation" (Rosenmeier 3). And just as her afflictions are of this world, so are her initial yearnings in this poem. Her oddly terse sermon that the one who lays her "goods in dust" is "just" is not at first effective; Bradstreet lingers on those earthly goods (292).   In apostrophizing and elegizing the dead house, she makes it human, a creative act that renders God's indirect brutality still more harsh. Savaged is not simply a shelter but a member of the family, a hospitable soul, an old friend, even a lover (a reference to the silenced "bridegroom's voice" seems to imply that even Christ has been lost here); Divine wrath has destroyed not simply clothes, books, and furniture but a fellow human being (293). Such an association increases the impact of God's fierce reminder (given also to Rowlandson) that "all's vanity" (293).

The final lines of Bradstreet's first stanza, according to Ellen Brandt, might indicate that "Fire is my Desire, [although] I let no man know it" (39). Brandt gives an erotic interpretation of this poem, in which fire is a "personal, albeit spiritual, rapine, in which devastation and a perverse pleasure are unmistakably intertwined" (39). Her argument might, I think, be pushed in a different direction: Bradstreet betrays a yearning for Divine violence, for the necessary mortification that must precede any pilgrim's ascent to that loftier home. In my reading, the pleasure is not quite so perverse. Rowlandson is powerfully cured of her fear that she might not receive enough affliction in this life. As a fellow Puritan, then, might not Bradstreet also recognize and even welcome the violence of Divine imperative and priority? In this peculiar embracing of such imperatives, I find a religious precursor to Marilynne Robinson's *Housekeeping*, though that novel's perspective is not, of course, Puritanical. Still, it might easily be subtitled "Adieu, all's vanity," with its evocative mixing of memory, loss, farewell, and the transience of all things— and of people. A kind of modern-day Bradstreet without the religion, Robinson's protagonist calls out, "Let them come unhouse me of this flesh" (159). Robinson echoes Bradstreet's emphasis on the ephemeral qualities of the corporeal through her own rhetorical linking of house and flesh.

Like Rowlandson, Bradstreet presents her personal spiritual torments through the image of one changed; indeed, both writers make effective use of the image of one made insomniac by reflections on an awful Divinity while everyone else sleeps. Even when safely returned to her community, Rowlandson is marked indelibly by her new knowledge: "when others are sleeping mine eyes are weeping" (120). Meanwhile, Bradstreet's first of "Several Occasional Meditations" notes that at night, while others have "at once both ease and rest," her eyes are "waking" and "open" (246). This image is in direct contrast with that of the thoughtless sleeper in "Upon the Burning," who is lulled by a falsely "silent night" (292). The pivotal image in each of these writings is eyes, open (and hence reflective, in both senses of the word, of God's presence and terrible potential) or closed (thereby foolishly insensible of same). Eyes are the instrument of witness. But what have they witnessed? Why are only *these* women awake? One very clear answer may be found in their similar obsession with acts of Divine violence in the material world.

Rowlandson cannot help but recall the acts of brutality presumably allowed, indeed—however indirectly—authored by her God. Bradstreet seems more willing to probe the effects of such brutality, going so far as to render the spirit's rebellion within her writing. This difference explains why Rowlandson seems overall less concerned than Bradstreet with trying to understand the workings of God. Bradstreet's witnessing takes on a more exploratory form. Yes, both women have been afflicted, and both bear witness to the Puritan world's most prevalent form of violence: God's testing. But Bradstreet's physical and spiritual trials are represented *solely* in her own words. That is, she does not rely on the biblical quotes and allusions with which Rowlandson so frequently braces her narrative. Of course, Rowlandson's motives in writing her narrative are bound up with the dual imperatives of providing a jeremiad for those sleepers who do not know enough to weep—yet—and also easing her return to a potentially suspicious community. Bradstreet, on the other hand, is creating her own art form and not a jeremiad, deliberately crafting a poem and not a captivity narrative. She shares with Rowlandson an abiding concern with the pilgrim's spiritual progress, but of the two writers, Bradstreet's engagement with the individual soul defines her work more strongly.   There is perhaps no more revealing vehicle for such engagement than the soul's responses to God's rigorous testing.

The notion of a useful Divine zeal often finds its rhetorical equivalent in Bradstreet's writing; for example, in the nineteenth of her "Meditations Divine and Moral," God "grinds [his servants] with grief and pain till they turn to dust" (275), while in her twentieth He heats them like iron in "the furnace of affliction and then beats them on His anvil into what frame he pleases" (277). Her husband is reminded, in "For the Restoration of My Dear Husband from a Burning Ague," that God "taught thee by His rod" (261). Such articulation indicates the violence of the spiritual struggle, as manifested in "The Flesh and the Spirit," wherein "Flesh" tries to persuade her sister, "Spirit," to indulge in this world's material stuff of honor, riches, and pleasure. Spirit turns on her sister with warlike words, promising to "see [her] laid in th' dust" (216) and promising her final exclusion from Heaven, as "things unclean" are prohibited there (215).   Spirit's vehemence is "theologically necessary," writes Hammond, "because she is fighting for her very existence" (128). Bradstreet's weapons here are only words, but they speak ferocity.

The issues of speaking and not speaking, in fact, largely defined Bradstreet's life as well as her work. Her sister, Sarah Dudley Keayne, had her child taken from her and was disinherited by her father because she insisted on preaching.[26] Susan Howe has observed that Bradstreet "seems to have persisted in her determination to keep on reading and writing by carefully controlling the tone of her rebellion," though on occasion her "cover slips and a voice of anger breaks out" (113). The elegy "In Honour of Queen Elizabeth," for example, insists on women's eminent ability "to play the rex," and reminds those men who would argue otherwise that to claim "our sex is void of reason" is "a slander now but once was treason" (196, 198). The threat beneath these lines is hardly veiled, since treason was a capital offense, punishable by death. In Bradstreet's "Contemplations," argues Rosenmeier, we hear a voice speaking of another type of violence, one that is neither human anger nor Divine punishment but, instead, a thinly veiled sexual violence. Casting the earth as female and the sun as male (and also as the Christlike "bridegroom"), the fifth stanza ends with that sun's heat "div[ing]" into nature's "darksome womb" (Bradstreet 206; Rosenmeier 149). I find Rosenmeier's reading of "rape," "damage," and "violence at the sexual core of that relationship" between the sun (divinity) and earth (nature) somewhat extreme. Nonetheless, I can see in it Bradstreet's acknowledgment of a forcefulness essential to human life and a sensual candor that might lead a twentieth-century audience to expect Puritanical condemnation.

As Hammond points out, however, Bradstreet's work "provoked not scandal but genuine pride among New Englanders" (4), much of it in the public record, as illustrated by the prefatory verses in *The Tenth Muse*.

Current scholarship tends to admire her for "her rebellion against religion and society," finding such dissent even in Bradstreet's determinedly autobiographical display; after all, "the mere self—one's private identity as a fallen individual—was precisely what Puritans wished to overcome" (Hammond 7, 23). Yet expressions of personal doubt and hints of rebellion were pivotal to Puritan spiritual ideology, contributing to Puritan modes of self-experience, and so were recognizable and accepted as part of the Puritan's progress. The violence of rebellion, therefore, like the violence of Divine corrective, serves a useful purpose in Bradstreet's poetry.

In discussing Bradstreet's critically "controversial" elegies on the deaths of her grandchildren, Paula Kopacz acknowledges the poet's distress but convincingly argues that she "deliberately vents her emotions" rather than denies them: "The task of the Puritan was not to repress emotions, but to direct them. . . . [w]hile modern sensibility sees 'tension' between emotion and doctrine, the Puritan viewed them as integrally related (182–83). Along these lines, we might read a necessary violence in Bradstreet's elegy for her grandson, "On Simon Bradstreet," which attests to the difficulties in grappling with God's will by re-creating the same kind of terseness displayed in "Upon the Burning of Our House" (and earlier in this study, in Rowlandson's descriptions of the initial Indian attack on her house). Her first line contains no subject but only verbs of a hasty departure ("No sooner came than gone"), as though anger, pain, and grief prevent any more direct reference to the child. He is the fourth grandchild she has lost, the third death of a close family member in less than half a year: her granddaughter Anne died in June 1669; her daughter-in-law Mercy in September; and Simon in November. Such a pattern not only bespeaks the realities of seventeenth-century life but also reads as a grim shorthand for what Kopacz has called "the two levels of time"—in this case, Bradstreet's earthly life span and her spiritual one (184). The suddenness of the poem's opening, as well as the curtness of the fourth line's "Cropt by th'Almighty's hand," rejects a lingering sense of mourning and instead emphasizes an abruptness imitative of the hand that so swiftly cuts down Bradstreet's "three flowers," continuing with a succinct (and, to many contemporary readers, unconvincing) "yet is He good" (237).[27] While Kopacz writes that such a phrase signifies the "eternal, enduring presence of His goodness [as] an undeniable fact," I see also in its quality of brevity the violence of Bradstreet's inner struggle (184). I agree with Kopacz that Bradstreet's use of the word "Let's" (as in "Let us") is exhortatory and not ironically speculative when she writes, "let's be mute," "let's not dispute," "Let's say" God is compassionate. Yet in its contracted imperative there is a tight-lipped vehemence that betrays what it costs Bradstreet to "reconcile [herself] to timeless existence" (Kopacz 185). As she remarks elsewhere, in a poem about being separated from her husband (titled simply "Another"), "Oppressed minds, abruptest tales do tell" (226).[28]

We have already seen that abrupt tale in Rowlandson's narrative. Now we see it in Bradstreet's struggle to reconcile herself to the brutalities inherent in Divine will and seventeenth-century life and death.   Form follows function for both writers; a notably violent existence leaves its traces in their work, in which we see repeatedly the brusque and broken pattern made when lives are jolted out of order or simply cut short.   Death, which came so early and so often cruelly to the Puritans, required proper interpretation in their writings, since, as Breitweiser observes, it was "Puritanism's area both of greatest bonanza and of greatest risk. . . . [Death] was not to be perceived as loss, as the human world's hemorrhage, but rather as transpositional or liminal event . . . [when] the soul returned to light or dark" (55).   Such an event demanded "constrained sorrow in response," yet the curt phrases of Rowlandson's narrative and Bradstreet's poetry themselves betray an anger and sorrow that refuses restraint (Breitweiser 55).   Understandably, then, the most prevalent form of violence in their work is the violence that emerges from conflict: between grief and anger's expression and their repression, between survival of the flesh and acknowledgment of the spirit, between Indians' insistence on their ties to the land and Europeans' insistence on their right to settle that land.   That conflicts should so characterize the writing of these women is even less unusual when we remember still another opposition: that between Puritanism's emphasis on public confession for members of its elect[29] and its general ban on women's public speaking.   A ban that both Rowlandson and Bradstreet managed to evade, it contributes to a centuries-long dichotomy between countless histories recorded by men and those remembered but withheld by women, a dichotomy that underlies so much of this study.

VIOLENT REFORM

It is a relatively short distance from Puritan captivity narratives and treatments of Divine wrath to nineteenth-century slave narratives, particularly those authored by women who make use of the sentimental novel's conventions.   While "the narratives of white women captives and black slaves [share] a familiar subtext of powerlessness" (Zafar 26), they also share a particular understanding of the uses of violence.[30]   This section explores three slave narratives, one fictional and two autobiographical: Harriet Beecher Stowe's *Uncle Tom's Cabin* (1852), Harriet Wilson's *Our Nig; or, Sketches from the Life of a Free Black, in a Two-Story White House, North; Showing That Slavery's Shadows Fall Even There* (1859),[31] and Harriet Jacobs's *Incidents in the Life of a Slave Girl* (1861).   Written primarily for white female audiences[32] and to aid the abolitionists' cause, they all rely heavily on the sentimental novel's deliberate appeal to strong emotion and are "aimed at socializing a murderously unjust society" (Armstrong 5).[33]   Of the several violent themes the three texts variously share, perhaps no other is so conspicuous as the wielding of violence in the name of social justice and reform.   In this section, I examine how each narrative explores in varying degrees a series of brutal domestic inversions, the theme of both human and

Divine vengeance, and the threat of sexual violence. Paradoxically, these authors manipulate the sentimental novel to highlight what nineteenth-century America sought to obscure: the brutal scaffolding beneath the sentimental ideals of female purity and piety, and domestic serenity.

Despite those professed ideals, the sentimental novel was perhaps not wholly unaware of what lay beneath them, especially when one considers the links between sentimental and gothic literary traditions, specifically in the form of often horrific inversions of the innocent and familiar to the wild and terrifying. A recurrent theme in all three of these narratives is such violent domestic inversion, all the more dramatic in the sentimental novels that helped to create and then reinforce the cult of true womanhood and valorization of domesticity. So much cogent scholarship has focused on the gothic elements and two main domestic inversions in *Uncle Tom's Cabin*, *Our Nig,* and *Incidents in the Life of a Slave Girl* that I need only outline them briefly here. Most commonly shared is the figure of the horrifically inverted Mother.[34] On the upright side, we have Stowe's Quaker mother, Rachel, who "rules [her] world" through Christian love and motherly gentleness, and (in *Our Nig*) Linda Brent's grandmother, called Aunt Martha, whose dignity and piety command respect from even the villainous Dr. Flint (Tompkins, "Sentimental Power" 519). On the underside, we have Marie St. Clare in *Uncle Tom's Cabin,* Mrs. Bellmont in *Our Nig*, and Mrs. Flint in *Incidents in the Life of a Slave Girl.* (As I discuss in later chapters, Toni Morrison and Gayl Jones revise and re-orient this notion of vampire-like, or dangerous, mothers, linking the danger to historical and social causes when the mothers are slave women who have increasingly complex reasons, if not justifications, for behaving dangerously to their own children.) We also have repeated inversions of domestic safety and nurturance. Stowe, for one, depicts the "slave-owning home as [a] gothic site" (168) precisely because of its openness to inversion: "the protective space called home, built by males, could soon prove prison, madhouse, seraglio, or charnel house to its female inhabitants" (Jenkins 168, 162).[35] Stowe's vivid gothic space is Simon Legree's house, with its miasma of unvoiced murders and hauntings; Wilson's is Mrs. Bellmont's torture chamber-kitchen, as well as the dark, close room where Frado must sleep; Jacobs's is the suffocating garret Linda Brent hides in, admittedly protected by her beloved grandmother's roof, but also forced to watch and unable to act as her son is bitten by a dog and terrorized by Dr. Flint.[36] Sanchez-Eppler, in fact, deftly interprets the kitchen cruelties of Mrs. Flint (who spits into kettles to keep slaves from eating from them) and Dr. Flint (who chokes the cook by cramming disliked food down her throat); "the kettle, instead of containing food for the body, becomes a receptacle for excretions from the body; the cook, instead of preparing the meal, is choked by it. Food withheld, contaminated, or crammed down the throat becomes punitive, its nutritive value perverted into a sign of dominance and submission" (n.16, 166–67). That no American home, North or South, was safe from the effects of slavery is made abundantly clear in these nineteenth-century narratives and echoed in such recent works as *Beloved* and *Corregidora*.

The slave narrative's "use" of violence and depictions of human suffering for the purposes of social reformation is an interesting twist to the notion of Puritanical "thriftiness," the concept that one can make good use of suffering. In these nineteenth-century narratives, however, the suffering is imposed by human, not Divine, law and is no longer "presumed to be an end in itself; it was thought to be the agonizing precursor of enduring moral and political victory" for abolitionists, who were, paradoxically, generally nonviolent (Wolff, "Masculinity" 602). Abolitionists both black and white shared a peculiar and protean relationship with violence, on both personal and political grounds. The national issues at stake were largely focused around violence and nonviolence. Even as they espoused the nonviolent position, abolitionists had to ask themselves if America "as a nation [should] engage in conquest and colonization" and whether "right-thinking men [should] engage in violent means of protest" against possible Constitutional support of slavery, and finally, if the nation as a whole should "engage in a civil war to settle the issue of slavery" (Wolff 603). Like the Quakers in Stowe's *Uncle Tom's Cabin* (and with the notable exception of the more recent convert, Phineas), abolitionists were usually "obliged to respond with only passive resistance" to even violent provocations (Wolff 603). If white abolitionists were occasionally displeased with William Lloyd Garrison's "inflexibly nonviolent posture," the black abolitionists were even more so (603; as Wolff notes, too, the Fugitive Slave Law only increased potential for violence, even among those pacific abolitionists).

In "Everybody's Protest Novel," James Baldwin passionately censures Stowe's "determination to flinch from nothing in presenting the complete picture" because, he argues, she does so out of sheer "panic of being hurled into the flames" of hell, rather than out of a sincere wish for blacks' equality with whites (496, 498). Although I find it somewhat excessive, Baldwin's argument does illuminate Stowe's ongoing theme of vengeance, both divine and human. As Joshua Bellin notes, *Uncle Tom's Cabin* indicates that Stowe "believe[d] that slavery could be abolished only by God" and, further, that because she was horrified at "the prospect of human—and especially black— violence," she felt obliged to "temper these uncontrollable powers by subsuming them in the Divine Plan" (283, 284). Whatever her fears, however, Stowe's text is as generous in its threats of human violence as any "impassioned pamphleteer" could wish (Baldwin 498), so much so that one of her contemporary reviewers (albeit a careless one) condemned Stowe for her "incitement to violence" when George Harris "murders" one of the slave catchers (Wolff 612–13). That George only wounds Tom Loker, and is even thankful that Loker survives, seems inconsequential. More powerful than the actual plot is the threat to which this reviewer responded. It is odd that such terrifying fantasies never struck slave owners without this model before them, since "in every moment of their lives . . . the masters [had] their slaves' blades at their throats," both figuratively (they might have had their houses burned down around them as they slept, or been poisoned by their cooks, or had their children murdered by their mammies) and literally, since a slave who shaved his master could easily let the blade slip (Accardo and Portelli 80–81).

The final, and perhaps most female-informed, element I want to discuss in these three narratives is the treatment of graphic violence, both sexual and generally physical. The ideals of the sentimental novel, highlighting as they did the purity of (white) American womanhood, offer a particularly sharp background against which the sexual violence of the slave narrative may be set. [37] Important to any consideration of the differences between Stowe's, Wilson's, and Jacobs's portrayals of sexual violence are their publication chronology and their separate relationships to fiction and autobiography. White author Harriet Beecher Stowe's fictional account of slavery, *Uncle Tom's Cabin,* preceded the works of two black authors: Harriet Wilson's ostensibly fictional (although really autobiographical) *Our Nig* and Harriet Jacobs's autobiographical *Incidents in the Life of a Slave Girl.* In the publishing world, Stowe's authority as a northern fiction writer composing a narrative about black slaves' experiences far outweighed that of two black women, both of whom experienced firsthand that which Stowe described. Harriet Wilson's narrative is followed by an appendix of three letters (at least two of which seem to have been written by white women) attesting to her real authorship and character, and Harriet Jacobs had to rely heavily on Lydia Maria Child to edit, publish, and finally authenticate her own narrative. [38] While her later *Key to Uncle Tom's Cabin* was intended to provide nonfictional documentation of that novel's fictional depictions of slavery, Stowe needed no initial testimonials to ensure that her book became the first American novel to sell over a million copies.

More relevant to my discussion than these differences in accepted narrative authority, however, is the progression from white-authored fiction to black-authored fiction (while Gates's introduction explores the connections between Wilson's life and her narrative, *Our Nig* was presented as a novel), and finally to black autobiography. The last written and thus, chronologically, the last to be accepted, is Jacobs's autobiography: the narrative that explores most openly and most probingly the sexual threat posed in black-and-white relations. I would argue that, in fact, only after Stowe's subtle and Wilson's overdetermined treatments of sexual violence, was the reading public able to accept Jacobs's more brutal depiction.[39] It is far different, of course, to read autobiography than to read fiction. In laying out the terms of sexual vulnerability for black women, Jacobs presented far more forthrightly than Stowe the sexual violence of miscegenation—essentially, white slave owners raping black women, as opposed to the prevailing white fear of black men raping white women.[40]

Any discussion of sexual violence in these three narratives must recognize that the sentimental novel, with its deliberate provocation of strong feeling, highlights a common danger in the relationship between audience and the writing of violence.   There is a fine line between using violence and experiences of physical and psychological suffering to evoke empathy, sympathy, and eventually action, and allowing violence to degenerate into titillation.   In the telling and the empathy lies also the temptation of sensationalism, perhaps the greatest pitfall in re-creating stories of violence. Anyone who thinks this too harsh a statement need only read Lydia Maria Child's 1860 letter to Harriet Jacobs, asking for more evidence of Southern brutalities on the heels of Nat Turner's 1831 slave rebellion:

You say the reader would not believe what you saw "inflicted on men, women, and children, without the slightest ground of suspicion against them."   What *were* those inflictions? Were any tortured to make them confess? And how? Were any killed? Please write some of the most striking particulars, and let me have them to insert. (*Incidents,* ed. Yellin, 244)

The most disturbing aspect of the breathless quality in Child's series of questions is its familiarity to any reader of these narratives.   Titillation is a grosser form of aesthetic indulgence: both deflect the reader's attention from the head-on confrontation with stark violence that ostensibly represents the author's subject.   For all its reliance on the cult of pure womanhood, domesticity, and the decency of the Christian family, the sentimental narrative was fully aware of the powers of violence and horror, powers that are easily corrupted by a demeaning form of excitement. Yet sentimental novels are not unique in their risk of cheapening history through the retelling of its brutality, as my later chapters show.   In particular, Cynthia Ozick's *The Shawl* and Leslie Marmon Silko's *Almanac of the Dead* both hazard this territory as they create art out of explicitly violent histories.   Unlike these earlier narratives, however, both *The Shawl* and *Almanac of the Dead* foreground this issue of art and brutality, making it inextricable from their larger historical concerns.

　　Graphic sexual violence was unspeakable in the cult of domesticity and notions about pure womanhood that prevailed in nineteenth-century American writing. Yet a skillful, covert allusion to sexual vulnerability and its consequent threat of sexual violence forged a link between depictions of black slave women and their white women readers.   After all, sexual vulnerability negatively defined the popular notion of American womanhood in the eighteenth and nineteenth centuries; in the popular literature of the time, if a woman were not scrupulously pure, she risked probable sexual victimization (and even death) at the hands of an unscrupulous man.[41] This muted awareness of sexual vulnerability, along with more conscious depictions of physical pain and suffering, occupies a perverse place of honor in sentimental narratives. As Fanny Nudelman writes, because pain can be "communicated quite easily," suffering in literature can "transcend physical boundaries, enabling a public recognition of private trauma" (946). If the sentimental novel sparks a sympathy through pain, then it may also invoke an empathy through its reiteration of women's vulnerability to sexual violence— a reiteration that increases markedly from Stowe's narrative to Jacobs's, with

Wilson's text providing a peculiar twist on that vulnerability. Too, physical suffering is comparatively glimpsed, rather than highlighted, in Stowe's novel, as opposed to the works of Wilson and Jacobs. Yet although *Uncle Tom's Cabin* does not dwell at length on the physical agonies leading up to Tom's martyrdom, it gives them more explicit attention than it does the sexual violence that menaces Eliza Harris, the "tragic mulatta" whose beauty and refinement make her a valuable figure to slave catchers Tom Loker and Marks (F. Foster 34). Stowe only hints at this type of vulnerability, as when mulatto Susan and her quadroon daughter, Emmeline, spend their last night together before the girl is sold to Simon Legree: Susan "knows that tomorrow any man, however vile and brutal, however godless and merciless, if he only has money to pay for her, may become owner of her daughter, body and soul" (383). This is precisely the kind of realization that will catalyze Sethe, in Toni Morrison's *Beloved*, to commit infanticide, after her own violation by her master's nephews; in Stowe's novel, Susan will only pray and grieve, and disappear from the story entirely five pages later. This line, along with the following description of George Harris's parentage, constitutes Stowe's most overt statement about black women's vulnerability to sexual violence: "George was, by his father's side, of white descent. His mother was one of those unfortunates of her race, marked out by personal beauty to be the slave of the passions of her possessor, and the mother of children who may never know a father" (134). For her part, Jacobs moves far beyond Stowe's veiled intimations, defining her experience of slavery most explicitly and most fully through her precarious position of vulnerability to Dr. Flint's continual sexual threats.[42] But *Our Nig* is remarkable for its deeply encoded treatment of sexual violence, a treatment that differs sharply from that of either *Uncle Tom's Cabin* or *Incidents in the Life of a Slave Girl*.

Harriet Wilson writes extreme variation on the theme of sexual violence, the very theme that initially seems to be lacking in *Our Nig*. We have no villain, only a villainess in the mother-turned-tyrant, Mrs. Bellmont. Like Stowe's Marie St. Clare, Mrs. Bellmont is a horrifically inverted mother—the devil in the house, as opposed to the angel. Unlike Marie, however, Mrs. Bellmont not only has the strength to do her own whipping, but also takes genuine pleasure in it. Indeed, the voraciousness and enthusiasm with which she attacks Frado is akin to sadistic sexual pleasure, as Wilson's narrative attests:

[Frado] was under [Mrs. Bellmont] in every sense of the word. What an opportunity to indulge her vixen nature! No matter what occurred to ruffle her, or from what source provocation came . . . a few blows on Nig seemed to relieve her of a portion of ill-will. . . . Mrs. Bellmont, enraged . . . kicked her so forcibly as to throw her upon the floor . . . [and] followed kick after kick in quick succession and power. (41, 43–44)[43]

Daughter Mary too seems prey to this gluttonous indulgence of vicious enthusiasm: "Taking a large carving knife from the table, she hurled it, in her rage, at the defenceless girl" (64). Both Mary and Mrs. Bellmont shriek, scream, and vent at Frado in what can only be read as an orgy of passion, providing ample illustration of what Stowe's Auguste St. Clare describes to his northern cousin Ophelia as the "great class of vicious, improvident, degraded people" thriving among slave owners (271).[44] Even St. Clare's less mild brother Alfred agrees that the system of slavery "gives too free scope to the passions, altogether" (313), even to the listless Marie St. Clare, who experiences a vicarious thrill in sending a pretty young slave out to be whipped: "now I'll bring her down—I'll make her lie in the dust! . . . I'll teach her, with all her airs, that she's no better than the raggedest black wench that walks the streets!" (372). Stowe shows that license extending further to those slaves who turn overseer for Simon Legree and take delight in hunting down and whipping their fellow slaves. Sambo first kicks an exhausted woman in the fields, then, "with a brutal grin," sticks a pin its entire length into her flesh (409). It is the grin, the enjoyment, that Wilson emphasizes in her depiction of Mrs. Bellmont:

It is impossible to give an impression of the manifest enjoyment of Mrs. B. in these kitchen scenes. It was her favorite exercise to enter the apartment noisily, vociferate orders, give a few sudden blows to quicken Nig's pace. . . . Excited by so much indulgence of a dangerous passion, she seemed left to unrestrained malice; and snatching a towel, stuffed the mouth of the sufferer, and beat her cruelly. (66, 82)

Mrs. Bellmont's interest in Frado is distorted and obsessive; after both Jack and James Bellmont comment at least twice on Frado's good looks, Mrs. Bellmont shaves off her "glossy ringlets" (68), as if to keep others from admiring her beauty. Shortly afterward, Frado is commanded to eat from Mrs. Bellmont's plate, in a kind of perverted familiarity (71). Significantly, Frado can bring herself to do so only after her beloved dog licks the plate clean; as James Bellmont astutely points out to his mother, Frado has not been "treated . . . so as to gain [Mrs. Bellmont's] love," so she rejects this freakish intimacy (72).

Stowe's portrayal of the sensual passions inflamed by slavery is muted, and Wilson's is admittedly metaphoric; Jacobs's is overt. Her experience of slavery is dictated by her sexual vulnerability and the sexual threats of her master, Dr. Flint, as well as the choices she must make to circumvent his untiring advances upon her. She also uses those elements of vulnerability and threat to connect with her (white) readers. With a series of negations, Jacobs draws a peculiar parallel between herself and white readers. In a passage that begins, "You never knew what it is to be a slave; to be entirely unprotected by law or custom . . . you never shuddered at the sound of [a white master's] footsteps, and trembled within hearing of his voice,"[45] Jacobs reiterates what her readers never experienced but could certainly imagine: the incessant threat of sexual violence that underpins the code of pure (white) womanhood. Such an imagining is a necessary link between the two posited figures in Jacobs's narrative: the teller and the listener. "[T]he threat of their similar sexual vulnerability" is deliberately wielded to join these figures (Sanchez-Eppler 104). The epidemic lynchings of black men during Reconstruction illustrate horribly the prominence of sexual vulnerability—particularly its defense by white men—to the white construction of pure, white womanhood.[46] Jacobs inverts this racial equation of attacker and victim with her portrayal of the white Dr. Flint, who fills the young mind of his black slave "with unclean images, such as only a vile monster could think of" (44), and makes her realize that her own beauty endangers her: "That which commands admiration in the white woman only hastens the degradation of the female slave. . . . [Flint swore] by heaven and earth that he would compel me to submit to him" (46). Granted, the stratagems of rape that Jacobs depicts are mild compared to those that Gayl Jones writes of in her 1975 *Corregidora*, in which women speak graphically of being raped, being locked in rooms and forced into prostitution, and of being beaten. Nonetheless, Jacobs is clear:

[R]eared in an atmosphere of licentiousness and fear . . . [w]hen a slave girl is fourteen or fifteen, her owner, or his sons, or the overseer, or perhaps all of them, begin to bribe her with presents. If these fail to accomplish their purpose, she is whipped or starved into submission to their will. (79)[47]

She also tells how, on one plantation, an overseer enters "every cabin to see that men and their wives had gone to bed together," because women must "continually increase their owner's stock" (76). As do the St. Clare brothers in *Uncle Tom's Cabin*, Jacobs stresses that slavery corrupts whites as well as blacks: "It makes the white fathers cruel and sensual; the sons violent and licentious; it contaminates the daughters, and makes the wives wretched" (81).

Wilson's and Jacobs's closer position to this kind of corruption allows them to move beyond Stowe's domestic agenda, which posits women as the United States's earthly saviors.[48] Marie St. Clare is the only villainess in Stowe's text, and even she does not inflict violence upon her slaves herself. On the other hand, Wilson reveals Mrs. Bellmont's sadistic pleasures, while Jacobs reverses the commonly feared threat of black male sexual violence wrought upon white women. The licentiousness of white masters extends not simply to their sons but sometimes to their daughters as well, as shown in the following peculiar twist on gender and racial power relations. A local plantation owner's daughter chooses "one of the meanest slaves on his plantation" to father her child; her selection is of "the most brutalized, over whom her authority could be exercised with less fear of exposure" (80). Because white fathers hold more power than white mothers, however, a baby with a white mother and black father is either killed instantly or exiled from the area, while a baby with reversed parentage is "unblushingly reared for the market" (81). Jacobs's concern with an "unblushing" portrayal of sexual coercion and violence lays the narrative groundwork for her decision to take the white Mr. Sands for a lover, so as to confound Dr. Flint's designs.

The bluntness with which Jacobs tells sexual violence extends, even increases, with her depictions of other forms of violence, particularly in the chapter entitled "Sketches of Neighboring Slaveholders." Stowe chooses to emphasize Tom's Christ-like suffering and endurance throughout his final beating on Legree's plantation, stating only that "[s]cenes of blood and cruelty are shocking to our ear and heart. What man has nerve to do, man has not nerve to hear. What brother-man and brother-Christian must suffer, cannot be told us" (475). Aside from a few references to "blood" and "degrading stripes" of the whip, this is all she has to say about the violence shown her hero. Wilson, for her part, focuses mainly on Mrs. Bellmont's sadistic relish. Out of all three, I think, Jacobs requires the most fortitude from her reader. After describing a favorite punishment of the planter Mr. Litch, who liked to roast pork fat over a man's naked body so that "scalding drops of fat continually fell on the bare flesh" (71), Jacobs refers to the bloodhounds who "literally tore the flesh" from the bones of runaway slaves (72) and then progresses to a whipping so severe that a man's "shirt was one clot of blood," removable "from the raw flesh" only with the application of lard (73). The worst tale is that of a man named James, beaten "from his head to his feet, then washed with strong brine, to prevent the flesh from mortifying," and imprisoned in a cotton gin "which was screwed down, only allowing him room to turn on his side when he could not lie on his back" (75). By the second day, the man is unable to reach the water just outside the cotton gin, and after four days he is found dead, "partly eaten by rats and vermin. Perhaps the rats that devoured his bread had gnawed him before life was extinct" (76). Compare the explicitness of this account to that of old Prue in *Uncle Tom's Cabin*, from whose agony we are triply distanced. First, news of her death is relayed not by the omniscient narrator but by a woman who appears but once in the entire novel and speaks only fifty words in total. The most important ones are these: "Prue, she got drunk agin,—and they had her down cellar,—and thar they left her all day,—and I hearn 'em saying that the *flies had got to her,—and she's dead!*" (Stowe 256). Second, we do not know precisely what has happened to Prue, except through Miss Ophelia's later summary that Prue has been beaten to death and Stowe's following elliptical phrase about the story's "most shocking particulars" (257). Third, Stowe redirects her reader's attention away from Prue and toward Eva, whose face is depicted in far more detail than are Prue's sufferings, with "her large, mystic eyes dilated with horror, and every drop of blood driven from her lips and cheeks" (256). Stowe veers her readers' attention to her characters' martyrdom, and Wilson focuses on the ostensibly fictional Frado's torments at the hands of Mrs. Bellmont, but I believe it is Jacobs who, in her close attention to detail, persuades her reader that "I draw no imaginary pictures of southern homes. I am telling you the plain truth" (56). The graphic violence that permeates her narrative attests to that truth.

OPEN SPACES, STIFLING INTERIORS

Willa Cather's 1895 observation that "geography is a terribly fatal thing sometimes" (*Courier* 8) might serve as an apt subtitle for *O Pioneers!* (1913) and *My Ántonia* (1918). It is an equally apt commentary on the fatalities of a far different sort of geography: the enclosed, stifling space of the nursery room/lunatic asylum that Charlotte Perkins Gilman depicts in "The Yellow Wallpaper," first published in 1892. Yet on the surface, Gilman and Cather have much to separate them, primarily in the area of feminism. Gilman's ardent polemics must have been precisely the kind of overtly political writing and thinking that Cather despised in the women's suffrage movement. Although Cather never publicly reviewed Gilman's work, she was clear enough in her stance on women's suffrage and wrote a scathing review of the second volume of *The Woman's Bible*, edited under the direction of Elizabeth Cady Stanton. As Sharon O'Brien has observed in *Willa Cather: The Emerging Voice*, Cather had little use for the Suffragists, since, unlike Gilman, "she did not question whether social institutions and expectations might have defined and confined women" (O'Brien 124). For Frances Kaye, Cather's declaration that "the world broke in two in 1922 or thereabouts" (*Not Under Forty* v) refers in part to the moment when she discovered an inhospitable world around her: "a world of woman suffrage and prohibition" that represented an attack on the male-dominated world of art in which she had done so well (111).

In contrast, Gilman's radical feminism permeated her art, emphasizing what Elizabeth Ammons has called "a tenacious nineteenth-century belief in the overt political—even evangelical—function of literature" (*Conflicting Stories* 34).[49] There is the separatist women's Utopia depicted in the 1915 *Herland*, as well as nonfiction such as *The Home: Its Work and Influence* (1903) and the sharp-witted *Women and Economics: A Study of the Economic Relation Between Men and Women* (1899), both of which explore the ways in which women (and to a lesser degree, men) are diminished by the former's socioeconomic dependence on the latter.

Despite their differences, nonetheless, the roles and fictional depictions of women illuminate two shared concerns in Cather's and Gilman's work: the destructive quality of heterosexual love, which so often turns to disaster, and each writer's navigation of violence within specific architectural or geographical spaces. The latter concern is truly linked to feminism in "The Yellow Wallpaper" (indeed, the word *feminist* does not apply to Cather), whose narrator is shut up in a room by her husband and forbidden to work, read, or write so that she might "recover" from postpartum depression. That threatened erasure of self recurs, in a far different context, within the violence that is inextricable from Cather's sweeping landscapes in *O Pioneers!* and *My Ántonia*.

For the narrator of "The Yellow Wallpaper" marriage is psychologically fatal: Gilman depicts a physician-husband turned jailer and his prescribed "rest-cure" turned imprisonment. The story is based on Gilman's experience under the care of the late-nineteenth-century nerve specialist, Dr. S. Weir Mitchell, who diagnosed her postpartum depression as nervous prostration, ordered a month's worth of complete abstention from intellectual and physical activity, and advised her never to "touch pen, brush, or pencil as long as you live" (Gilman, *Living* 96). She very nearly went mad. "The Yellow Wallpaper" is her story, replacing her husband, Charles Stetson (with whom she said she was genuinely happy, although they eventually divorced), with "John," a condescending, selfish doctor who smothers his wife into insanity. As Hedges has observed, Gilman's narrative bespeaks her sense of being "trapped by the role assigned the wife within the conventional nineteenth-century marriage," wherein "marriage meant children and too many children meant incapacity for other work" (46). An indictment of the white, middle-class social system that made women utterly dependent on their husbands, violence in "The Yellow Wallpaper" is of the psychological kind, stemming from mental constraints and imprisonment in a nursery whose barred windows and nailed-down bed suggest a mental asylum.

Cather's treatment of heterosexual love generally culminates in more physical destructiveness than Gilman's.[50] For her characters, that love turns either to ruin and exile (if only temporary—Ántonia virtually disappears from the middle of her self-titled story, once she reaches sexual maturity and comes to grief because of it); or to rape—witness Wick Cutter's attempted attack on Ántonia and his subsequent beating of Jim; or to maddened jealousy and carnage, as with the fatal triangle of Emil Bergson and Marie and Frank Shabata. No matter what, it seems to promise sheer agony for all concerned. In *O Pioneers!* Carl Linstrum suggests that Marie is "cut to pieces" by her love for Emil Bergson, and certainly the murderous fallout of this love nearly destroys Alexandra, Emil's sister and Marie's close friend.[51] Additionally, Marie is the one whom Alexandra—and Cather, too, perhaps—sees as responsible for the double murder: "She blamed Marie bitterly. And why, with her happy, affectionate nature, should she have brought destruction and sorrow to all who had loved her [?]. . . . There was Emil, in the Norwegian graveyard at home, and here [in prison] was Frank Shabata" (115–16). Beyond the guilt that Alexandra attributes to her, Marie is no longer in her thoughts; not even her gravesite is mentioned. Emil and Frank are rendered practically innocent, victims of female passion, while Marie is the blight of their lives. In *My Ántonia*, however, the fusion of passion and violence is gender blind: when "Crazy Mary" Benson's husband moons over Lena Lingard, the enraged older woman chases Lena with a corn knife, threatening to "trim some of that shape off you" (82);[52] and Wick Cutter nearly rapes Jim before realizing he is not Ántonia, then beats him severely. Like Marie Shabata, Ántonia Shimerda is held responsible for her (would-be) attacker's violence, since Jim blames her for "let[ting] me in for all this disgustingness."[53] Kaye argues that the reader's "sense of indignation" is, like Jim's, "dislocated" to the extent of believing that "the intended victim . . . somehow brings about the crime" (101). The violence of Frank's lethal jealousy in *O Pioneers!* that ends with his killing Marie and Emil is tempered in *My Ántonia*, but only just: replacing it are attempted rape, disgust and horror, and physical disfigurement, the last a telling item for an author who abhorred illness and any type of physical unsightliness (Kaye 101–2). Yet for Cather, those whom love does not destroy (namely, Ántonia and Alexandra), it strengthens, whereas Gilman's heroine in "The Yellow Wallpaper," transformed into a furiously "creeping" woman, is defeated by her encounter with heterosexual love.[54]   What saves Cather's heroines, finally, is their abiding connection with Nebraska's ferocious terrain; what helps to undermine Gilman's is her terrible geographic and spatial isolation.

For Cather, the images of violence that stem from nature are linked quite closely with the fear of being sucked into, made null and void by, the landscape. Not coincidentally, the opening setting of *O Pioneers!* and Jim's initial response to the Divide in *My Ántonia* strongly resemble Cather's own remembrance of arriving in Webster County, Nebraska, at nine years old: "I felt a good deal as if we had come to the end of everything—it was a kind of erasure of personality. . . . [although] I had heard my father say you had to show grit in a new country. . . I thought I should go under" (*Kingdom of Art* 448; qtd. in O'Brien 63).   That potential for obliteration recurs in *O Pioneers!*: Hanover, Nebraska, is "trying not to be blown away" at the very beginning of the book, and the houses are "haphazard on the tough prairie sod. . . . None of them had any appearance of permanence, and the howling wind blew under them as well as over them" (1); "the vast hardness" of "the stern frozen country" looms over "a sod house crouching in a hollow. . . . The great fact was the land itself, which seemed to overwhelm the little beginnings of human society that struggled in its sombre wastes. . . . Men were too weak to make any mark here" (5).   Finally, Jim's introduction to the landscape in *My Ántonia* initially resembles these two responses, though it changes swiftly to an awed acceptance:

There was nothing but land: not a country at all, but the material out of which countries are made. . . . I had the feeling that the world was left behind, that we had got over the edge of it, and were outside man's jurisdiction. . . . Between that earth and that sky I felt erased, blotted out. I did not say my prayers that night: here, I felt, what would be would be. (7)

Here, the human experience of Nebraska's geography approaches something like a resigned comfort, and even that comfort has a submissive quality, a capitulation to the raw forces of nature big and indifferent enough to swallow him whole.   Even the God of humanity seems powerless out here, since prayers are useless, and "what would be would be."

Jim's is a quickened journey from fear to calm assent, the same course that Cather charts in *O Pioneers!* and again in *My Ántonia*.   Nebraska's brutally indifferent landscape finally evokes an acknowledgment of nature as a force that subsumes humanity in death without struggle or pain.   What is seen as violent in some instances—the landscape threatening to subsume the humans, to erase their personalities, to annihilate them—is turned, in Cather's art, to the kind of serenity that Marilynne Robinson's Ruth echoes in *Housekeeping*, as she muses on how the dead truly do become part of the earth and water surrounding us. After the shock of Emil and Marie's murder, Alexandra comes to her own understanding of death, shot through with natural imagery:

After you once get cold clear through, the feeling of the rain on you is sweet. . . . It carries you back into the dark, before you were born; you can't see things, but they come to you, somehow, and you know them and aren't afraid of them. Maybe it's like that with the dead. If they feel anything at all, it's the old things, before they were born, that comfort people like the feeling of their own bed does when they are little. (111)

The only man-made image—the bed—is used as a simile, while the rest of the writing creates a mythic connection between the rain soaking clear through the skin and memories of "before you were born." Similarly, Sharon O'Brien aptly connects Cather's feared "erasure of personality" with Jim's acceptance of it; he evokes Alexandra's primeval memories as he lies back in Grandmother Burden's garden, when he wants to be nothing more than "something that lay under the sun and felt it. . . . Perhaps we feel like that when we die and become a part of something entire, whether it is sun and air, or goodness and knowledge. At any rate, that is happiness; to be dissolved into something complete and great" (12). Cather's understanding of humans' standing within an often violent geography illuminates her negotiation of self-erasure within the vast plains of Nebraska, the sense of being pulled into something larger than oneself. For Cather, that something larger is the landscape. For Gilman, even in her most creative work, "The Yellow Wallpaper," it means the economic and social position of women (albeit white, middle-class or working women). Certainly, for a woman, understanding social causes and consequences (as Gilman wrote so much about), rather than individual privileges (of the kind Cather had enjoyed), also signifies seeing oneself as part of something larger. Neither writer can negotiate this relationship between self and that "something larger" without also waging the violent struggle against submersion. In Cather's case, that struggle is against a fiercely cold rain that "soaks you through" or a bleak, flat plain that threatens to consume one's personality; in Gilman's, against a brutally repressive social system that drives a woman over the brink into madness.

Cather's wide-open spaces may dwarf her human characters, and even threaten to swallow them whole, but they are not carefully, even maddeningly, controlled the way nature is in "The Yellow Wallpaper." As Jean Kennard notes, "The only access to nature [Gilman's] narrator has is to a carefully cultivated and confined garden. [Sandra] Gilbert and [Susan] Gubar point out that in contrast the idea of 'open country' is the place of freedom" (Kennard 81). Just as the hostile landscape imprints itself on Jim Burden and the readers of *O Pioneers!* and Cather herself, so too does the wallpaper in Gilman's abhorrent nursery make its malevolence known.   The color infuriates, but the design goes one step further, with its "defiance of law" that echoes Jim's concept of a land beyond "man's jurisdiction" and its mind-torturing pattern: "You think you have mastered it, but . . . It slaps you in the face, knocks you down, and tramples upon you" (25). This wallpaper is nature identified, with an evil twist: it reminds "one of a fungus . . . an interminable string of toadstools, budding and sprouting in endless convolutions." Whereas Nebraska intimidates through its defiant barrenness, this internal space is defined by a revolting fecundity—what Annie Dillard has called "the teeming evidence that birth and growth, which we value, are ubiquitous and blind, that life itself is so astonishingly cheap" (163). There is, nonetheless, a similarity between the prairie and the larger space—house and gardens—inhabited by Gilman's narrator: the feeling of being cut off from others.[55] In "The Yellow Wallpaper" this sensation is man-made rather than nature imposed, since the space itself is divided and enclosed by "hedges and walls and gates that lock, and lots of separate little houses for the gardeners and people" (11). The effect of such separations is clear, as the narrator believes that she would recover faster "if I had . . . more society and stimulus" rather than so much isolation (10).   The Divide's inherent "Genius . . . unfriendly to man," its wild "ugly moods" as seen by John Bergson in *O Pioneers!* (8, 7) corresponds to the "strange, provoking . . . figure, that seems to skulk about" within the wallpaper pattern (18). Just as John Bergson sees a menace within the land's unfriendly spirit, Gilman's narrator sees an unhappy and ominous projection of herself, a woman trapped in a pattern of dependency and enforced inactivity that defies common sense, with a husband who treats her like a little girl and prescribes imprisonment, isolation, and total idleness for her mental health. The violence of this type of paradox becomes the spirit of the wallpaper, the Genius unfriendly to woman trapped in Dr. S. Weir Mitchell's maddening rest-cure. When the narrator slips and says the woman shakes "the bars" (never before mentioned) in the wallpaper, her own identity as prisoner is clear (30).

Seemingly without editorializing, Gilman's narrator lists an increasingly restrictive series of imprisoning devices, when she explains that John refuses to "give way to" her nervous fancies about the wallpaper by refusing to re-paper the room he has forced her into: "He said that after the wallpaper was changed it would be the heavy bedstead, and then the barred windows, and then that gate at the head of the stairs, and so on" (14). Her bed cannot be moved, the windows are barred so she cannot escape, and the stairs too are gated. Just after this list, of course, the infuriating husband notes, "You know, the place is doing you good" (15). The stifling controls of "The Yellow Wallpaper," manifested in the room, house, and grounds, contrast with the fierce openness of the Great Divide in *My Ántonia*. Jim's killing of the giant rattler leaves him and Ántonia feeling exultant, newly seeing Nebraska as "big and free" (26).   Yet this very sense of "freedom," emphasized by Jim's seeing in Nebraska "not a country at all, but the material out of which countries are made," hides another kind of violence, as Mike Fischer points out. *My Ántonia*'s temporal setting, presumably the mid-1880s, indicates that the twenty-four-year-old snake Jim kills would have been born just before the 1862 Homestead Act, which opened up Nebraska to widespread white settlement. Fischer notes that Jim's killing the snake "represents a metonymic displacement of the true genealogy of Nebraska's white settlement: the Indian Wars of the 1860s that were planned in conjunction with the passage of the Homestead Act and that made its implementation possible" (Fischer 36).[56] Still, despite the historical context surrounding and ignored by Cather's narrative, the prairie offers a compensatory wild freedom in its terrifying vastness.

Such geographical freedom from "the jurisdiction of man" exacts its price, however, as Jim soon discovers during his first winter in Nebraska. Winter exposes the bare skeleton beneath the transient finery of green, lush vegetation, the violent underside of spring and summer:

The pale, cold light of the winter sunset did not beautify—it was like the light of truth itself . . . [as if to say]: "This is reality, whether you like it or not. All those frivolities of summer, the light and shadow, the living mask of green that trembled over everything, they were lies, and this is what was underneath. This is the truth." (85)

This obvious image of death repeats Cather's motif of self-erasure, of "reality, whether you like it or not." It is an image that Marilynne Robinson returns to in *Housekeeping*, when Ruth imagines bones buried in the snow and houses reduced to their skeletal frames. Too, the figure of a something lurking just below the surface also appears in "The Yellow Wallpaper," whose narrator peels away the wallpaper to uncover the "creeping" woman beneath; in this case, a realization not of death but rather of an oppressive, maddening cultural system emerges from hiding.

Finally, the brutal underside of nature often gives way to human violence, as though to indicate a contagion of atmosphere. The ravaged nursery of "The Yellow Wallpaper" bespeaks inarticulate rage: "The floor is scratched and gouged and splintered, the plaster itself is dug out here and there, and this great heavy bed . . . looks as if it had been through the wars" (17). The imprisoning atmosphere of the room apparently has driven others to the same fury that afflicts the narrator herself, who claws at the paper and in frustration bites at the bedstead, becoming "angry enough to do something desperate," such as leaping out of the third-story window (34). Such infection by environment marks one of *My Ántonia*'s most famous "inset stories," that of the Russian Peter and Pavel, who flee to Nebraska after sacrificing a bride and groom to a pack of hungry wolves. Theirs is a story with a "profound sense of exile and alienation," the inevitable result of what happens when humans succumb to the ferocious imperatives of landscape (Peterman 159). Peter and Pavel become like wolves themselves, single-mindedly rapacious. They too have a desperate survival instinct in a bleak territory. Within the tale, human and terrain become literally one, when the sledge containing the groom's family overturns and the wolves attack: "The black ground-shadows were already crowding over the heap in the road" (31). Suddenly all the players in this scene become part of landscape—neither animal nor human, but instead a tableau of shadow and form. As if to emphasize this loss of humanity, Pavel's act of tossing the bridal couple out to the wolves is followed by the sound of their own village monastery bells, summoning people to morning prayer. The wild landscape is shattered by the reverberations of a "civilization" from which Peter and Pavel are now forever excluded, due to their experience of and violent response to the former. Tellingly, the Russian and American geographies become fused in Jim's fantasy, as late at night he imagines himself "in a sledge drawn by three horses, dashing through a country that looked something like Nebraska and something like Virginia" (32). Too, when he hears coyotes howling near the farm, "their hungry, wintry cry" inspires Jake and Otto Fuchs to tell stories "about grey wolves and bears in the Rockies, wildcats and panthers in the Virginia mountains" (35). Thus does Cather remind us that nature cannot be wholly appeased, even by exile and relocation; the Russian wolves, like the Russian murderers, reappear in the mountains and plains of America.

As with Peter and Pavel, the suicidal tramp's story is one of intermingled humanity and landscape. However, their tragedy is that they mirror all too well their terrain. The tramp's tragedy is that he does not; quite simply, he does not fit in with Cather's country of resiliency, acceptance, and immigrant culture. His gruesome death is triply foreshadowed in ways that emphasize his ostracism within an unfriendly landscape. First, Ántonia describes a hellish heat, an apocalyptic sun that threatens to destroy the world. Second, the tramp asserts that he is not in step with the changing country when, following Ántonia's reference to Bohemians and Norwegians, he replies, "I thought this was Americy" (87). Finally, his death wish reveals his sense of territorial exclusion, as he laments that the drought has so reduced the ponds that "a man couldn't drownd himself in one of 'em" (87). Even his last-ditch attempt to fuse literally with the landscape—to turn himself into wheat, as it were—is unsuccessful; after he leaps head first into the threshing machine, he jams it so that it never works properly again. Out of the three suicides in *My Ántonia*, only the tramp's illustrates what becomes of those who do not harmonize with Cather's landscape: Wick Cutter's murder-suicide is isolated from the prairie and is clearly embroiled in "man's jurisdiction," since he planned and carried it out through sheer, legal-minded spite. Mr. Shimerda's suicide, though initially grisly, quickly vanishes into his grave, a gentle site of tranquillity on the plain, and evokes not horror but rather a mournful violin requiem. The tramp's suicide, however, is marked by exclusion on two counts: by his xenophobia and by the land itself. The clues to this exclusion are in his pocket: the man-made penknife, indicating utility, and also human violence and power; the chicken bone, indicating both natural sustenance and the power of human dreams and hopes, since one pulls on the bone to make a wish; and the worn copy of a sentimental poem, "The Old Oaken Bucket," indicating human art. In short, work, food, and spirit all prove useless to this exile, this wanderer who does not even realize that glorious summer is not the appropriate time for suicide (winter, as Ántonia elliptically points out, makes far more sense, since it is a time of death; that is when her father committed suicide, after all and, as Jim Burden has noted, that is when the earth itself seems dead). Unlike the gentle Mr. Shimerda, the tramp is forever etched in the reader's mind as waving psychotically and diving into the threshing machine, a violently depicted role of the territorial pariah.

Emil and Marie's murder results in a far gentler version of immersion within the landscape and also foreshadows the oddly peaceful suicides and deaths of *Housekeeping*. Like the muted violence of Mr. Shimerda's suicide, which slips into a grave "like a little island" of clemency and softness (59), Emil and Marie become forever connected to landscape. The two are deeply associated with their surroundings even before death, from Marie's mulberry tree to Emil's stile, but Cather's depiction of their murder scene literally, and literarily, inscribes the landscape with blood: "The story of what had happened was written plainly on the orchard grass, and on the white mulberries that had fallen in the night and were covered with dark stain" (106). Marie imprints her part of the story by bleeding into the soil and grass where she has dragged herself to the hedge and then back to Emil, whose hand she marks with "dark stains, where she had kissed it" (106). Here, she and Emil become one with the landscape, through the leveling medium of blood; they are inseparable from the stained mulberries and grass, and their bloody murder transmogrifies them into two white butterflies who dive and soar up into the sky, while "the last wild roses of the year opened their pink hearts to die" (106). Presaged here is Alexandra's serene notion of death as merged with rain and time immemorial, and Jim's warm surrender to the vegetative state of growing things that merely exist, rather than struggle and ask why. Like Ruth in *Housekeeping*, who imagines the skeletons of her grandfather and mother in Fingerbone Lake as a reminder that even in death we are not perished, like Sethe in *Beloved* who sees one daughter born into the Ohio River and must let another vanish into the woods and her watery remembrance of the Middle Passage, like Rosa in *The Shawl* who watches her daughter turn butterfly at the exact moment of death, like the Laguna Pueblos in *Almanac of the Dead* who understand that "man was too insignificant" to desecrate the earth (762), Cather's characters too come to terms with their reabsorption into the landscape, the erasure of self that the vast plains of Nebraska signified. That relationship between self and landscape, finally, is envisioned and re-envisioned throughout more than three hundred years of American women's writing.

This chapter closes with a discussion of our spatial relationship to violence because, in part, that is how it began. Mary Rowlandson's negotiation of her "removes" deeper and deeper into what she saw as a savage landscape informed by physical and spiritual brutalities is also notable for its disclosure of cross-cultural confrontations and clashes: a violence that has informed United States history from its inception. The sense of journeying mirrored in Rowlandson's narrative re-appears in Anne Bradstreet's poetry, which navigates the difficult terrain between the physical and spiritual worlds of the seventeenth-century Puritans. She too has her "removes," as she tries to comprehend the actions of a religious system wherein violence is meted out both as a means of punishment and a mark of Divine election. For the nineteenth-century slave narratives of Harriet Wilson and Harriet Jacobs and the sentimental abolitionist novel of Harriet Beecher Stowe, the journey is more physical than spiritual. Their stories tell of finding their way in a country literally divided in two parts: spaces marked by slavery and indentured servitude, such as Dr. Flint's and Simon Legree's plantations, and Mrs. Bellmont's household, and those marked by freedom and escape. Tellingly, only the white-authored *Uncle Tom's Cabin* has such spaces, and they are located not in the United States but in Canada and Africa. For the heroines of *Incidents in the Life of a Slave Girl* and *Our Nig,* such spaces offer only temporary shelter, since both black authors could not truthfully say they themselves had found permanent freedom in this country. Similarly, Charlotte Perkins Gilman's narrator does not close her tale with a successful negotiation of the territory, because she too is speaking to reveal the flaws within the system. Happy endings or no, all of these spatial navigations are pivotal to women's writing in the United States, so much of which concerns finding a place, marking out a territory, laying claim to a home. As the next chapter contends, Toni Morrison's *Beloved*, with its stunning reenactment of the Middle Passage and its depiction of a people re-writing their own immigration narrative, is one such story.

NOTES

1. This particularized reading of violence applies not only to the works of Rowlandson and Bradstreet but also to Marilynne Robinson's *Housekeeping.*

2. Their conscious, deliberate acknowledgment of the politically catalyzing forces of violence in American history makes these three narratives pivotal in this chapter; such acknowledgment forges perhaps the strongest, and most overt, link between them and the contemporary novels I discuss. As examined more thoroughly in the following chapter, Toni Morrison's *Beloved* pays homage to the nineteenth-century slave narrative form, as well as fleshing out the particularly brutal, little-known history of Margaret Garner, a slave mother who saw a choice between life and freedom for her children. For further information about this woman, see Cynthia Wolff's "Margaret Garner."

3. The groundbreaking study of the relationship between sexuality and the development of Cather's voice is Sharon O'Brien's *Willa Cather: The Emerging Voice.* Other works that address this issue are Judith Fryer's *Felicitous Space: The Imaginative Structures of Edith Wharton and Willa Cather* and Judith Fetterley's "*My Ántonia*, Jim Burden, and the Dilemma of the Lesbian Writer."

4. I have found Richard Slotkin's 1973 *Regeneration Through Violence: The Mythology of the American Frontier, 1600–1860*, while a more cultural than strictly literary study, still an excellent guide for this line of thought.   He sees in Rowlandson's captivity narrative an archetype, "the first coherent myth literature developed in America for American audiences" (95). Yet, as Christopher Castiglia points out in his 1996 *Bound and Determined: Captivity, Culture-Crossing, and White Womanhood from Mary Rowlandson to Patty Hearst*, Slotkin gives short shrift to later women's fictional narratives and seems to repeat Roy Harvey Pearce's 1947 claim that the captivity narrative "enters literary history proper in [Charles Brockden Brown's] *Edgar Huntly*" (Pearce 1, qtd. in Castiglia 195 n.2). Castiglia concludes that, according to Slotkin and Pearce, "[a]fter the Puritans, then, the captivity narrative apparently disappeared, to emerge again most importantly in the pages of male authors" (195n.2).

5. See Kolodny (*Land Before* 17), Howe 112–21, and Rosenmeier 92–94 for a discussion of the various reprimands, silencings, excommunications, banishments, and/or "madnesses" of Anne Hutchinson, Mary Dyer, Anne Hopkins, and Sarah Dudley Keayne.   These are a few of the women who were silenced after the Antinomian controversy of 1637–1638, sparked by Hutchinson's public preaching. See also Logan 260–62 and Margaret Davis 49–50. Mitchell Breitweiser qualifies this "mistrust of women's writing," however, noting that it is approved when "confined to the minor or supplementary genres," as opposed to major doctrinal works of Puritan ideology and history (18), and also when it can be used to "lend a powerful assistance to male theorization" (101). Tellingly, the malformed fetuses of Mary Dyer and Anne Hutchinson become "emblems" of the women's public heresies in the writings of John Winthrop and Cotton Mather (209 n.55).

6. Kolodny is only one of several scholars who posit that Rowlandson's "overlay of religious interpretation" stemmed largely from her preacher-husband's reading—and writing—over her shoulder (*Land Before* 6), while critics such as Teresa A. Toulouse, Breitweiser, and Tara Fitzpatrick find in Rowlandson's religious models of martyrdom and providence a means for her reestablishment within the Puritan community after her return from the Narragansetts.

7. Nancy Armstrong has written that Rowlandson seems to represent "English culture itself . . . under assault" (9). See also her book, co-written with Leonard Tennenhouse, *The Imaginary Puritan: Literature, Intellectual Labor, and the Origins of Personal Life.*

8. As the greatest authority in her experience, the Bible obviously lends some of that authority to her own narrative, as does the preface by Per Amicum (most likely, Increase Mather).

9. Mary White Rowlandson. *The Soveraignty and Goodness of God, together with the Faithfulness of His Promises Displayed; Being a Narrative of the Captivity and Restoration of Mrs. Mary Rowlandson, Commended by her to all that Desire to Know the Lord's Doings to, and Dealings with Her, Especially to her Dear Children and Relations* (Cambridge: Samuel Green, 1682), rpt. as *A Narrative of the Captivity and Removes of Mrs. Mary Rowlandson* (Fairfield, WA: Ye Galleon P, 1974) 34. Subsequent quotations from this work are cited in the text.

10. Such religious beliefs, of course, worked concurrently with the justification of less spiritually motivated differences of opinion: land contestations. See Slotkin 42, 67, 78–81, in particular, as well as Castiglia 2–3, 58, 123; Fitzpatrick 20–21; Ann Kibbey's *The Interpretation Of Material Shapes in Puritanism: A Study of Rhetoric, Prejudice, and Violence*; Sacvan Bercovitch's *The American Jeremiad* and *The Pur-*

itan Origins of the American Self; Richard Drinnon's *Facing West: The Metaphysics of Indian-Hating and Empire-Building*; Roy Harvey Pearce's "The Significances of the Captivity Narrative"; Richard VanDerBeets's *The Indian Captivity Narrative: An American Genre*; as well as Perry Miller's *Errand into the Wilderness* and *The New England Mind: The Seventeenth Century*.

11. While the French Jesuits tried to persuade the Indians to convert, the Puritans were "inclined mainly to force," and even when the Puritans did attempt conversion, their goal was to eradicate Algonquian cultural identity through excessive regulations and prohibitions of even the most basic hygienic practices (e.g., the use of body grease) (Breitweiser 137, 179). Significantly, the Indians' approach to war was marked by difference from the white colonists; the Indians conceived of war as limited, episodic, and ritualistic violence, rather than the Puritans' protracted battle, which "aimed at cultural destruction—abstract war" (Breitweiser 138–40).

12. The irony of this juxtaposition is not lost on Howe, who reminds us that "in the first paragraph of the first published narrative written by an Anglo-American woman, ostensibly to serve as a reminder of God's Providence, guns fire, houses burn, a father, mother, and sucking child are killed by blows to the head" (95). That the authority Rowlandson relies on also constrains and represses her truths is clear from her continuous shifts from brutal experience to the Wonder-Workings of Providence (see Howe 100, for example).

13. Connections between Indians and Puritans were complicated rather than simplified by rigid Puritan typology.   From John Winthrop to Increase Mather, Indians were classified as solid evidence of God's displeasure with backsliding Puritans: "You were attacked *by* the Indians because you had become *like* the Indians" (Breitweiser 86). In accordance with this typology, one could not detest the Indians without detesting one's own responsibility in bringing on their torments— read, God's punishment (see 134).

14. Granted, this is a twentieth-century interpretation of the situation, since the resources of sixteenth-century America were hardly overtaxed. Indeed, Rowlandson's contemporaries, coming as they did from an overcrowded England, saw only a land of plenty, despite its cruel winters.

15. This particular passage is significant in terms of Rowlandson's own bereft maternity, as she ingests a mother's young and finds it "very good." Breitweiser does not mention this specific meal but does allude to her "hideous reassimilation of that which has been torn from her" (142).

16. Rowlandson, *The Sovereignty and Goodness of God. . .* "Preface to the Reader"; rpt. in *So Dreadfull a Judgment: Puritan Responses to King Philip's War, 1676–1677*, ed. Richard Slotkin and James K. Folsom (Middletown, CT: Wesleyan UP , 1978) 318; qtd. in Breitweiser 134–35.

17. Her doing so situates her narrative historically as much as the events she records, since she sees Providence, whereas a late-twentieth-century reader like Susan Howe sees the very real possibility of a random, chaotic universe: "At sun-rising, on a day of calamity, at the inverted point of antitypical history, Mary Rowlandson looks out at the absence of Authority and sees we are all alone. In a minute death can and will come. All collectivities will be scattered to corners" (Howe 94).

18. See Toulouse 660 and Breitweiser 111. The latter does assert that Joslin's choosing gestation (hardly a "mere whim") over providence (waiting) presents a viable "challenge to the moral integrity of the instigating type" (112).

19. See also Howe 49 and Kolodny, who notes that "the pattern of capture and suffering followed by redemption might signify a promise that New England's current

problems . . . were similarly a divinely mandated 'scourging,' at once justified by the community's momentary backsliding but essentially temporary in nature" (*Land* 20). Breitweiser sees in Rowlandson's personal war experiences the creation of her new identity: she undergoes a purging fire to transform her from minister's wife to "an object of awe, a sacred object, a talisman, something fantastic and maybe a little repellent in the midst of the ordinariness being reconstructed after the war" (81).

20. As Slotkin has remarked, Rowlandson's organizing scheme is one of location rather than temporality. Time often seems to fuse with place, as Rowlandson tells time not by "Day One, Day Two," and so on, but instead by the Indians' continuous movements throughout the largely unfamiliar and hostile (to her) landscape. This notion of interval marked by space recurs in the important Middle Passage section of Toni Morrison's *Beloved*, and I return to it in my next chapter. Suffice it to say here, however, that the experience of captivity—the abrupt sundering of self from home—lends itself to such a violently upturned way of marking time.

21. In "Why Our First Poet Was a Woman: Bradstreet and the Birth of an American Poetic Voice," Patricia Caldwell aptly links Bradstreet's gender with her situation as a "first-generation poet in the New World"; the struggle to articulate identity influences both conditions (2). See also Hammond (139–40).

22. In *Anne Bradstreet Revisited*, Rosamond Rosenmeier writes that recent studies of Puritanism acknowledge that the English Puritans' regional differences crossed the Atlantic with the early colonists. We should therefore conceive of Puritanism "not [as] a monolithic belief system as much as a loose association of threads" (xii). Qualifications should also extend to Bradstreet's purported "rebellion" against that belief system, adds Rosenmeier, who alludes to Cheryl Walker's observation that "far too much has been made of Bradstreet's rebellion against the Puritan God" (Walker 14; see also Rosenmeier 2–4).

23. For the purposes of my study, a focus on these two poems is most fruitful; however, Bradstreet's work does recognize other types of violence. "The Four Monarchies," for example, not only provides evidence that, as Jane Eberwein writes, "women, like men, live out the effects of public actions," but also chronicles a series of "selfish, barbaric, and devastatingly destructive acts" (125, 132).

24. *The Works of Anne Bradstreet*. Ed. Jeannine Hensley (Cambridge: Harvard UP, 1967) 292. Subsequent quotations from this work are cited in the text.

25. While apocalyptic imagery is not the focus of my study, I would be remiss if I did not acknowledge such imagery's popularity in American writing. As Douglas Robinson points out in *American Apocalypses: The Image of the End of the World in American Literature*, "the very idea of America in history *is* apocalyptic, arising as it did out of the historicizing of apocalyptic hopes in the Protestant Reformation" (xi).

26. Bradstreet's father was brutal at Anne Hutchinson's trial, too, accusing her of depravity (corrupting all the ministers) and "venting" her "strange opinions" (*The Antinomian Controversy, 1632–1638: A Documentary History*, ed. David Hall; Middletown, CT: Wesleyan UP, 1968: 318; qtd. in Howe 111; see also Rosenmeier 92–94).

27. Ann Stanford reads this poem as being "close to blasphemy" (114), while Ellen Brandt argues it reveals Bradstreet's "incipient hatred for a sometimes cruel" God (42).

28. Along a slightly different trajectory, Rosenmeier sees in Bradstreet's terseness both a "poetic method [that] has its roots in biblical proverb or parable" and (specifically in her marriage poems) a rhetorical image of the poet's sorrowful muteness in her husband's absence (120–22).

29. Despite the strict ban on women's preaching, nearly half the recorded

confessions at Cambridge's Church of Christ were women's (Howe 63).

30. The slave narratives replace the early American captivity narratives' portrayal of "savage heathens with portraits of equally savage Christians," according to Zafar, depicting "the fiendish enemy as the figurative, if not actual, descendants of the white Christian captives; putative Protestants become positive Pharaohs" (32).

31. As Hazel Carby notes in *Reconstructing Womanhood*, *Our Nig* can easily be read as "an allegory of a slave narrative," since Wilson's mulatto protagonist is treated like a slave even in the "free North" (43).

32. As sentimental novels, *Uncle Tom's Cabin*, *Our Nig*, and *Incidents in the Life of a Slave Girl* belong to "a genre . . . whose chief characteristic is that it is written by, for, and about women" (Tompkins, "Sentimental Power" 504).   As Hortense Spillers remarks, however, all the black women in Stowe's text are flat images, "carnivalesque propositions of female character," and the women to whom Tompkins refers "so elid[e] with a *revoked* adjectival marker named 'white' that we barely notice" ("Changing the Letter" 551).

33. See Kaplan 109–10, and Fox-Genovese, "To Write" 166–69.   For a discussion of how Stowe imposed the construct of family feeling and women's power in the domestic sphere to wage political battle, see Tompkins's "Sentimental Power: *Uncle Tom's Cabin* and the Politics of Literary History," and her *Sensational Designs* 140–41, and also Amy Schrager Lang's *Prophetic Woman*, especially 193–214.

34. See, for example, Jenkins, Gwin, Cynthia Davis, Nudelman, Stern, Halttunen, and Ammons ("Stowe's Dream").

35. This is a concept that foreshadows my following discussion of Charlotte Perkins Gilman's "The Yellow Wallpaper." For studies of the gothic elements of the sentimental tradition, see Halttunen, and Stern, especially 439–40, and 447–51. The image of Simon Legree's house reverting to the wild nature surrounding can be read as a gothic version of the idea repeated in Marilynne Robinson's *Housekeeping*: that what is man-made eventually succumbs to what is not (see chapter 5).

36. Similarly, while Valerie Smith (*Self-Discovery and Authority*), Houston Baker (*Blues, Ideology and Afro-American Literature*), William Andrews, and Jean Fagan Yellin make claims for Linda's effective subversive strategies against Dr. Flint during her months of hiding and later flight to the North, Carla Kaplan argues instead that "Jacobs is at great pains to dramatize Brent's *inability* to 'subvert' her status, 'assault' her master's domination, wage 'effective' combat, or 'reverse' the power structures which bind her" (103).

37. A very brief list of works that explore the sentimental literary tradition are Barbara Welter's *Dimity Convictions: The American Woman in the Nineteenth Century*, Nancy F. Cott's *The Bonds of Womanhood: "Woman's Sphere" in New England, 1780–1835*, and Ann Douglas's *The Feminization of American Culture*. See also Nina Baym's *Woman's Fiction: A Guide to Novels by and about Women in America, 1820–1870*, Hazel Carby's *Reconstructing Womanhood: The Emergence of the Afro-American Woman Novelist*, and Mary Helen Washington's *Invented Lives: Narratives of Black Women, 1860–1960*.

38. Harriet Wilson, *Our Nig; or, Sketches from the Life of a Free Black, in a Two-Story White House, North, Showing That Slavery's Shadows Fall Even There. By "Our Nig,"* ed. Henry Louis Gates, Jr. (1859; reprint, New York: Random House, 1983) 133–40; see also "Notes to the Text" viii–x. Subsequent quotations from this work are cited in the text. Jacobs's book enjoyed some visibility for a time, but Wilson's "never received even *one* review or comment," according to Gates ("In Her Own Write" xii). Both Gates and Jean Fagan Yellin have been instrumental in

"rediscovering" and authenticating these pivotal texts (see Yellin's "Written by Herself" and Gates's edited version of *Our Nig*).

39. Jacobs had initially asked Stowe to write her story but was offended when Stowe first contacted Jacobs's employer, Mrs. Willis (Mrs. Bruce in the novel), to authenticate the story, and then offered merely to cite Jacobs's experience in her *Key to Uncle Tom's Cabin*, as a means of substantiating her own fiction (see Yellin, Introduction, *Incidents* xix, and also Nudelman 955).

40. See "In the Quiet, Undisputed Dignity of My Womanhood" in Carby's *Reconstructing Womanhood*, especially 109–14 and 141.

41. Susanna Rowson's 1791 seduction novel, *Charlotte Temple*, which "enjoyed enormous popularity for decades," offered one such scenario (Doriani 204).

42. See Karen Sanchez-Eppler 83–84, 92; Valerie Smith's *Self-Discovery* 28; and Houston Baker's *Blues, Ideology* 52, which suggests the universality of this sexual violence for slave girls.

43. I had already formulated my interpretation of Wilson's narrative before I read Julia Stern's "Excavating Genre in *Our Nig*," in which she marks Mrs. Bellmont's brutal and gothic inversion of maternity, observing that while the text depicts no sexual assaults upon Frado, Mrs. Bellmont's looming "'over' Frado in 'every sense' evokes images of unspeakable violation, a rape of the spirit if not quite of the body" (453). Stern astutely explains Mrs. Bellmont's brutality as her horrified response to the fact that she and the mulatto girl she despises are connected through race and gender (441, 444). My reading diverges from that of Stern's, however, in that Mrs. Bellmont seems to me to take a kind of sexual pleasure in torturing Frado, while Stern argues that Mrs. Bellmont needs "to see Frado as devoid of erotic appeal" so that the older woman remains "the most compelling female in her household" (460 n.18, 444). See also Cynthia Davis's "Speaking the Body's Pain: Harriet Wilson's *Our Nig*," which posits a metonymic link between pain and sexual exploitation in the depiction of Frado's abused body.

44. This violent worldview is not exclusive to slave owners, as St. Clare compares his and Ophelia's fathers: hers chose to stay in New England and "rule over rocks and stones, and . . . force an existence out of Nature," while his chose to dominate over human beings (262). Robinson's *Housekeeping*, as I later discuss, focuses on the pitfalls and illusions of the former choice.

45. Harriet Jacobs, *Incidents in the Life of a Slave Girl, Written by Herself*, ed. Jean Fagan Yellin (1861; reprint, Cambridge: Harvard UP, 1987) 55.

46. This construction also provided a front for "an excuse to get rid of Negroes who were acquiring wealth and property," as turn-of-the-century black political writer Ida B. Wells put it (*Crusade for Justice* 64; qtd. in Carby 109).

47. In Louisiana plantations, and most likely elsewhere, there still exist small cabins attached to the main houses, called *garçonierres*. These were built for the purpose of "breaking in" sexually the young white men of the house, who were tacitly encouraged to take slave girls there, far from the white mistress's gentle sensibilities.

48. See Ammons, "Stowe's Dream" for an intriguing interpretation of Uncle Tom as a maternal savior figure.

49. Christopher Wilson makes a compelling argument for Gilman's fusing her ideology with her aesthetics and literary style, particularly in *Herland* (see "Charlotte Perkins Gilman's Steady Burghers," especially 278–90).

50. See Blanche Gelfant's pivotal essay, "The Forgotten Reaping-Hook: Sex in *My Ántonia*," which investigates that novel's uneasiness with sexuality.

51. Willa Cather, *O Pioneers!* (1913; New York: Dover Publications, 1993) 120. Subsequent quotations from this work are cited in the text.

52. Additionally, Mary's "proud exhibition of the sharpness of her knife's blade suggest[s]," according to Paula Woolley, a violent refutation of "femininity and an attempt to appropriate male power" (178 n.17).

53. Willa Cather, *My Ántonia* (1918; New York: Dover Publications, 1994) 121. Subsequent quotations from this work are cited in the text.

54. While several feminist critics in the late 1970s, such as Gilbert and Gubar, Annette Kolodny, and Elaine Hedges, read the narrator's madness as a kind of triumph over her insanely oppressive situation, I agree with Jean Kennard that it is only "the interpretation of madness as a higher form of sanity that allows feminist critics finally to read this story as a woman's quest for her own identity" (82). See especially Gilbert and Gubar, *Madwoman* 89–91; Kolodny, "Map for Rereading" 457–58; and Hedges 49–53.

55. Julieann Fleenor traces in three of Gilman's stories the ways in which "female exclusion, women denied the opportunity to work, or their imprisonment behind four walls, led to madness" (120). She also discusses Gilman's recurring theme of fatal or "diseased" maternity (123, 128; see also Ammons's *Conflicting Stories* 36).

56. In his *Willa Cather in Context: Progress, Race, Empire*, Guy Reynolds takes a somewhat different approach, reading in Cather's opposition to the "melting pot" version of Americanization her argument that "the later a civilization . . . the more inferior it is" (61; see also 77–79, 87).

Chapter 3

Passages Home, Journeys Outward: A Reading of Toni Morrison's *Beloved*

As a response to the question, "How do you deal with a survivor from the Middle Passage?" (P. Smith 63), Toni Morrison's novel *Beloved* (1987) exposes the hypocrisy in the selective promise of self-creation and re-creation for those who come to the United States. Itself a conjunction of journeying, arrival, and history, *Beloved* explores a brutal, perverse variation on two peculiarly "American" themes: immigration—through the abduction of African slaves—and assimilation—through the efforts of succeeding generations to establish themselves in generally hostile country. Current scholarly interest in cultural and ethnic identities must embrace new, even unlikely, approaches to immigration and assimilation histories.[1] Morrison's emphasis on the Africans' agonizing bodily experience of the Middle Passage, and her depiction of the improbable domestic space of a decrepit lean-to by the Ohio River, occupied by two runaways, constitute such an approach, as she rewrites a long-cherished American story of immigration and resettlement by linking place, passage, and violence and by traversing the border between home founding and a recurring sense of homelessness.

In *Beloved*, the Middle Passage and a pregnant, battered slave woman's flight north resonate in each other, the former a violent transport of Africans from home to diasporic separation and the latter a journey that initiates a process of belonging and becoming. A search for place, vital to all of Morrison's work, informs the brief meeting of two transients when the slave woman, Sethe, meets a homeless white girl near the abandoned lean-to that becomes a temporary domestic space of healing, birth, and communion. Because one of the text's principal moments of violence springs from maternal love (in Ohio, Sethe will murder her child, Beloved, to save her from Schoolteacher, a vicious slavemaster), it is not surprising that *Beloved*'s confluence of space, history, and violence is infused with maternity.[2] While the lean-to witnesses an instance of maternal nurturing as Amy heals Sethe, Morrison's Middle Passage section echoes a child's agonized yearning for its mother. Space, violence, and parental protectiveness meld in Sethe's belief that her children will be safe if she kills them: "My plan was to take us all to the other side where my own ma'am is."[3] A "composite" of the murdered baby and also Sethe's mother,[4] Beloved returns in the body of an eighteen-year-old woman, accusing Sethe of abandonment.

Beloved's recurrent longing of children and mothers for each other bespeaks the disruption of families both during and after the Middle Passage; Schoolteacher tries to dehumanize Sethe specifically as a mother by having his nephews hold her down, suck the milk from her breasts, and then (after carefully digging a hole for her pregnant belly) whip her with cowhide until the skin of her back is permanently deadened and scarred. The abruptness of the Middle Passage itself, termed a "kidnapping" by Morrison ("Unspeakable Things" 32), lies behind *Beloved*'s bewildering first line—"124 was spiteful" (3)—which jerks the reader, like the captured Africans, "into an environment completely foreign . . . without preparation and without defense" ("Unspeakable Things" 32). Recasting her audience as abducted, unwilling "immigrants," Morrison prepares us for her reclaimed American history of violent kidnapping and ruptured families.

Since Morrison sees houses as both "an increasingly complex measure of individual well-being" and "the basic unit of the community" (Scruggs 170), the activities enclosed in domestic space, the identity of those who are sheltered and those who are not, and the vulnerability of "home" to violent destruction comprise much of *Beloved*.[5] Sethe's journey is framed between two houses, as she flees the ironically named Sweet Home plantation in Kentucky and heads north to Ohio, where her mother-in-law and children live at 124 Bluestone Road. Sweet Home, a brutal economic institution that owns and controls black lives,[6] is first run by the relatively benevolent Garner and then by his sadistic brother-in-law, Schoolteacher, who starves, beats, and finally kills most of the slaves there. Morrison's depiction of Schoolteacher and Garner, who are two sides of the same figure, shatters the myth of the kindly slave owner. 124, the haunted house that opens each of *Beloved*'s three sections, is marked, like the slaves and ex-slaves who people this text, by a long and various history. A former way station on the underground railroad, it becomes a spiritual haven under the authority of a freed slave woman called Baby Suggs, then the isolated home of her daughter-in-law Sethe, and her granddaughters Denver and Beloved—all of whom are still caught in what Mircea Eliade has called "the terror of history" (qtd. in Scruggs 186).

The spatial and temporal distance between these houses is a strong component in the novel's narrative frame; Morrison was thinking about Ohio, Kentucky, and the river between them long before she wrote this book, observing in a 1976 interview that Ohio's position between Kentucky and Canada makes it "an interesting state from the point of view of black people" because it bridges the distance between slavery and freedom ("Intimate Things" 215). Functioning as a tangible "passage" between the slave state Kentucky and the free state Ohio, the Ohio River also connects with the waters of the Middle Passage, since it flows south via the Mississippi to merge with the Gulf of Mexico and thereafter the Atlantic Ocean. The interconnectedness of these waters evokes a space of freedom and the remembered history of slavery; Denver is born in the Ohio, and the re-incorporated Beloved emerges from a stream that feeds the river. This association of water and Beloved's return owes much to what Morrison calls "rememory": a West African–influenced belief that the dead and such vanished places as the cramped, fetid hold of the slave ship on the Middle Passage can return.

Although situated on "the bloody side of the Ohio," the leaf-filled shack Sethe finds during her near-fatal flight to Cincinnati witnesses her experience of nurturing and healing (31). It is a place of simultaneously acknowledged and diffused boundaries between the wild and the domestic, as well as between races, for here Sethe meets another outlaw female figure, Amy Denver, an uneducated, unenfranchised white. While Sweet Home is divided between illusory benevolence and real brutality, the lean-to has neither divisions nor pretense. In recognizing the conditions of the human world for what they are and going on from there, Sethe and Amy play a biracial variation on the theme in African American literature that Michael Cooke calls "intimacy," when they move into "an unguarded and uncircumscribed engagement" with each other beyond prescribed codes of behavior (9). Refugees from violence when they meet, both women defy the rigid boundaries imposed by their racial difference in a domestic space that, even while shadowed by that violence, affirms their connection.

Despite the importance of Sethe and Amy's exchange, however, *Beloved* focuses primarily on black communities. Before the two women meet, Morrison invokes a community of precursors for Sethe. The text's allusion to earlier black women authors through the trope of a snake exemplifies what Karla Holloway has called the recursive element in black women's writing. Positing continuity rather than utter solitude, recursion layers memory and "the mythic figures within language and culture until each is folded into the other" (Holloway, *Moorings* 13). When Sethe hears Amy Denver's footsteps, she expects a white man: "something came up out of the earth into her—like a freezing, but moving too, like jaws inside. . . . 'I was hungry to [bite him]. Like a snake'" (31). Invoking two black women's texts—a nineteenth-century slave narrative and a twentieth-century novel— Morrison revisits the snake-filled swamp featured in both Harriet Jacobs's *Incidents in the Life of a Slave Girl* (1861) and Zora Neale Hurston's *Their Eyes Were Watching God* (1937).[7]   Jacobs writes that "even those large venomous snakes were less dreadful to my imagination than the white men in that community called civilized" (116), while Hurston's character Nanny flees to save her baby from a venomous mistress. Like Sethe, she is sore and tired: "Ah knowed mah body wasn't healed [from childbirth], but Ah couldn't consider dat. . . . Ah knowed de place was full uh moccasins and other bitin' snakes, but Ah was more skeered uh what was behind me" (Hurston 34–35). Morrison's recursive use of the snake pays homage to earlier literary figures of escape and endurance, even as her snake is a figure of defense rather than the lesser of two evils. That is, unlike Jacobs and Nanny, who prefer the snake's violence to that of whites, Sethe becomes a violent snake; she defines herself as the subject (not the helpless object) of ferocity, asserting a subjectivity that foreshadows her stunningly fierce love for her children.

Amy Denver is, however, neither a snake nor a selfless white angel who puts everything in order before a graceful exit.[8] Despite her "outlaw" status as a penniless, uneducated white woman who helps a runaway slave, Amy voices the dominant ideology of her time: she is racist, blunt, and cruel even as she massages Sethe's feet back to life. In a story of survival, recovering history, and working towards intimacy, Amy Denver is a figure of possibility who calls Sethe out of her deathlike stupor and into "a full and unforced communication with the given, the available, and the conceivable in human experience in a particular time and setting" (Cooke x). At the same time, her whiteness acknowledges and suggests the possibility of transcending the fixed and violent social realities permeating Morrison's text.

Racial boundaries are not all that *Beloved* navigates. Since Morrison's recovery of a repressed history must also span temporal boundaries, the novel's circular time frame shortens the distances between present and past, between the living and their ancestors. Such connection is imperative for Morrison's shell-shocked black characters to "imagine a future" (Bowers 61) and is exemplified by a place where opposites meet: a shelter filled with the outdoors in the form of dead leaves and rocks. In this space Sethe's past and future converge, alongside the river whose waters symbolically merge Denver's birth and Sethe's mother's passage.   The lean-to's diffused boundaries are foreshadowed through Sethe's attempts to fuse inside and outside at Sweet Home, where unless she picks "some pretty growing thing" and takes it into Mrs. Garner's kitchen, her work goes badly and sickens her; the "brine in the barrel blister[s] her arms" (22). Her efforts to "cure" herself through nature presage her experience in the shelter, where she is healed when Amy brings nature inside specifically to rejuvenate Sethe, soothing her maimed back with spiderwebs, making a bed of leaves and rocks for her swollen, infected feet.[9] These crossed boundaries sketch out more than physical space. Nearly as fluid as the Ohio River are the parameters of identity, which meet but do not merge in the disenfranchised characters of Sethe and Amy, "two throw-away people, two lawless outlaws—a slave and a barefoot whitewoman with unpinned hair" (84–85).[10] As Amy's nursing parallels Sethe's previous work at Sweet Home, the two women cross their identities precisely at the point of domestic work. Amy, in fact, must do most of the work here, in effect taking Sethe's role. Rather than patiently waiting all night for Lillian Garner's fretful call, Sethe is the patient whose back and swollen feet are treated by Amy's "good good hands" (35). Amy's "weaving about the lean-to" is telling (80); like the Delaware weaver who rescues Paul D, the last of the Sweet Home men, during his flight to freedom, Amy also repairs human beings shattered by the abuses of slavery.

Complicating Amy and Sethe's convergence at the point of domesticity is their mutual experience of violence; each woman is fleeing insupportable brutality.[11] Sethe is running to get milk to her baby girl who is safe in Ohio, but she is also escaping Schoolteacher, who has had her beaten and violated.[12] Amy is leaving the ironically named Mr. Buddy, who has kept her since birth as a servant to pay for her mother's passage to the United States. As she tells Sethe, her body has been whittled down by beatings, near starvation, and solitary confinement: "I used to be a good size. Nice arms and everything. . . . That was before they put me in the root cellar" (34). Her first response upon viewing Sethe's maimed back is to see a chokecherry tree, but her second is to identify herself as another battered woman: "I had me some whippings, but I don't remember nothing like this" (79). In the lean-to and a nearby rowboat where Denver is born, these two women cross the socially constructed boundaries of their black and white identities in an act of faith and compassion. Rather than sinking her teeth into Amy, as her first impulse dictates, Sethe trusts her; and rather than turning Sethe in to the authorities or abandoning her, Amy takes care of her, as the two women work together "appropriately and well" when Sethe's water breaks in a leaky rowboat (85).

Through water and maternity, Morrison connects Denver's birth with the Middle Passage and all the ferocious history that the resurrected Beloved signifies. In merging with the Ohio, Sethe's amniotic fluid also connects with the waters of her mother's journey and is later recalled by her when she breaks water upon first seeing the returned Beloved. *Beloved*'s focus on the maternal medium of fluidity offers an alternative to what Mae Henderson calls history's "dominant metaphor" of white paternity, which Morrison refigures in the image of a pregnant black woman (76).[13] A maternal image reflecting an African memory of "rivers whose resident ladies (goddesses) hold the promise (or denial) of fertility," the Ohio embodies a kind of ancestral figure that "reconstructs an imaginative, cultural (re)membrance of a dimension of West African spirituality" (Holloway, *Moorings* 61, 2). The Ohio's role as co-midwife reinforces this identification: "When a foot rose from the river bed and kicked the bottom of the boat and Sethe's behind, she knew it was done" (84–85). Born amid bluefern seeds "in which the whole generation sleeps confident of a future" (84), Denver herself is simultaneously the seed of a free generation and a link to the past, through the combined waters of the Ohio, the Gulf of Mexico, and the Atlantic.[14]

Despite her brief appearance, her verbal cruelty, and her racism, Amy Denver's moment of communion with Sethe is essential to *Beloved*'s scheme of journeying and resettlement.   Morrison has Sethe name her daughter Denver. Sethe's choice of name makes Amy "part of [Sethe's] history but not its center" (C. M. Hennessy 13) by recalling the two women's fleeting cross-racial intimacy.   Still, in naming Denver after a white girl, Morrison recognizes, even while revising, the experiences of Africans on the Middle Passage, whose names (and thus, ties of kinship) were lost or ignored; even those who survived lost their families twice over when their true names were replaced with meaningless tags, like Baby Suggs's "Jenny Whitlow," a name "denoting ownership, appropriation . . . deny[ing] group identity and African origins" (Rigney 40).[15]   Denver's name also reflects Morrison's under-standing that any kind of alliance, even temporary, is born "not in the violence of benevolent rhetoric, but in work and struggle and labor" (C. M. Hennessy 14).   Through Denver's birth, Amy and Sethe forge the temporary alliance that, like the lean-to, offers Sethe a respite from the violence she is leaving and the violence she is going to: Beloved's murder.   With its gestures of signifying, recursion, and intimacy, the lean-to section locates a necessary place for endurance and compassion, however fleeting, in *Beloved*'s brutal, recovered history.

Because blacks have, until recently, been inscribed as "nonparticipants" in United States history (Brenkman 98), Morrison reimages the Middle Passage, the historic moment of African arrival, to answer this question: If a principal part of the American story is one of immigration and assimilation, how and where do black Americans fit in?   Relating an immigration vastly different from all others in its explicit absence of choice and exploring a type of assimilation that demanded not adaptation but cultural and self-annihilation marked by "lynchings and torture, family members sold away, degradation, and cumulative loss" (Bowers 67), *Beloved* probes one of America's most painful and repercussive histories.   This is why Morrison must draw her readers into her text.   Having admitted that *Beloved* is "about something that the characters don't want to remember, I don't want to remember, black people don't want to remember, white people don't want to remember" (Angelo 120), she devises a strategy that reenacts black literature's focus on "shared ways of saying" between writer and reader (Holloway, *Moorings* 7).[16] The book's perplexing structure demands unraveling, leading its audience into the "compelling confusion" of a complex, layered text of variously remembered and retold events ("Unspeakable Things" 33).   Paradoxically, the difficulty of reading this text makes it more bearable; the gradual revelation of so much fearful violence helps to soften *Beloved*'s history for the reader.

While Morrison's version of the Middle Passage appears initially "to be an unintelligible experience, a story of images which the reader must grope" to decipher (Horvitz 162), it is essential to unraveling Beloved's identity, a collective of returned ghosts that include Sethe's daughter and mother, as well as countless unremembered dead Africans who did and did not survive their journey to America. It is difficult to place these ghosts into a literary history built carefully around their absences, which are "so stressed, so ornate, so planned, they call attention to themselves . . . like neighborhoods that are defined by the population held away from them" ("Unspeakable Things" 11). Morrison uses that difficulty to shape the language of her Middle Passage section by discarding the conventions of syntax and punctuation and, most important, by paring down and fusing spatial and temporal indicators, the usual cognitive markers relied on by readers.

Mikhail Bakhtin's term *chronotope* refers to literature's melding of time and space into a "concrete whole" in which time "becomes artistically visible" and space "becomes charged and responsive to the movements of time, plot and history" (84). While Bakhtin differentiates between the epic, whose places are abstract and whose time has neither biological nor maturational duration (countries are interchangeable; heroes do not age), and the novel, which is spatially as well as temporally specific (90, 119), Morrison's Middle Passage section alternates between specificity and abstraction. Since at least two thorough explications of this passage have been published,[17] I will not replicate their work; what interests me is how *Beloved*'s chronotope re-creates the abrupt sundering of a people from their historic time and place. Bakhtin's discussion of "the idyllic chronotope" emphasizes the "unity of place" that is violated by the Middle Passage and the subsequent experiences of African slaves in the United States: "a grafting of life and its events to a place, to a familiar territory. . . . Idyllic life and its events are inseparable from this concrete, spatial corner of the world where [one's ancestors] lived and where one's children and their children will live" (224, 225). Although Bakhtin observes that within this unity of place, individual lives and "various phases of one and the same life" tend to merge (225), it is the violent disruption of that unity that blurs individual life spans and memories in *Beloved*. The force of the Africans' kidnapping, followed by dispersion and the shattering of families, constitutes a memory so terrible that it defies telling and must be repressed, until it erupts through Beloved's multiple voices.[18]

To depict the overwhelming confusion of the Africans on the Middle Passage, who knew neither the language of their captors nor the destination and duration of their journey, Morrison creates a narrator who thinks in a kind of prelanguage—a child so young, or a girl so traumatized,[19] that she does not conceive of herself as separate from her mother, whom she calls "the woman with my face" (211). Couched in Beloved's inchoate thoughts,[20] time during the Middle Passage fluctuates between the ordinariness of daylight and storms and the peculiarly mythic evocations of "the beginning," "always now," and "forever" (210). But in the suffocating hold of a slave ship, time has a dimension beyond the mythic and the diurnal; it becomes physical as Beloved distinguishes the long days and nights only by "the crouching that is now always now" and the times when she "cannot fall because there is no room to" (211). This fusion of the temporal and the spatial also has precedence in African transformation tales, which "dissolve considerations of time and space" (Jones, *Liberating* 183). Time "thickens, takes on flesh" (Bakhtin 84), first, through Beloved herself, who on one level physically embodies the memory of months that were never recorded, and, second, through the way in which she "tells time" in a stunningly communal way, stemming from her spatial relationship to others: "at night I cannot see the dead man on my face daylight comes through the cracks and I can see his locked eyes" (210). Similarly, when storms rock the ship and "mix the men into the women and the women into the men[,] *that is when I begin to be on the back* of the man *for a long time I see only his neck and his wide shoulders* above me" (211, emphasis added). She knows of a man's attempt to die only through her sense of touch; the "trembling" she "can feel . . . over here" continues for an undetermined length of time, until she realizes that "there is no room to tremble so he is not able to die" (210–11). And always during this passage, Beloved (most likely speaking as Sethe's mother) identifies herself in relation to her mother, first declaring that "I am not separate from her   there is no place where I stop   her face is my own," and then, after her mother leaps off the ship, longing for "the hot thing" (210)—a shared "wish to join, merge, and fuse with the lost mother" (Horvitz 163). Mingling time and space to create a physical, communal history, Morrison shows that even in the hold of a slave ship, what Africans brought to the United States was their own "best thing" (273): themselves.

Beloved's reminders of the Middle Passage build a defining impulse towards community, as Morrison redeems a painful history of upheaval by re-creating and then transforming the Africans' corporeal experience in the airless cargo space of a slave ship. This historically fraught sensation of massed bodies, later reproduced as the women's rescue party, is the means by which Sethe is eventually reincorporated into her community, just as her moment of healing in the lean-to occurs in the presence of the significant waters of the Ohio. Similarly, just as Beloved is time made flesh, so too is the group of thirty women that walks down Bluestone Road to rescue Sethe from Beloved's lethal voracity.   Whereas Beloved embodies only the past, however, these women embody the present. Their appearance is a physical protest against "past errors taking possession of the present" (256) as they confront the insatiable demands of history incarnated by Beloved. No matter how fluid, temporal boundaries finally must be recognized as boundaries; Ella, the group's leader, "didn't mind a little communication between the two worlds, but this was an invasion" (257). To actualize itself, this community of African Americans must enfold splintered-off individuals like Sethe, an act that acknowledges but then exorcises the kind of invasive force that Beloved represents.[21]

Morrison deliberately evokes the Middle Passage to introduce the scene

of Sethe's reintegration into the community of the present.   Conjuring the
closeness and despair of a ship's cramped hold is the summer air: hot, moist,
and fetid, stinking of death from Cincinnati's slaughterhouses.   Having
invoked a subconscious communal recollection of the Middle Passage
through the deathlike stench of "hanging meat and things rotting in jars,"
Morrison then begins redeeming this shared memory as she shifts her
emphasis from the forced crowding of abducted Africans to a gathering
defined by celebration (259).   When the women arrive at 124, they recall the
party thrown eighteen years ago to celebrate Sethe's safe arrival in Ohio:

the first thing they saw was not Denver sitting on the steps, but themselves. Younger,
stronger, even as little girls lying in the grass asleep. . . . They sat on the porch, ran
down to the creek, teased the men. . . . There they were, young and happy, playing in
Baby Suggs's yard. (258)

Morrison's homage to the women's solidarity thus comprises two collectively
remembered pasts, each illustrating the sensate experience of "rememory."
These signposts point to a still more concrete evocation of the Middle
Passage, whose meshing of time and physicality surfaces when Sethe is
literally embraced back into the African American community.   Beloved's
prelanguage remembrance of the journey foreshadows the women's wordless
singing: "In the beginning there were no words.   In the beginning was the
sound, and they all knew what that sound sounded like" (259).   The fluidity of
this sound now encircles Sethe, signifying for her the twenty-eight days of
community she had earlier shared with these women:

it was as though the Clearing had come to her with all its heat and simmering leaves,
where the voices of women searched for the right combination, the key, the code, the
sound that broke the back of words. . . . It was a wave of sound wide enough to sound
deep water and knock the pods off chestnut trees. It broke over Sethe and she
trembled like the baptized in its wash. (261)

Like the Ohio's waters, which simultaneously embrace the newborn Denver
and fuse with the sea route of the Middle Passage, the women's liquid call
bathes Sethe in a communion of nurturing and collective history.
        The most emphatic redemption of the bodily experience of the Middle
Passage appears through Beloved's perspective, reaffirming the terrible cost
of Sethe's reincorporation in her community, when she watches Sethe running
"into the faces of the people out there, joining them and leaving Beloved
behind. . . . Away from her to the pile of people out there. They make a hill.
A hill of black people, falling" (262). Not understanding that Sethe has gone
to kill the man she believes is Schoolteacher, Beloved sees her mother's flight
as yet another abandonment and disappears, but not before she witnesses a
reenactment of the massing of flesh that constituted much of the Middle
Passage: the "hill of black people" grouped together. This time, however, the
focus is not on Beloved's sensation of being crushed and smothered under the
inert bodies of abducted Africans who are crammed together involuntarily.

Rather, Sethe is overwhelmed by the bodies of the community who save her from murdering Edward Bodwin, their white benefactor, an act of violence that would destroy not only her but also them. The women now mass their bodies together willingly, falling together upon Sethe to protect her. Beloved's vision of massed flesh completes Morrison's refashioned moments of the Middle Passage, whose most tangible outrages are remembered and redeemed in a strikingly physical reenactment.

As I mention in my introduction, Toni Morrison sees an unhealthy relationship between Americans' (often faulty) sense of history and will to believe in the American dream: "We live in a land where the past is always erased and . . . the slate is clean. . . . [Our historical] memory is much more in danger now than it was thirty years ago" (qtd. in Gilroy 222). In *Beloved* it is as dangerous to engage with memory as it is to lose it. Sethe and Paul D (and to a lesser extent, Denver) are imperiled by their violent confrontations with Beloved's history-made-flesh. Risk also extends to *Beloved*'s witnesses, or readers, and to Morrison herself, all of whose reluctant involvement with this furious history is easily understood. The process of remembering, retelling, writing it all down, and then offering it up to be read demands an intense connection to this novel's inherent brutalities. In one of *Beloved*'s most vicious scenes, Sethe recalls Schoolteacher's nephews stealing her breast milk while he stands "watching and writing it up" (70). The role of one who witnesses such atrocities, through either writing or reading, cannot be a simple one in any case, but must be particularly complicated when witnessing occurs through fictional narrative, a genre that acknowledges certain pleasures in the telling and reading of stories.[22]

Certainly, as Paul Ricoeur has noted, "human lives need to [be] and merit being narrated. . . . The whole history of suffering cries out for vengeance and calls for narrative" (62). Yet how can we possibly reconcile the pleasures of narrative with such abhorrent subject matter? I frankly admit that the urge to make something useful out of violence, or to make violence useful, has dominated much (perhaps too much) of my thinking about *Beloved*; at the same time, the fact that Morrison's subject matter constitutes one of North America's most repellent histories nearly insists upon a guarded engagement with the novel. Because the psychic, physical, and cultural violence of slavery continues to cut deep, continues on some levels to be real in the United States, much as Beloved herself becomes "real" in the novel, even fictional approaches toward that violence require caution. To paraphrase (and take somewhat out of context) James Phelan, perhaps right now it is more helpful to shift from "explicating [the violence in *Beloved*] to explaining the purpose of its recalcitrance" (715). Morrison never smoothes down the brutalities of her narrative, nor does her closing passage neatly wrap up all loose ends.

On the positive side, through her narration of a people's sundering from their homeland Morrison evokes the communal in the unlikely spaces of a slave ship and a crumbling lean-to and then affirms it through the confrontation between past and present, between an outcast and the people who come to reclaim her. There, in the bodily contact between one person and the group, Morrison discovers a culture's flexibility and resiliency, along with "the imagination, intelligence, and necessity available for the journey" ("Unspeakable Things" 33). That resiliency, however, has a price. Immediately after the tableau of Paul D and Sethe's putting their stories together in Baby Suggs's house, Beloved roams out of the novel entirely, actively disremembered by the larger community and seen by those who knew her, like all other fiction, as nothing more than somebody's imagined words. *Beloved* ends with neither a man and woman holding hands nor the assertion that a sense of community can survive a forced uprooting. Rather, it ends with a return to forgetfulness, the very kind of forgetfulness that indirectly split apart the black community so pivotal to this novel. Morrison's refrain that Beloved's is "not a story to pass on" contains both recognition and warning: recognition of the anguish and repulsion intrinsic to her story, and warning against forgetting "not only the footprints but the water too and what it is down there" (275). In that water are suspended the bitter stories of abduction, forced immigration, disease, and death—yet also the seeds of a new culture, one as integral to the formation of the United States as any of our more official histories. The characters in *Beloved* believe that remembering is "unwise" (274). The readers of *Beloved*, importuned by the now-invisible Beloved for a kiss, do not have that option.

NOTES

1. See Gates's "Culture Wars," especially 11; see also Magdalena Zaborowska's 1995 *How We Found America: Reading Gender Through East European Immigrant Narratives*.

2. As Sally Keenan has written, Morrison's choosing a pregnant slave woman for her heroine "defies the limits of empirical history"; Deborah Gray White's research shows that slave women were underrepresented among escapees precisely because of their role as mothers. But "in combining in one event both the woman slave's fierce desire for freedom and the fierce devotion to her children, [Morrison] figures something that the historiography has largely been unable to represent" (Keenan 64).

3. Toni Morrison, *Beloved* (New York: Penguin Books, 1988) 203. Subsequent quotations from this work are cited in the text.

4. As Horvitz notes, Beloved also represents a long line of African and African American women who were "cruelly severed from their mothers and daughters" (163).

5. Compare this theme with the brutal domestic inversions enacted in the nineteenth-century sentimental narratives of Harriet Beecher Stowe, Harriet Wilson, and Harriet Jacobs (see chapter 2). Scruggs also supplies a brief though detailed analysis of houses in Morrison's *The Bluest Eye* (1970), *Sula* (1974), *Song of Solomon* (1977), and *Tar Baby* (1981) (see 169–70).

6. As Fox-Genovese notes, the plantation was not defined by the nineteenth-century northern bourgeois cult of female domesticity (*Plantation*, 31–38; see also Giddings 41).

7. Likewise, Gates traces the "trope of the swamp" in *Their Eyes Were Watching God* and DuBois's *A Quest of the Silver Fleece* (*Signifying* 193). Useful to my argument is his discussion of signifying as the revision of "key tropes and rhetorical strategies received from other precursory texts" ("Blackness" 242). Tellingly, slave owner Marie St. Clare in Stowe's *Uncle Tom's Cabin* does not understand the significance of the swamp, as she describes "a man that was so lazy he would . . . lie round in the swamps. . . . That man was caught and whipped, time and again . . . and the last time he crawled off, though he couldn't but just go, and died in the swamps. There was no sort of reason for it, for father's hands were always treated kindly" (Stowe 272).

8. Calling Sethe a "nigger," Amy asks if she plans to "just lay there and foal," and warns her not to "up and die on me in the night, you hear? I don't want to see your ugly black face hankering over me" (32–33, 82). Nonetheless, since she does not betray Sethe, Amy's character violates "the rules of interracial interaction with which [Sethe's] fellow blacks are familiar" (T. Harris 165).

9. In stark contrast to Schoolteacher, who has a hole dug to protect his "stock" in Sethe's womb, Amy also fashions a bed of leaves for the baby.

10. Although Sethe and Amy navigate their social roles, they remain distinct from each other; a complete blurring of identities would betray the historical realities *Beloved* so clearly documents. As Mary Poovey has noted, "there *are* concrete historical women whose differences reveal the inadequacy of th[e] unified category [of "woman"] in the present and the past" (60).

11. See C. M. Hennessy 10–11. Racial boundaries also meet at the combined points of violence and healing when Paul D and his escaped chain gang are taken in by a group of sick Cherokee who are "decimated" by the policies of Andrew Jackson (111–13).

12. Morrison's recognition of the methods by which slavery chipped away at the black family, and particularly black motherhood, finds its illustration in Sethe's remembrance of her obscenely enforced role as wet nurse: "two boys with mossy teeth, one sucking on my breast the other holding me down, their book-reading teacher watching and writing it up" (70). Morrison's substitution of grown men for white babies is an indictment of the "Mammy" function thrust upon slave women, in what Judith Wilt has called "demonic nursing" (159). This picture also gives weight to Sethe's continual obsession with having enough milk for all her children, as well as to her memories of hungry infancy, when her own mother, sent out to the fields, could not nurse her and she was forced to wait until the wet nurse Nan had already fed the white babies. Typical in Morrison's fictional vision, what was formerly assumed to be wholly natural and innocent—nursing an infant—is rendered brutally violent in slavery's most unnatural context. See also Omolade 363–64, and Wilt 154–66.

13. Henderson's discussion is problematic for me in its neglect of black *paternity*, particularly regarding her notion of Sethe's "immaculate conception" ("Re-Membering" 76). Also Halle is an integral, albeit briefly played, part of *Beloved*'s history.

14. It would be a mistake, however, to frame Denver's birth in solely positive terms. As the Fugitive Slave Law and Denver's inability to leave her mother's yard will prove, being born cannot be equated with "claiming ownership of [a] freed self" (95). Denver does not lay claim to her self until quite late in the novel's temporal frame, after she has worked through her own processes of memory and storytelling (see *Beloved* 78, and Rimmon-Kenan 112–13).

15. In this respect Sethe resembles her strong-willed mother, who, as Sethe is told, named her daughter herself, after Sethe's father (62). See also Pérez-Torres, and Benston (in Gates's *Black Literary Theory*, especially 152).

16. As Rimmon-Kenan aptly points out, the tension between repressing and narrating this history extends to *Beloved*'s characters themselves, from Paul D's tobacco tin heart and Denver's deaf spell, to Baby Suggs's notion of the "unspeakable" past (120–21).

17. See Horvitz 162–65, and House 18–22.

18. As Aldon Nielsen observes in *Writing Between the Lines: Race and Intertextuality*, our national repression of African Americans' slave experience has a cultural dimension as well.   Right now we have no museum devoted to commemorating the culture that Africans created during their sojourn in slavery; Nielsen adds that the Middle Passage "may be the great repressed signifier of American historical consciousness" (101).

19. As Sethe's mother, the speaker would have to be old enough to conceive, since she was "taken up many times by the crew" and "threw away" the baby engendered by rape (62).

20. In a recent essay Walter Benn Michaels asks how "texts [can] transmit rather than merely represent 'horror'" (9).   Discussing the relation-ship between writing and bearing witness, he explicates Shoshona Felman's argument that in order for "the act of reading literary texts" to be related to the act of facing horror, "language must break down to avoid becoming mere reportage" (Felman 2, qtd. in Michaels 9). See also Michaels 8–11.

21. In one of several interesting analyses of *Beloved*'s uses of psychoanalytic discourses, Jennifer Fitzgerald calls this moment in the text an act of "communal mothering" (683).

22. I take up the difficulties inherent in representing horror more fully in my discussion of Cynthia Ozick's *The Shawl*.

Chapter 4

When Legacy Meets Desire:
The Blues in Gayl Jones's
Corregidora

In her recent critical work, *Liberating Voices: Oral Tradition in African American Literature*, Gayl Jones observes that most Third World writing links storytelling with "the sense of whole being" (179). American writing, of course, has a long tradition of staking claim to one's self by telling one's own story, with examples ranging from the autobiographical (Benjamin Franklin, Harriet Jacobs, and Maxine Hong Kingston) to the fictional (Huck Finn, Holden Caulfield, and Janie Woods). Yet Jones's own 1975 novel, *Corregidora*, problematizes this connection. Exploring the generational passing down of a rigid and unforgettably brutal family history, *Corregidora* discloses how a prescriptive form of storytelling leads not to a whole sense of self but rather entombs that self in the wearisome sameness of an externally defined identity. Dealing with four generations of black Brazilian-American women who are strictly defined initially by a slave owner and then by themselves, the novel challenges its readers to think about how the system of slavery reifies a concept of black women as hypersexual by regarding them as property. Great Gram Corregidora charges her daughter and granddaughter to "bear witness." The meaning of the phrase is literal: there must be an ongoing line of children to memorize her old slavemaster Corregidora's atrocities and recite them at the Last Judgment, when all questions about injustice and evil will be asked.[1] Hence, these women replace their sexual commodification with deliberate, vengeance-motivated self-definition. But as

Ursa (a childless blues singer and the youngest Corregidora) discovers, this resolve has two drawbacks: the Corregidoras' agenda severely limits their sexual identities even as, cyclically, that limitation incites domestic violence.

Scarred by their family history, Mama and Ursa can neither accept nor refute their mothers' belief that all men are rapists. Their ambivalence finally provokes their husbands to the point of violence, which, though it stems indirectly from old Corregidora's sexual abuse, is not excused by it.[2] Using the doubled lens of blighted sexuality and domestic assault, Jones argues that despite its goal of autonomy, political self-objectification is a flawed step toward the empowerment of these women.[3] Not solely focused on violence and retribution, *Corregidora* also asks how a woman can renegotiate her sexual desire when she descends from a long line of abuse and rage.

Ursa Corregidora's sexuality has been silenced first by her family's outrageous history and then by their vow of retribution. She breaks that silence when she discovers her own voice and art through the African American tradition of the blues song—a tradition whose performer "is not only the victim but also, by virtue of the performance itself, [holds] the ultimate power" (Byerman 179). This kind of dialectic extends to Gayl Jones herself, who refuses to depict only what she calls "positive race images" in her work (Tate 97). Arguing that "there's a lot of imaginative territory that you have to be 'wrong' in order to enter," Jones applauds but also criticizes certain techniques for black female self-authorization (Jones, "Work" 234).

In *Corregidora*, mothers perpetuate as well as suffer from violence. Even as Gram and Great Gram speak vengeance through their memories, their stories resurrect the image of their abuser and, paradoxically, allow him in some measure to dominate the lives of their daughter and granddaughter. In politicizing the bodies of themselves and their daughters as maternal breeding grounds for retaliation, the Corregidora women transform those bodies into public spaces. In seeking to avenge the wrongs done them, they also, however unwittingly, visit those wrongs on their children. Thus does politicization become betrayal. A significant question for a slave mother— "What notions of identity and culture could [she] transmit to the daughter whom she had enslaved by the very fact of giving birth to her?" (Keenan 53–54)—becomes more complex when it pertains to the twentieth-century freed black women of *Corregidora*.

Ursa's familial project of passing judgment infuses her very surname.[4] As Melvin Dixon notes, *corregidore* means "judicial magistrate" in Portuguese: "by changing the gender designation, Jones makes Ursa Corregidor*a* a female judge charged by the women in her family to 'correct' (from the Portuguese verb corrigir) the historical invisibility they have suffered" (239). Additionally, *Ursa* is the Latin word for "bear." Strictly speaking, this term signifies the animal rather than the act, but the associative meaning is undeniable.[5] Rendered sterile when her husband pushes her down a flight of stairs, Ursa must bear witness through her art, the blues. She also bears witness that she has a place beyond retribution and vengeance. Finally,

Ursa bears a literary connection through her first name. In 1859, "one of the first two black women to publish a novel in any language" was Maria F. dos Reis, whose novel *Ursula* appeared in Brazil the same year that Harriet Wilson's *Our Nig* appeared in the United States (Gates, "Introduction," *Our Nig* xiii).

Old Corregidora not only turns Great Gram's sexuality into a product but also fathers her daughter and her granddaughter, who then become living emblems of both violence and survival. Each woman in this family gives birth to a daughter who must memorize and testify to her mother's brutal, angry history.[6] Ursa's grandmother explains the need for this human evidence, speaking of the official abolition of slavery in Brazil: the officials burned all written documentation of slaveholding "cause they wanted to play like what had happened before never did happen." Gram must substitute flesh for official paper evidence in her project of bearing witness (79). "What had happened before" was the violent reduction of women to objects of exchange. In the abusive economy of old Corregidora's Brazilian plantation, Great Gram and her daughter are regarded solely as valuable sexual entities; a woman's vagina equals her economic value, and that economic value equals her essence. As old Corregidora's favorite "gold piece," Great Gram is used for both his profit and his pleasure until she flees to Louisiana, temporarily abandoning their daughter, who must deal with Corregidora unaided. His definition of slave women does not die with him, however; it crosses time and place to surface in Ursa's first marriage. Ownership based on sexual relations informs her marriage to Mutt Thomas, whose great-grandfather, an ex-slave, bought his wife's freedom, only to lose her when he fell into debt. Marked by his own family history of slavery and ownership, Mutt identifies Ursa as "his pussy," a term that signifies for him a faithful and loving wife (46; see also S. Robinson 154–56). Possession is as important to Ursa's husband as it was to her great-grandfather, whose name Ursa still bears, to Mutt's anger: "You Corregidora's, ain't you? . . . You ain't my woman" (61). Ursa remembers Mutt's asking to see "his pussy. Let me feel my pussy" (46). In Mutt's time, the emphasis is not on economic value (Corregidora's "gold piece") but rather on sexual fidelity; he asks Ursa repeatedly to confirm that "[i]t's my ass, ain't it? Ain't no other man had it, or have they?" (164) Caught up in the political agenda of her mother, grandmother, and great-grandmother (herein called *mothers*), Ursa initially allows Mutt to own her body and soul; according to Corregidora's rules a woman is wholly defined by her vagina and her womb.

Working towards self-realization in the mid-twentieth-century United States, Great Gram and Gram transform—but do not abandon—Corregidora's objectifying code. In their philosophy, a woman's body is never her own, and a child is never a person in her own right. "Self-appointed griots," they tell and retell an invariant history whose "power to obliterate personality"—and desire—is remarkable half a century later (Kubitschek 146–47). Sexual violence doubly limits desire and pleasure for these women. First defined as "pussy," they are now self-defined as womb. The function of woman's body therefore is single-minded still; no longer a sexual commodity, it has become a political commodity. Until Ursa can reclaim her desire and sexuality, until she breaks free of the constraints of the story her mothers have told and retold, she cannot redeem her legacy of abuse. As Patricia Hill Collins notes, supplanting "negative images with positive ones can be equally problematic if the function of stereotypes as controlling images remains unrecognized" (106). Even the powerful mantle of an avenger can become a straitjacket.

Perhaps *Corregidora*'s most uncomfortable aspect for the reader is its refusal to submerge desire under a history of abuse. Although Jones neither exonerates the old slavemaster's atrocities nor depicts rape as anything but vicious, we must remember that *Corregidora* works against smothering sexuality beneath a political veil. Jones is concerned with how Corregidora's victims discover the capacity for sexual pleasure in their own lives. Mama tells Ursa that Martin, her husband and Ursa's father, was bold enough to ask Great Gram and Gram what she had always been too intimidated to ask: "How much was hate for Corregidora and how much was love?" (131). While the deliberately raw narratives of Great Gram and Gram dispel the image of Corregidora as romantic lover, Martin's question forces Jones's readers to examine the highly disconcerting coexistence of desire and abuse.

While Ursa's mothers speak freely about sexual assault, sexual yearning appears only furtively in their narrative.[7] Ursa is therefore led to muse about the possibility of pleasure for her mothers: "And you, Grandmama, the first mulatto daughter, when did you begin to feel yourself in your nostrils? And, Mama, when did you smell your body with your hands?" (59) *Corregidora* is at its riskiest in hinting that desire can exist in even the most abusive situations. Jones notes that her readers are often "bothered by the fact that the author doesn't offer any judgments or show her attitude toward the offense, but simply has the characters relate it" (Tate 97). Like Jones, Ursa does not judge Gram and Great Gram but only puzzles over their desire:

They were with him. What did they feel? You know how they talk about hate and desire. Two humps on the same camel? . . . Still, there was what they never spoke. . . . How all but one of them had the same lover? Did they begrudge [Mama] that? (102–3)

These questions are enormously difficult, perhaps unanswerable. Jones's insistence on asking them reveals the complexity of desire, as well as the inevitable confusion resulting from linking sexuality with personal and political revenge.

Fully as important, Jones delineates the extent to which Ursa's mothers have been cheated. The novel shows that even when desire sprouts between the cracks of a thwarted life, it may never truly thrive. No one can forget Corregidora's identity as rapist and slave breeder, yet he also provides Great Gram and Gram with their only sexual experiences: experiences of fear, rape, and incest. In a deeply twisted sense, Corregidora is the only "lover" they ever have (*lover* connoting regular involvement),[8] yet their memories of him have maimed their desire as surely and as viciously as Mutt's attack has maimed Ursa's body. She cannot conceive a child, while her mothers cannot conceive of sexual love; Corregidora's forcing them to sleep with whomever he pleased left them incapable of loving (104).

Although the Corregidora women struggle to bear witness rather than human units of labor for their slavemaster, slavery was certainly a formidable opponent. Patricia Hill Collins points out that controlling black slave women's reproduction was a good business decision for slave owners: "Every slave child born represented a valuable unit of property, another unit of labor, and, if female, the prospects for more slaves" (76). As Collins and Hazel Carby have noted, the justification for "breeding" black slaves is inextricable from nineteenth-century ideologies of white and black womanhood. The "cult of true womanhood" was a whites-only club, and membership required a suppression of sexuality. Black women remained outside the doors, forced not only to provide further units of property and labor for slave owners but also to bear the image of "Jezebel, whore, or sexually aggressive woman," an image that rationalized so many sexual attacks on black slave women by white men (Collins 77; see also S. Robinson 138–48, as well as D. White and J. Jones). Thus, a racist agenda has historically associated "overt, rampant sexuality" with African American women (Carby, *Reconstructing* 27). "The matriarch" and "the welfare mother," two images of black women fabricated by contemporary white culture, continue this association, the former representing a woman whose sexual aggressiveness "emasculates Black men because she will not permit them to assume roles as Black patriarchs, and the latter, a woman whose "low morals and uncontrolled sexuality" have ensured her poverty (Collins 77, 78).

These distortions of black female sexuality reverberate in nineteenth- and twentieth-century black women's fiction. In grappling with their exclusion from the cult of true womanhood, black women writers also worked to separate themselves from "a persistent association with illicit sexuality,"[9] which entailed deleting sexuality from their representations of black women:

The long history of the exploitation of black sexuality led to the repression of passion and the repression or denial of female sexuality and desire. . . . Racist sexual ideologies proclaimed the black woman to be a rampant sexual being, and in response black women writers either focused on defending their morality or displaced sexuality onto another terrain. (Carby, *Reconstructing* 32, 174)

Collins identifies "the need to reconceptualize sexuality with an eye towards empowering African-American women," noting that "sexuality and the erotic [are] a domain of exploration, pleasure, and human agency." In challenging instead of fleeing "Eurocentric notions of unrestrained Black sexuality," *Corregidora* insists that the erotic is a legitimate dimension of black women's experience (Collins 164, 166, 192). Ursa's struggle to voice her own desire inevitably leads her to that realm.

As Hortense Spillers has written, the concepts of sexuality and desire were "thrown into unrelieved crisis" within the bizarre dictates and arrangements of slavery ("Mama's Baby" 76). Seen in the context of that crisis, the youngest Corregidora woman may not wholly renounce her familial identity of woman-as-womb, but she does begin to change the terms of her self-definition by acknowledging pleasure, in however a limited way. Unlike her mothers, who try to substitute rage for gratification, Ursa focuses her sexuality on her clitoris rather than her womb. The work of Gayatri Spivak and Hélène Cixous, each with her own emphasis on the specificity of the body, is helpful in evaluating this localized reclamation of sexuality.[10] In "French Feminism in an International Frame," Spivak describes the clitoris as something suppressed or effaced in the interest of defining "woman as sex object, or as means or agent of reproduction" (151). Since female sexual pleasure has nothing to do with reproduction, the clitoris is what Spivak calls "women's excess in all areas of production and practice" (82). Ursa centers her pleasure precisely on the point that "exceeds" both Corregidora's racist appropriation and her mothers' political objectification of the female body. In doing so, she takes her first step towards reclaiming her entire body from an initially racist, politically motivated agenda.

Like Spivak, Hélène Cixous also discusses desire; however, Cixous locates female sexual pleasure all through the body rather than focusing on a "phallic" point, such as the clitoris.[11] As long as Ursa confines her pleasure to a singular, finite location, she is still limiting her desire, still defining her sexual self in narrow terms. Obviously biological determinism is a tricky launching pad for any feminist discussion. Nonetheless, Gayl Jones's physically oriented focus on female pleasure necessitates a careful look at the body. Cixous's emphasis on the multiplicity of female pleasure is relevant to my discussion precisely because it works against that narrowing definition. Cixous visualizes a "woman's body, with its thousand and one thresholds of ardor" and its "profusion of meanings that run through it in every direction" (315), while Ursa's limited sense of desire leads to her difficulty in "feel[ing] anything" sexually. That difficulty haunts her through the novel and is largely responsible for destroying her two marriages. More important, it reinforces her belief that she is somehow flawed as a woman and feeds into her family's code of objectification. In the logic of her mothers, without a womb, how can she function as a woman? Ursa's sterility tortures her with the knowledge that she can no longer fulfill her mothers' expectation. She cannot forget what she thinks of as a dry, barren space within her and bemoans the "[s]ilence in my womb" (99).

Corregidora's emphasis on the body ties in with Cixous's and Spivak's perspectives on female desire, which oppose what Elizabeth Spelman calls white feminism's "somatophobia": "fear of and disdain for the body" (126). Alluding to Simone de Beauvoir's observation that women have been "regarded as 'womb,'" Spelman connects feminism's "negative attitude toward the body" with "the idea that the work of the body and for the body has no part in real human dignity" (127). From Jonathan Swift's scatological poetry to Claude Lévi-Strauss's research on the significance of women's menstrual cycles in "primitive" cultures, women (but not most men) are indeed represented as having lives "determined by basic bodily functions. . . . Superior groups, we have been told from Plato on down, have better things to do with their lives" (127).[12] As Spelman rightly points out, when this disdain for bodies divorces "the concept of woman . . . from the concept of woman's body," it posits a kind of ahistorical woman, one who

has no color, no accent, no particular characteristics that require having a body. . . . And so it will seem inappropriate or beside the point to think of women in terms of any physical characteristics, especially if their oppression has been rationalized by reference to those characteristics. (128)[13]

In short, there would be no difference between the lives of a black woman of 1890 and a white woman of 1990. *Corregidora* successfully avoids this difficulty by making the physicality of its black women paramount.

The Corregidora women's repression of desire for political reasons can be read as a response to slavery's capitalist control of black women's sexuality. Their consistent self-identification with reproductivity is a stunning variation on Gayatri Spivak's Marxist discussion of women within a framework of production. While women biologically "produce" children, Spivak notes that, socially speaking, "the legal possession of the child is an inalienable fact of the property right of the man who [biologically yet also legally] 'produces' the child" (79).[14] This emphasis on property and production intersects with the experience of black slave women squarely at the crossroads of reproduction and desire. Designated as breeders, slave women were, in Harriet Jacobs's words, "'considered of no value, unless they continually increase their owner's stock'" (49, qtd. in Carby 54). Their denigration made them vulnerable to rape and commercial exchange. It also thwarted their sexuality. As Spivak notes, this theory of product and ownership leaves no room whatsoever for sexual pleasure. Naturally, she adds,

One cannot write off what may be called a uterine social organization (the arrangement of the world in terms of the reproduction of future generations, where the uterus is the chief agent and means of production) in favor of a clitoral. The uterine social organization should, rather, be "situated" through the understanding that it has so far been established by excluding a clitoral social organization. (152)

That is, recognition of women's sexual desire alongside their "value" as (re)producers is one way of empowering them as subjects of pleasure rather than passive objects of exchange. Women's "pleasure-as-excess" thus finds an appropriate "sign" in the clitoris—a sign that Ursa acknowledges in her rejection of her mothers' imposed self-definition.

That sign also defies women's relegation to an inferior status in Freudian terms. When Hélène Cixous attacks the notion of what she calls "the supreme hole," she refers to both the "lack" of a phallus in women, as perceived by Freud, and the literal cavity of the vagina and womb.[15] Focusing on woman's "lack" results in the consistent identification of the "female" with "the negative"—an absence and a deformity. Instead, Cixous prefers to focus on female desire. She locates a woman's pleasure throughout her body, arguing for the "nonexclusion either of the difference or of one sex" and "the effects of the inscription of desire, over all parts of my body and the other body" (314). Cixous visualizes multiple sites of female pleasure, while the Corregidora women see a chance to create a tabula rasa on which they can inscribe their story of sexual violence and rage. But is that all they see? The enforcement of a singular, fixed meaning on their sexuality would seem to shut out desire from their lives. Still, Jones's careful and persistent questioning about their "hate and desire" suggests that the issue of vengeance is not so clear-cut as it first appears.

En route to reclaiming her sexuality from this political agenda, Ursa recognizes her family's rigid code of binary oppositions between male and female. Their history categorizes each sex, both black and white. All men are rapists; all women, victims who sustain themselves on their anger. Fashioning old Corregidora's sexual commodification of their bodies into political self-commodification, Ursa's mothers turn his racist, oppositional perspective to their own advantage. In doing so, however, they insist on what Keith Byerman calls a "dualistic universe" of victims and rapists (180). Historically, this mode of "either/or dichotomous thinking" has fed racist as well as sexist objectification; both Collins and Barbara Christian have observed how easily white culture's concept of black women as "Other" leads to forms of manipulation (see Collins 68–69, and Christian, *Perspectives* 160). (As I will soon argue, Ursa empowers herself by moving beyond this victim/victimizer worldview.)   Toni Cade Bambara points out that "stereotypical definitions of 'masculine' and 'feminine'" oppose "what revolution for self is all about—the whole person" (qtd. in Collins 184–85). The men who marry Mama and Ursa try to fight against their imposed definition as rapists.   As Corregidora's legacy wins out, however, their frustration leads to domestic violence against their wives. Martin beats Mama until her face is swollen and discolored. Mutt Thomas drunkenly pushes Ursa down a flight of stairs, killing her fetus and leaving her sterile. Ursa must resolve both the racist brutality of her mothers' lives and the limitations of their response to that brutality. Until she can do so, she remains subject to the violence engendered by old Corregidora's atrocities. Familial memories distort her sense of self, and both her husbands victimize her in part (but only in part) because she sees herself as a victim. Ursa needs to transcend the cycle of violence that her mothers have unknowingly passed on to her. To some degree, she can do so by fully understanding her sexual self.

Ursa's identity as a daughter is pivotal to this understanding, as she realizes her increasing need to locate her own mother's personal remembrances of Martin (104). With her accident and two failed marriages behind her, Ursa visits her mother to learn about her parents. She needs to see herself as a child born of love rather than of rape. Asking about her father for the first time in her life, she tells her mother that Mama and Martin's history was always more significant to Ursa than anything she had ever learned about Corregidora (111). Ursa's mother is not a victim of rape or incest when she marries Martin. Identified by both herself and her mothers as a walking womb, however, she still categorizes her husband as a tool for vengeance, telling Ursa that while she was not interested in a man as such, her "whole body *wanted* you . . . and knew it would have you, and knew you'd be a girl" (114; emphasis added). Because Mama's body wants a daughter—not a man, not a lover—that body enacts an emotional form of parthenogenesis: although she needs a man to conceive a daughter, Mama has no desire for a lover himself (101). Ursa reflects that her mother was so thoroughly drilled by *her* mother and grandmother that she felt no real need of Martin after she had gotten pregnant (101). Denied a sense of herself as a private and sexual being, Mama always hears the angry voices of her mothers and their rapist when she closes her eyes. Aware of her own complicity in this denial, she remembers her first sexual experience: suddenly "it was like I felt the whole man in me. . . . *I wouldn't let myself feel anything* [else]" (117–18; emphasis added).

Mama's familial identity as angry victim not only thwarts her sexuality but also reinforces Martin's sense of powerlessness and frustration as a black man in twentieth-century North America.[16] The pernicious legacy of slave owners like Corregidora has contributed to the "existing gender ideology concerning Black masculinity and Black femininity" (Collins 164). Sexual violence committed against black women also affects black men. As Carby notes, "Black manhood . . . could not be achieved or maintained because of the inability of the slave to protect the black woman in the same manner that convention dictated the inviolability of the body of the white woman" (35). Although Mama and Martin have never been slaves, this ideology of black sexuality permeates their relationship. Living with him in her grandmother's three-room shotgun house,[17] Mama rarely sleeps with Martin, telling him her mothers' presence inhibits her, until her familial agenda comes full circle, realizing a self-fulfilling prophecy of abuse and victimization as Martin's angry frustration leads first to his disappearance and then to violence. Believing that the only relationship between men and women by Corregidora standards is that of prostitute and client, Martin beats his wife when he next sees her, and her response is, tellingly, no response at all: knowing that she neither could nor would do anything in response to his violence, she "carried him to the point where he ended up hating me. . . . That's what I knew I'd do with any man" (120, 121). Mama's self-identity as inevitable victim is thus even more malignant, because it is more powerful, than Martin's rage.

Frustration and violence emerge in Ursa's own marriage when Mutt pushes her down a flight of steps. Certainly Mutt is accountable for his brutal behavior, but Ursa also recognizes that the raging memories of her ancestry have infected her marriage. Mutt cries that he is weary of her recurring litany of abuse and rage and does not understand her imperative of memory as far as Corregidora is concerned (154). In part, Mutt's own slave ancestry explains his possessiveness, but it is also Ursa's inability to feel anything sexually that drives him to wild speculations about men continually staring at her. And in some peculiar way, Ursa is constantly under scrutiny—not from living men but from the "remembered" visage of Corregidora himself. She even keeps a photograph of him. Mutt tells Ursa that neither he nor she is "them," referring to all of their slave ancestors (151). But Ursa is them, and will be them for as long as their memories confiscate her body as a witness.

Often she wonders just whose body she inhabits: hers or the collective body of the Corregidora women. Great Gram and Gram re-tell their history so effectively that Ursa's mother memorizes it verbatim; in fact, through repetition and familiarity, *their* memory becomes *hers* (129). At one point her mother's narrative merges so strongly with Great Gram's that it seems to Ursa that she hears not her mother's voice but Great Gram's instead (124). Staring at a photograph of herself, Ursa realizes that despite her earlier belief that she was different from her mothers, she now knows that, like them, "I had it" (60). *It* refers to Corregidora's blood, but also to the horrific remembered lives of Ursa's mothers. She is so forcibly identified with her family that she has no privacy from their relentless memories. While her mother is at work, her grandmother tells her stories of the past; when her mother returns, she too tells these stories; when Ursa herself returns home from school, she is greeted with still more memories (101). These stories, terrible and essential, become her mothers' wedding gift to her.

Such a gift not only sexually constrains but also silences—a silencing that *Corregidora* undermines through the blues song and the oral narrative. It is no coincidence that Ursa can voice her desire through the blues; Jones has explained that *Corregidora* is a "blues novel" because "blues acknowledges all different kinds of feelings at once" (Harper 700).[18] If a woman's voice and power are equated solely with her reproductive capacity, she is rendered silent and powerless when she will not or cannot bear children. Because she is sterile, Ursa becomes a cipher in her familial code of vengeance. But Jones's deliberate choice of an oral art form for her narrator shatters the silence of a peculiarly "female" identity. Ursa's artistry is separate from childbearing yet equally valid when she finally sees herself not as an empty womb but a powerful blues singer instead. Jones thus contributes to black feminism's "overarching theme of finding a voice to express a self-defined Black women's standpoint," a theme prevalent in other feminist contexts as well (Collins 94).

The Corregidora women's political agenda offers this choice: sing the note of vengeance or not at all. Addressing these issues of speech and silencing through a deliberately oral narrative, *Corregidora* weaves a pattern out of the blues and colloquial speech. Jones calls this pattern a "ritualized dialogue": "you create a rhythm that people wouldn't ordinarily use. . . . [by taking] the dialogue out of the naturalistic realm" (Harper 699). Ritualized dialogue calls attention to speech itself, emphasizing the ways in which language can transcend a rigid, calcifying identity. In one such dialogue, Ursa confronts her own desire and conflicts of power and powerlessness in a dream. She and Mutt voice a pattern of imperative, pleading, and response. Mutt's lines appear in the following order, punctuated only by Ursa's concise "Naw": "Come over here, honey"; "I need somebody"; "I said I need somebody"; "I won't treat you bad"; "I won't make you sad"; "Come over here, honey, and visit with me a little"; "Come over here, baby, and visit with me a little" (97–98). The novel's final, somewhat ambiguous, dialogue is also ritualistic. Three times Mutt and Ursa chant, respectively: "I don't want a kind of woman that hurt you" and "Then you don't want me." The pattern changes slightly but powerfully with Ursa's last reply: "I don't want a kind of man that'll hurt me neither" (185).[19] Jones's deliberate use of repetition and rhyme, her decided focus on orality, illuminates the two ways out of Ursa's repetitive familial narrative: the blues song and her verbalized anger.

Mama calls the blues the music of the devil, a label whose associations with sinful chaos evoke Ursa's nearly hysterical anger after her accident. Her delirious cursing in the hospital—so memorable that several characters later refer to it—heralds her refusal to be hemmed in by the violence of her family and her husband. Her rage has become more personalized after her hysterectomy, resulting in a fury so virulent that her second husband, Tadpole, tells her she has terrified even the most hardened of city nurses with words they had never heard before (8). Ursa's narrative is deliberately raw, as her words echo what Ralph Ellison once said about the blues: "They at once express both the agony of life and the possibility of conquering it through sheer toughness of spirit" (qtd. in Jones, *Liberating* 160). Early on in her marriage to Mutt, however, she is disturbed by his profanity until she learns to respond in kind, comparing him to Corregidora, whose own example taught her great-grandmother how to swear (153). Great Gram's stories have been repeated so that her daughters will memorize them and absorb her identity, but Ursa now creates her own version of her family history that denies neither the violence behind her objectification nor the bare fact of Corregidora's paternity.   Janice Harris astutely writes that without Corregidora, Ursa "would have nothing to bear, no past or present to sing about, no notes, no lyrics. She is and is not one of Corregidora's women" (4). Ursa therefore cannot deny the violence of her familial history because to do so would silence her art. Rather, she counters the political agenda that silences all voices except the one screaming for retribution.

Jones does not quite turn her sword into a plowshare when she turns Ursa's rough language into art; *Corregidora* does not entirely renounce violence. Instead, Ursa uses the language of her own rage to transform violence into violent art. Mutt's violence forever alters Ursa's ability to bear witness, and her ensuing anger forever alters her singing voice. Her friend Cat notices the change, telling her that her voice now evinces a kind of raw experience (44). Acknowledging the brutality in both her mothers' lives and her own, Ursa's voice becomes the medium through which she empowers and redefines herself.

As Christine Brooke-Rose notes, women who speak too much or too openly are "usually castigated as too close to both nature and truth for comfort, in other words, as witches, and in more 'scientific' times as hysterics" (309). When for Ursa, nature and truth are transformed by Mutt Thomas's act of violence, she too becomes a kind of hysteric.[20] The violence of her husband converges with that of her mothers' histories, circumscribing Ursa's identity more tightly than ever. Her fetus is destroyed, as are her chances for bearing any future generations who could give evidence of her familial past. Conceived to bear witness to a brutal past that she herself cannot claim, Ursa is now bereft of both child and purpose. She has been groomed for one kind of role in the "theater" of her mothers' past, only to discover that she cannot play—or sing—it. In order to sing at all, she must abandon "hysteria" for an artistry of unlimited possibility. The extemporaneous quality of the blues enables Ursa to begin improvising an alternative to sheer rage, ending with the novel's confluence of ambivalence and hope.[21]

Regaining her tongue in her art form, Ursa relocates her creativity from womb to throat, an act of redemption foreshadowed in her reflections on sterility. She compares herself first to something without seeds and then to a broken banjo or guitar (46). Ursa's art thus becomes far more important than her ability to "make generations." As a singer who sees herself as a broken harp string, Ursa must eventually abandon her damaged self-definition in order to sing at all. To surmount her legacy of abuse, Ursa must do more than recover her sexual desire. She also needs to recognize her own potential for ruthlessness in what Gayl Jones calls the "blues relationship" between men and women. Claudia Tate writes that *Corregidora* explores "what is required to be genuinely tender. Perhaps brutality enables one to recognize what tenderness is" (98). Tenderness and brutality coalesce in the novel's ambivalent closing scene between Ursa and Mutt. Twenty-one years after Ursa's accident, Mutt appears, and the two reunite. Still, Ursa's initial thoughts are violently retributive even during a moment of intense sexual intimacy. She knows that just before fleeing the plantation, Great Gram did something to Corregidora that simultaneously enraged and obsessed him. Only now does she understand what it was: "A moment of pleasure and excruciating pain at the same time, a moment of broken skin but not sexlessness . . . a moment that stops before it breaks the skin" (184). During fellatio Ursa retreats from "broken skin" to stopping just "before"—she does not castrate Mutt. The point is that she *could* have done so.[22] She empowers herself in this sexual union, however violently, by becoming an active agent, someone who wanted this also instead of the passive one who must always say she wants to "*get* fucked" (89, emphasis added). Here, at the very end of Corregidora, Ursa takes an important step toward rescuing herself from her family narrative of abuse.

In order to abandon her enforced role as victim, Ursa acknowledges her own power to hurt, a power that is a point of connection for her and Mutt. She traces a line of cruelty and brutality down from Corregidora first to her parents' treatment of each other and then to what she and Mutt have done to each other (184). By recognizing herself and Mutt in these "others," Ursa also recognizes the pattern of mutual abuse that she must break in order to salvage desire. Mutt, too, must resolve his own troubled relationship with possessiveness, by acknowledging and then transforming his history as he recalls his great-grandfather's insanity after losing his wife: he first ate onions to keep people away from him and then, desperately lonely, ate peppermint to call them back. When Mutt attempts this practice, however, he only becomes sick (183–84). Still, Mutt shakes Ursa by the shoulders even as he voices his own desire to turn away from violence. The novel closes with Ursa's realization of her own potential as an abusive agent. It also points towards another potential: that of a woman who can reclaim her body and her desire.

Through her honest treatment of Ursa's familial politics, Jones herself resists an imposed definition: that of a "representative" black woman writer. Unwilling to be pigeonholed as a speaker for her race, Jones agrees with Claudia Tate's observation that many readers object to her depiction of characters "who do not conform to positive images of women or black women," and that "they want to castigate Eva [of *Eva's Man*] and Ursa as some sort of representative black female" (97). *Corregidora* anticipates this question posed by Jones in a later essay, "About My Work":

Should a Black writer ignore [problematic black] characters, refuse to enter "such territory" because of the "negative image" and because such characters can be misused politically by others, or should one try to reclaim such complex, contradictory characters as well as try to reclaim the idea of the heroic image? (233)

Certainly, Jones does not deny that political strategy may be helpful to a writer, but she is alarmed by its potentially rigid constraints, warning that an agenda can also "tell you what you cannot do" ("Work" 233). In choosing to enter the "territory politics won't allow you to enter" and to ask the "questions politics won't allow you to ask," as *Corregidora* makes clear, Jones places herself on the side of risk ("Work" 233).

Hence, Jones's choice to write about a blues singer is double-edged, enabling her to depict "the simultaneity of good and bad," since blues music "doesn't set up any territories. It doesn't set some feelings off into a corner" (Harper 700). Here she foreshadows Houston A. Baker's 1986 observation about the blues, whose "instrumental rhythms suggest change, movement, action, continuance, unlimited and unending possibility" (8). Jones is careful to separate herself from narrators like Ursa Corregidora, but the sign of the blues singer—a woman who often asks the "wrong" questions—does evoke the author's presence as storyteller and blues singer herself.[23]   Jones "sings the blues" when she creates characters who are not inherently "positive race models."   Although she argues that "I do not have a political 'stance'," her writing is political in its refusal to be compartmentalized as "positive" African American work, and in its denial that an African American woman writer can be only one kind of artist (Jones, "Work" 234).

Corregidora's system of slavery and prostitution depends on the silence of women. Also silenced for and by Ursa's mothers, however, are the voices of desire and love—any voice, in fact, that does not speak vengeance. In this way, Jones argues that women as well as men are agents of silencing. For many black American women, speech signifies power and rebellion against the notion of a "mute ideal" (Brooke-Rose 310). Ursa's doubled voice as hysteric-singer eventually undoes her enforced muteness, as does Jones's creation of a "blues novel" whose multiple forms of orality and acceptance of both "good and bad" allow the author to speak freely. Corregidora's deliberately colloquial narrative evokes what Jones calls an "up-close" perspective, a direct relationship "between the storyteller and the hearer" (Harper 692, 698). That relationship is perhaps the most appropriate vehicle for Jones's courage in asking such difficult, even unpopular questions about how the political commodification of women's bodies forecloses the real simultaneity of "correct" and "incorrect" desires.

NOTES

1. Gayl Jones, Corregidora (Boston: Beacon, 1975) 41. Subsequent quotations from this work are cited in the text. Most of the textual references are paraphrased because, for now, Gayl Jones denies permission to quote more than 300 words from all her works, excluding Song for Anhillo.

2. Both Collins and Carby offer excellent arguments about how race, gender, and class oppressions contribute to but do not justify domestic violence against African American women.

3. In doing so, she centers her work firmly within certain traditional American quests for self-definition. Collins traces the "journey from internalized oppression to the 'free mind' of a self-defined, Afrocentric feminist consciousness" in black women's writing (93–106).

4. Not incidentally, the novel emphasizes Corregidora's unending hold on Great Gram, Gram, and Mama by giving as their only formal designation their rapist's surname.

5. Interestingly, the animal-based names Jones chooses for her major characters can be neatly organized according to gender. The men's names—Mutt and Tadpole—have powerless or diminutive associations, while the women's names—Cat and Ursa—denote grace and strength.

6. In this, Jones's narrative contrasts sharply with Harriet Jacobs's Incidents in the Life of a Slave Girl, wherein Linda/Jacobs sees her mulatto children solely as "object[s] of maternal nature" rather than as proofs of sexual coercion (Sanchez-Eppler 102).

7. At one point, Great Gram recalls Corregidora's "digging all up in me till he got me where he wonted me" (125). The enigmatic "where he wonted me" might be read as a moment of either pleasure *or* pain.

8. Desire's fusion with hatred is made clear in Melvin Dixon's identifying Corregidora as "the lover and husband [?] of all the women" (241).

9. Think, for example, of Frances E. W. Harper, Pauline Hopkins, and Jessie Fauset. See also Christian's *Black Women Novelists*, McCullough, and Carby, especially 167–68.

10. While Cixous's theory of female desire is problematic in its essentialist assumption that "the body" is that of a white, middle-class woman, her emphasis on *any* body at all is valuable because it undermines feminism's tendency toward somatophobia (fear of and contempt for the body), which reinforces Western oppositions between body and mind. Cixous's theory of the multiplicity in female desire, with its focus on the physical, provides a good (albeit limited) perspective on Jones's recovery of black female sexuality. See also Spelman 126–31, and Collins 68–69.

11. Certainly I cannot ignore Cixous's biological and racial essentialism. Cixous's (and Irigaray's) theories do not ask "to what extent the body—whether male or female—is a cultural construct, not a 'natural' given" (Suleiman 14), nor do they acknowledge the effects of race and class. See also Christian, "Race" 233. Nonetheless, Cixous's notion of the subversive capacity of female pleasure is helpful in illuminating *Corregidora*'s negotiation of desire.

12. Wendell Berry makes a similar point about race and manual labor in the United States (112–14). As for women's persistent association with the body, Lévi-Strauss's *L'Origine des manières de table* describes two equally terrible possibilities:

> either that the rhythm of [women's] periods slow down and immobilize the course of events; or else that it speed up and throw the world into chaos . . . [one] can as easily imagine that women cease to give birth and have periods or that they bleed endlessly and give birth on any plot of grass. (qtd. in Clément and Cixous 29)

In an entirely different light, Paula Gunn Allen also discusses the menstrual "power" of women in *The Sacred Hoop*.

13. See also Diana Fuss's *Essentially Speaking*, in which she writes that "it is not merely that to be a 'Negro' . . . is to possess a particular genetic or biological make-up; it is, rather, to *be* the biological" (75).

14. She cites the current battle over abortion rights as proof of "this unacknowledged agenda" (79–80). See 78, 81–83, for more of her qualified Marxist analysis. See also Hyman 42–45 for an interesting Marxist reading of the Corregidora family.

15. Along similar lines, Hyman notes the problematic nature of Lacanian analysis, which posits women as transmitters of the phallus from father to son; a woman must "obtain" a phallus through heterosexual intercourse and "then pass it through herself to her male child." After giving birth, the woman is again granted an inferior status "that is defined in terms of her lack of the phallus" (41).

16. Collins has a provocative section regarding abusive relationships between black women and men, culminating in an analysis of Zora Neale Hurston's *Their Eyes Were Watching God* as illustrating "the process by which power as domination . . .

has managed to annex the basic power of the erotic" in black heterosexual relationships (179–89).

17. A "shotgun" house, like a railroad flat, is notable for its lack of privacy; each room follows the other with no intervening hallway, so that a bullet fired through the front door would exit straight out the back door.

18. After a long silence, Jones published not another novel but a book of literary criticism, *Liberating Voices: Oral Tradition in African American Literature* (1991); in it, she continues her discussion of blues, as well as other forms of orality. See especially her chapter on Alice Walker's *The Third Life of Grange Copeland*, in which she traces "the dramatic and tonal patterns for the novel and its emotional and thematic content and progression from blues to spiritual, opening to hope and possibility" (151).

19. As I soon mention, however, she admits this only while Mutt shakes her by the shoulders.

20. In a limited sense, Ursa assumes the role of "hysteric" as defined by Catherine Clément: a woman "whose body is transformed into a theater for [her own] forgotten scenes, [who] relives the past, bearing witness to a lost childhood that survives in suffering" (5). Ursa differs from this woman in that she must relive her *mothers'* scenes because they can never be forgotten.

21. Perhaps the best description of this "blues moment" in *Corregidora* comes from Jones herself: "a blues in which the spiritual is also contained" (*Liberating* 160).

22. Published one year after *Corregidora*, *Eva's Man* takes this moment to its brutal conclusion: Eva Medina murders, then orally castrates her lover.

23. Janice Harris notes that singing the blues "permits a remarkably open expression of being oppressed . . . [through] its linguistic license and freedom to improvise" (4–5). Still, Harris's limited association of the blues with oppression ignores their celebration of the self, a celebration noted in "The Blues Roots of African American Poetry" (Harper and Stepto).

Chapter 5

Beneath a Layer of White: Violence and Nature in Marilynne Robinson's *Housekeeping*

Ruthie Stone, the narrator of Robinson's *Housekeeping*, describes the furniture ornamented by her grandfather, Edmund Foster: "Each of these designs had been thought better of and painted out, but over the years the white paint had absorbed them, floated them up just beneath the surface."[1] Like those designs, violent physical and psychological undercurrents run just beneath the surface of *Housekeeping* itself, in which the catalytic events are a fatal train wreck and a mother's suicide; a series of abandonments by fathers, husbands, mothers, daughters, and sisters; and finally, the destruction of several houses by fire, water, snow, and ice. These last calamities herald the fierce presence of nature, which Joan Kirkby calls "a living force, organic, animistic, driven by powerful energies which the human world finds menacing" (99). Yet in her perception of nature, Robinson deliberately submerges this natural violence "just beneath" the white paint of Ruth's imperturbable narrative.

Traditionally, most Americans have been taught that nature is a malevolent wilderness that only our human ingenuity can beat back, a belief that reinforces the "nature-culture dichotomy characteristic of much American thought" (Kirkby 91).[2] As early as 1782, Crèvecoeur's *Letters from an American Farmer* describes what happens to settlers living beyond the civilizing influence of "fair cities [and] substantial villages": they become "ferocious" and are "no better than carnivorous animals of a superior rank, living on the flesh of wild animals" (Letter III).[3] *Housekeeping* undermines this dichotomy by slipping, water-like, through the oppositional framework that pits humans against nature. Robinson erases the usual battle lines drawn between human society and natural forces; each permeates the boundaries of the other like the ubiquitous waters of Fingerbone Lake. Ruth is a witness to nature's power of mutability, to the relentless transformation of all living things by the forces of entropy. She accepts rather than fights those forces, and her acceptance is communicated by a narrative leveled flat of all violence.

Like *Beloved*, which explores the boundaries between home and wilderness, and *Corregidora*, which questions the dominant ideology's creation of self and other, *Housekeeping* recognizes the role of violence in challenging received ways of knowing the world. However, while the violence Morrison and Jones depict is graphic and shocking, one can read the submerged (and less explicit) violence of *Housekeeping* in two ways. First, if one bears in mind traditional Western notions of nature, this text illustrates that natural violence is a disturbing yet necessary undercurrent of human existence to be accepted, not an opponent against which to prove oneself. Second, through its images of whiteness, *Housekeeping* can be read as illuminating how racial privilege conceals the ways in which violence underpins wealth and power.

The latter part of my argument is overdetermined, since *Housekeeping* never explicitly mentions race. Yet that very ability to ignore race signifies a kind of privilege, particularly when examined alongside novels like *Beloved*, *The Shawl*, and *Almanac of the Dead*, which seemingly have no such option.[4] Susan S. Lanser writes that white feminist scholars must

stop reading a privileged, white, New England woman's text as simply—a woman's text. If our traditional gesture has been to repeat the narrator's own act of *under*reading, of seeing too little, I want now to risk *over*reading, seeing perhaps too much. (424)

Like Lanser, I want to risk an overreading and ask if Robinson challenges America's materialist notions of survival from a place of white racial and economic privilege.[5] Ruth's rite of passage is not a struggle to position herself, to speak, to be seen. Rather, she works to slough off, to become invisible. She and her Aunt Sylvie abandon houses, worldly possessions, and even their own subjectivity to become transients;[6] but people can surrender only what they already have. Ruth and Lucille inherit a house and orchard, plus a small financial legacy, from their grandmother; they are property owners even as they are orphans. If Ruth embodies Thoreau's observation that "we are often imprisoned rather than housed in" our homes, we must remember that she is imprisoned beneath a roof she *owns*, not that of an employer (76).[7] She defects from the "material world" at a place where the privileges of race and economics (though not of gender) intersect, privileges that bring us back to Edmund Foster's painted designs. I read the white paint covering *Housekeeping*'s violent undertones as Ruth's own—albeit limited—racial privilege, which shields her from certain kinds of violence even as it imprisons her.

At the same time, I believe that *Housekeeping* finally, and deliberately, works *against* that privilege. Casting off her comfort and protection amid a constant refrain of loss, Ruth conjures an existence in which privilege is hollow. In reminding her readers that in the end "even our bones will fall," Robinson directs us to a place where the social constructs of privilege, respectability, and wealth mean nothing.[8]

THE MUTING OF VIOLENCE

In their discussion of materialist feminism, Judith Newton and Deborah Rosenfelt write that what "a literary text does not say" is "as interesting as what it does say," arguing that an author's work is necessarily but unintentionally limited by her historical time and ideology (xxiii).[9] Yet there is a way in which *Housekeeping* deliberately "does not say" violence because it is consciously revising a typically violent worldview. Martha Ravits, for example, sees *Housekeeping* as a feminized American heroic quest, noting that the book reworks a white male ritual "often typified by some form of competition, hunting, or violence in American fiction" (659). One particular masculine quest posits the landscape as either brutal and subject to human mastery, or feminine, seductive, and open to sexual aggression.[10] In part, Robinson "feminizes" this tradition by submerging its violence within the emotionally murky voice of her narrator.[11]

Ruth Stone narrates several disastrous, often fatal events in language marked only by sorrow and mild surprise. Even her second sentence, a litany of death and abandonment, is strangely calm: "I grew up with my younger sister, Lucille, under the care of my grandmother, Mrs. Sylvia Foster, and when she died, of her sisters-in-law, Misses Lily and Nona Foster, and when they fled, of her daughter, Mrs. Sylvia Fisher" (3). As Siân Mile points out, "There is no passion in the book because nothing is any more or less important than anything else. . . . [Ruth's voice] assures us that there will be no pits or falls, only flat, passionless lives" (Mile 133).[12] A suicide's daughter, Ruth broods on broken families, the fragility of the body, and the slender lines we draw between domestic safety and howling wilderness, yet her very voice seems to elide the ferocity inherent in nature. She accepts, rather than fights against, the catastrophic events that shape her destiny as a transient.[13]

Ruth's is an underwater voice. A quiet, lyrical quality permeates the violence of her story, blurring the boundaries between life and death, nurturing and abandonment. Rather than pitting opposites against each other, Robinson sinks them into the fluid medium that overruns all perimeters. Thus the Fosters' two most violent deaths occur within the waters of Fingerbone Lake: Edmund Foster's train wreck and his daughter's suicide. The depiction of the Fireball's plunge is remarkably peaceful; Ruth likens the train's movement off the bridge and into the lake to a weasel's "sliding off a rock" (5–6). Instead of plummeting or even splashing, the train seems to glide effortlessly into the water in the middle of a moonless night. Train wrecks are generally noisy occurrences, yet Robinson chooses to leave out the screams, the crash of steel cars piling against one another as they pitch into the lake. Moreover, the event is described by a series of opaque speculations, not positive facts. No one sees anything; no one hears anything; no one even finds anything, except for a seat cushion, a suitcase, and a head of lettuce.

Rippling outward from the immersed violence of her father's death, Helen Stone's suicide acknowledges an inner wilderness that is hidden yet powerfully destructive. Although she appears peculiarly serene prior to her death, her calm is finally exposed as "slight as the skin on water" (197), and her self-destructive core later emerges in her daughter, who pleads, "Let them come unhouse me of this flesh" (159). In submerging this menacing undercurrent of violent self-destruction beneath the surface of Ruth's narrative, Robinson reveals the tenuous balance between seeming tranquility and secret violence.

Helen reenacts Edmund's accident in her own collision between man-made vehicle and water: borrowing a neighbor's car she "sailed in Bernice's Ford from the top of a cliff . . . into the blackest depth of the lake" (22).[14] The verb Ruth applies to Helen's death, *sailed*, is a holiday word of cheery abandon. Indeed, Helen's abandonment of her children and her life seems almost light-hearted here. For Ruth, Helen is a peaceful, abstracted figure remarkable for her calmness and the "elegant competence of her slightest gesture." Only much later does Ruth note the "hush and solemnity of [Helen's] incipient transfiguration. . . . I remember her, grave with the peace of the destined, the summoned, and she seems almost an apparition" (196–97). Finally, however, Ruth understands that her mother's "calm sustained her as a coin can float on still water" (197). These significant images of perilous delicacy lead to Ruth's meditation on the explosive nature of loss itself: "she left us and broke the family and the sorrow was released and we saw its wings and saw it fly a thousand ways into the hills" (198). Helen does not sail across a meadow; she erupts. She is a woman about to break apart. Her suicidal desperation lurks beneath her serenity, and her poise skates with misleading ease upon her fragile skin. Her daughter inherits this poise in the form of a self-destructive acquiescence. Waiting for real or imagined wild children at an abandoned mountain cabin, Ruth silently asks for death: "Let them come unhouse me of this flesh, and pry this house apart" (159).

In undermining the usual Western relationship between humans and nature, Robinson explores the inevitable presence of death in life and decay in beauty. As Anne-Marie Mallon writes, *Housekeeping* posits "transience, not fixity, [as] our natural human condition, and it offers us the opportunity to see that truth . . . as a constant source of power and possibility" (97–98).

Housekeeping refuses to organize natural forces into binary oppositions such as benevolent and malevolent; rather, the risings and fallings of nature are leveled to an equal value, as we see prefigured in Edmund Foster's paintings of mountains, which lack a traditional sense of perspective. Several critics simply dismiss Edmund as the industrialized patriarch who must be killed off before the feminized heroic quest can begin.[15] In part, this is true. Yet in a novel of blurred distinctions, he is also a visionary along the lines of Ruthie, Sylvie, and Robinson herself. His art defies gravity in its depiction of trees, each standing "at right angles to the ground, where it grew exactly as the nap stands out on folded plush . . . every fruit and bird was plumb with the warp in the earth" (4). Leveling vegetation and animals to the same size and importance, Edmund's art embodies his search for something different, if not better, in his quest to break out of a sod house built like a grave.

Robinson's visionary leveling also appears during Edmund and Sylvia's mountain hikes, where they encounter several combined images of life and decay. The wind smells both "sweetly . . . and rankly of melting snow"; rare wildflowers grow from insect burrows, bear excrement, and the decaying of "perished animals"; the air is "sour with stale snow and death and pine pitch and wildflowers"; soon, "all dormant life and arrested decay would begin again" (16). The conjunction *and* connects everything and subordinates nothing. Rotted flesh and spring greenery grow out of, rather than work against, each other. These early images determine not only the tone but the epistemological world of the novel. Ruth acknowledges forces that kill, drown, freeze, and putrefy, but she does not respond to them as threats, flying "into a frenzy of activity to insure that her human presence is feared and respected" (Aldrich 136).

Such acknowledgment on Robinson's part makes possible the leveling vision of Edmund Foster's paintings, the smell of greenery and decay all on the same wind, and the doubled role that Fingerbone Lake plays in *Housekeeping*. For Ruth the lake is not just a communal grave but also the only place from which resurrection is possible. In its waters, as Martha Ravits notes, Ruth sees "possibilities of restoration. . . . Water that can swallow up the living can also cast up the dead" (Ravits 651–52). Ruth envisions Lake Fingerbone providing a resurrection "general enough" to contain her mother and grandmother (96). For her, the essence of mortality is simply part of nature—something inevitable but also regenerative. The title *Housekeeping* is especially fitting in its association with thriftiness. In nature, nothing (and no one) is ever wasted; nothing ever disappears. To understand nature's intrinsic violence and inclusion of death, one must also understand its renascent possibilities.

With its endless associations of renewal, water permeates this text as thoroughly as it saturates the flooded houses of Fingerbone, Idaho. Even Sylvia Foster's dramatic aging (her hair and flesh seem to recede from her skull, leaving her, says Ruth, vaguely monkey-like) and nondramatic death become watery in Ruth's account. Ruth and Lucille find her corpse, but Ruth does not say, "It was horrible." She does not even say, "We were frightened." Instead, she envisions Sylvia's death as reunion:

It was as if, drowning in air, she had leaped toward ether. What glee there must have been . . . when my grandmother burst through the spume . . . And how [the dead] must have rushed to wrap their coats around her, and perhaps embrace her . . . [while she searched] the growing crowds for familiar faces. (164–65)

Like water, the narrative submerges any repulsive details of Ruth's story, turning the gruesome images of decay into whimsical poetry. She imagines her grandfather as a long-time train passenger in his berth, able to look out his window and see, up through the waters of the lake, "the daylit moon, a jawless, socketed shard, and take it for his image in the glass" (150). Trying to excavate the ruins of the mountain homestead, Ruth fantasizes about finding dead children and seems to anticipate discovering "the rain-stiffened hems of their nightshirts, and their small bone feet, the toes all fallen like petals" (158). Even these images of empty eye sockets and broken bones do not deter Ruth; decomposition turns into composition, becoming the mutable, redemptive stuff of art. Ruth gently creates her stories of "natural regenerative decay," turning skeletons into flower petals and fleshless skulls into moons shining at midday (Kirkby 106). All of these images are transient; like Sylvia Foster, they simply exchange one mode of being for another. They turn monkey, or flower, or moon. Whatever their shape, they continue: they are, as Ruth murmurs, "not perished" (160).

Pervading *Housekeeping* down to its religious framework, this sense of continuance reimagines the Puritanical deity of white America's literary beginnings. In Robinson's text, Eve and the wives of Lot and Noah are cast as victims—not sinners—in the hands of an angry God. But then Robinson transforms that God from an angry being to an indifferent, simultaneously dangerous and preservative natural force, so that the Great Flood (a famous example of divine wrath) not only destroys people but ensures that they become forever part of the natural world:

Let God purge this wicked sadness away with a flood, and let the waters recede to pools and ponds and ditches, and let every one of them mirror heaven. Still, they taste a bit of blood and hair. One cannot cup one's hand and drink from the rim of any lake without remembering that mothers have drowned in it, lifting their children toward the air. . . . Nothing is left of [them] after so many years but a certain pungency and savor in the water, and in the breath of creeks and lakes, which, *however sad and wild, are clearly human.* (193; emphasis added)

Ruth moves from the biblical to the personal, still along the watery lines of death and memory, when she adds that she cannot take a drink of water without remembering that "the eye of the lake is my grandfather's, and that the lake's heavy, blind, encumbering waters . . . stopped [Helen's] breath and stopped her sight" (193).

Here, violence and death compose life. To drink is to sustain life, but there is nothing one can drink that does not taste of mortality. The trope of the Flood makes clear that people and nature are fused. The earth's water will always taste of that early race drowned by human sin and sacred rage. In Judeo-Christian mythology, as in *Housekeeping*, water has the doubled figure of life and death, of nourishment and murderous anger. Its liquid blurs the boundaries between sinner and sinned against, the living and the dead, natural forces and the strongholds of civilization. The flooded lake that accompanies Sylvie's arrival in Fingerbone reminds the reader of human ephemerality. Sofas, tin cans, and books are awash in water that is "full of people" (168). It might just as well be full of tears. The borders between love and loss are bound with sorrow, not anger, as told by Ruth's grieving voice. Still, it is that voice that also calmly catalogues the violent potential of time and weather.

Perhaps more so than any other work in my discussion, *Housekeeping* tells violence but tells it slant. In moving beyond the traditional white American dichotomy of humanity versus nature, Robinson circumvents a direct confrontation with the violence of nature itself. She also circumvents conclusiveness. *Beloved* and *Corregidora* do not end with finality, nor does *Housekeeping*. In each instance, open-endedness is a deliberate move within a strategy of questioning certain culturally defined identities in America. Each book refuses to prescribe or proscribe.[16] *Housekeeping* may, however, be the murkiest of all three texts. For Joan Kirkby, the book illustrates that no one can tell what "forms [life] will take" once we shed our "culturally defined notions of the human" and "open ourselves to those very forces we have been trying so hard to deny or control" (Kirkby 107).[17] Opening up to nature requires a redefinition of violence. Mainstream American culture needs to repudiate its vehemently oppositional stance to "wilderness" and to acknowledge the violence inherent in all of us. This acknowledgment marks the final dialogue of Jones's *Corregidora* and turns Morrison's Sethe into a powerful (however flawed) figure instead of merely a victim. The theme of violence redefined emerges through Ruth's extraordinarily self-abnegating narrative, a narrative that returns over and over to the transience of the physical by reminding us that "it is better to have nothing" since, finally, we too will be nothing (159). Robinson refuses to curtail possibility in our relationships with the natural world, even at the risk of saying "nothing" definitive about them.

THE WHITENESS OF THE TEXT

If we can imagine Ruth's first sentence as a revision of *Moby-Dick*'s opening line, we might also imagine a subheading that paraphrases one of Melville's chapters: "The Whiteness of the Text."[18] While in *Moby-Dick*, the whiteness (of the whale) ostensibly denotes nature's terrifying indifference, in *Housekeeping* it signifies concealment.[19] There is the white paint of Edmund Foster's furniture, the white frost blanketing the abandoned mountain homestead, the white salt covering Ruth's imagined landscape of Carthage, and the white snow in the apocryphal tale of the mountain family's wintertime survival. In each instance, whiteness is simultaneously transformative and terrifying, nurturing and sterile. In the example of Edmund's furniture, however, I read whiteness as embodying two concepts. First, it represents an ordered civilization that tries to obliterate the rebellious art of a visionary. Second, while the association may not be premeditated on Robinson's part, this paint can signify racial (albeit qualified) privilege.

Look again at Edmund Foster's designs:

All three pieces were painted creamy white, and would have been completely unremarkable, except that my grandfather had once ornamented them. On the doors of the wardrobe there appeared to have been a hunting scene, turbaned horsemen on a mountainside. On the head of the bed he had painted a peacock, hennish body, emerald tail. On the dresser he had put a wreath or garland, held in the hands of two cherubs who swam in ether, garments trailing. (89–90)

Only the drawings make this furniture remarkable. In fact, they make it art, evoking an earlier, non-Western human history (the turbaned hunters are obviously not European), nature's own art, and spirituality. The exotic images reflect Edmund's artistic vision. Even the handmade furniture they ornament is, like the house Edmund has built, off-center; some legs are longer than others to accommodate the sloping floors. Edmund himself, halfway between "civilization" and *Housekeeping*'s slanted perspective, works on the railroad that disrupts Hawthorne's pastoral garden,[20] and he is often formal in "suspenders and his Methodism." Yet at other times, he forgets all this and is more like Sylvia's imagined "dark man" with a sunken belly, a "soul all unaccompanied" (17).[21] In this respect, Edmund begins the journey that his daughter and granddaughter will eventually undertake, his visionary importance underlined by the failure of the white paint to obliterate his art.

Before I turn to the relationship Ruth, Lucille, and Sylvia share with the text's images of whiteness, however, I want to suggest that Edmund's role as visionary artist offers still a third possible reading, this time in the current historical context of *Housekeeping*'s audience. Recent years have seen a rise in literature and scholarship about cultural notions of what it means to be white. The scholarship is not limited to literary discussion (such as Edward Said's *Culture and Imperialism*), but extends to sociology (as in Ruth Frankenberg's collected interviews of white women in *White Women, Race Matters: The Social Construction of Whiteness*) and history (David Roediger's *The Wages of Whiteness: Race and the Making of the American Working Class*). A certainly accurate common denominator in many of these studies is the experience of whiteness as racism, knowing or ignorant, and privilege, recognized or unacknowledged. For instance, Roediger's analysis of nineteenth-century Irish-American workers pivots on those workers' insistence on their own (white) supremacy over the black workers with whom they shared an abundance of manual, unskilled jobs, as well as contempt from nonimmigrant whites. Often called "white slaves" or "white niggers," the majority of Irish-American workers of this time period, according to Roediger, felt challenged to "get out from under the burden of doing unskilled work in a society that identified such work and (some craft jobs) as 'nigger work'" (150).

Roediger's highly complex chapter on Irish-American workers resonates with many other studies of whiteness. Certainly any accurate discussion of American whiteness must consider the influences of racism; as Julius Boeke put it, "Europeans did not sail to the Indies to collect butterflies"—they went to colonize nonwhites (qtd. in Cox 6). *Housekeeping*'s Edmund, however, climbs mountains to gather wildflowers, insect nests, and eggshells, if not butterflies precisely. Despite his work on the railroad (in a sense, an established, powerful means for subduing nature), he is neither colonizer nor enslaver. Rather, as artist, he imagines a world that operates outside the realm of either/or.

When one thinks within the framework of traditional binary oppositions (oppression versus victimization, colonizer versus colonized), conceptions of black and white are forced into the same rigid definitions. On a social and historical level, undoubtedly they must be. On an artistic level, however—say, the level of fictional narrative—it is possible to try to move outside such a framework. In keeping with the novel's leveling perspective, Edmund's topsy-turvy worldview suggests one way to do so. His role as visionary artist—what I have earlier called his search for something different—offers at least the glimmer of a new outlook on what whiteness might mean. Rather than seeing only oppression or even privilege (although the latter cannot be ignored in the case of Ruth, Lucille, and Sylvie, as I soon discuss), we might through Edmund's eyes begin to see a vision of whiteness that defies our current perspective as startlingly as his painted trees defy gravity—a vision that refuses to be pulled into the old story of persecution.

And what of the white paint itself? Ruth imagines herself, Lucille, and Sylvie as the cherubim on the dresser drawers, pulled by Edmund's vision to a "bitter, moon-pulled lake" and hovering on "the rim of the vortex that would drag them down out of that enameled sky, stripped and screaming" (149).[22] In language more violent and frightening than she generally uses, Ruth fantasizes about being dragged out of a white-painted sky—perhaps a sky of money, land, houses, and a particular sense of belonging. The whiteness that covers Ruth and Sylvie is a privilege as well as a suffocating blanket, providing them with home, orchard, books and furniture, and Edmund Foster's pension.

Simultaneously, the lyrical evasiveness of Robinson's narrative may be read as another kind of privilege that Ruth retains—one of invisibility.[23] Confessing that she does not know what she thinks, Ruth sees her confusion as "a source of both terror and comfort"; and in return for her threatened loss of subjectivity, her making "no impact on the world," she is "privileged to watch it unawares" (105–6). In *Beloved*, Sethe correlates invisibility with safety: "feel how it feels to be a coloredwoman roaming the roads with anything God made liable to jump on you" (68). While Ruth and Sylvie are subject to legal trauma, ostracism, and, finally, separation, they appear to be protected from the brutal physical attacks that *Beloved*, *The Shawl*, and *Corregidora* depict so frequently. Their whiteness lets them fade into a white culture rather than stand out against it; a humanized version the white paint coating of Edmund Foster's furniture hides them even as it hides the real human violence of their world.

When Ruth speaks of Fingerbone's high percentage of freight-train hoppers and indigents, people whose faces reflect their hard histories (178–79), when Sylvie tells stories about people who are *not* privileged, who are homeless, cold, lonely, crazy, and hungry—here are figures who evoke for the reader the terrors of vacating privilege. Robinson's text addresses the social inequity of homelessness even while remaining generally silent about the privileges her main characters enjoy. This leads Marilee Lindemann to argue that although Robinson might appear to be indulging in "whimsical flights of fancy" within a "lily-white" world, she explores that world "with a set of concerns and strategies that clearly connect her to those whose artistic territories are fraught with more overtly violent racial or sexual tensions" (117). Reinforcing such a view, we might ask: Just how extensive *is* Ruth and Sylvie's privilege after all? Legally, they are both voiceless, nonconformist women, one underage and the other a freight-hopping transient, who waver precariously between privilege and disenfranchisement. Yet their position all the while is informed by choice; in choosing to abandon the house Ruth owns, they can prevent their separation by the probate court. It is indeed a "terrible thing to break up a family" (190), a terrible thing to forsake one's home; still more terrible is to have no say in the matter of one's broken family or one's homelessness. Hence, while their possibilities are circumscribed by their own social eccentricities and by "the representative of the State, the sheriff, the probate judge" (Kirkby 97), Ruth and Sylvie's option of transience is itself a kind of luxury.

Still, that luxury is qualified and pared down through *Housekeeping*'s moments of whiteness—snow, frost, salt—which, if they seem barren initially, finally come to signify redemption through loss. In a text that crosses and re-crosses the constructed divisions between insiders and outsiders, Robinson also creates an undercurrent of leveling that brings us to a place of mortality and regeneration: a place where privilege means nothing, where status, wealth, and race disappear beneath what one might call the Great Leveler—nature itself. Immersed in that medium, salt, frost, and snow first threaten with annihilation, but then they nurture:

It was as if the light had coaxed a flowering from the frost, which before seemed barren and parched as salt. . . . Light would force each salt calyx to open in prisms, and to fruit heavily with bright globes of water—peaches and grapes are little more than that, and where the world was salt there would be greater need of slaking. (152)

Snow both imprisons and nourishes, providing a trapped family with drinking water and "stew" conjured out of of old shoe leather.   These images, simultaneously bleak and sustaining, acknowledge the text's paradoxical thematic union of destruction and sustenance.

When Ruth sojourns at the abandoned homestead in the mountains, she weaves an intricate story about its long-gone family. Most remarkable for its circuitous journey from whiteness to loss and, finally, to redemption, Ruth's soliloquy closes with an elegiac longing for death and her mother: "It is better to have nothing, for at last even our bones will fall. . . . [Helen] was a music I no longer heard, that rang in my mind, itself and nothing else, lost to all sense, but not perished, not perished" (159–60). The associations of whiteness with privilege lead us to the novel's true source of grief: Ruth's dead mother, whose desertion and subsequent omnipresence point to a common human fate of bereavement.

Spiraling out of nature, mortality—loss—transcends respectability, transience, and privilege.   Domestic comforts exclude neither grief nor loss; Ruth says the most bitter sorrow "is that every soul is put out of house" (179). When neighbors visit Sylvie and Ruth with casseroles and concern and note Ruth's sorrowful face, Sylvie's matter-of-fact response is, "She should be sad . . . who wouldn't be?" The realization of the abiding importance of families connects these seeming opposites: Sylvie in a stained raincoat with fish in her pockets and the solid, respectable Fingerbone matrons with their freshly baked pies. They tell her, "Families are a sorrow, and that's the truth"; "I lost my girl sixteen years ago in June and her face is before me now" (185–86). Too, Fingerbone itself is marked by loss.   Surrounded by natural and "man-made" violence, Fingerbone is an impermanent establishment: "There was not a soul there but knew how shallow-rooted the whole town was. It flooded yearly, and had burned once" (177). The reminder that lives on in Fingerbone, with its "tolerance of transience," is the realization that the shadowy hobos and freight-train hoppers who move through Fingerbone are "not very different from us" (179, 178). Perhaps Sylvie keeps her house dark at night to avoid flaunting her status as a house dweller by "counterpoising a roomful of light against a worldful of darkness" (99). Ruth is haunted by the faces and voices of phantom homeless children, by the images of those who must stand outside in the cold, watching others eat inside a clean, well-lighted place. Finding points of connection rather than of "difference" and hence, in this case, exclusion, *Housekeeping* repeats its song of "nothingness" and forsaken subjectivity.

If Sylvie is something of a Marxist in her refusal to recognize property boundaries ("borrowing," for example, someone else's rowboat),[24] Ruth is a variation on someone who lives with one foot in the grave. Her awareness of change keeps before her the specter of death and loss; the trappings of privilege mean nothing to her because "in the end even our bones will fall." She opts for what Ravits calls "the unsettling, austere condition of transiency" (666).   Robinson does not focus on the joys of having but instead illustrates how ownership can lead to constraint. This text was published in 1980—coincidentally, the year Americans elected Ronald Reagan over Jimmy Carter, who went on to become deeply involved with Habitat for Humanity, a group that builds houses for poor people, while Reagan's inauguration ushered in over a decade of escalating prosperity and poverty. Although set in the 1940s or 1950s, *Housekeeping*'s issues are those of contemporary America: the failure of the ethics of accumulation and the terrible division between those who have so much while others go without. One of the text's few distinct expressions of violence stems from this division, when Ruth observes, "Perhaps all unsheltered people are angry in their hearts, and would like to break the roof, spine, and ribs, and smash the windows and flood the floor and spindle the curtains and bloat the couch" (158).

There is also the violence with which Sylvie and Ruth redefine the notion of family and join those unsheltered people. Setting fire to the house built by Edmund, they try to release the "spirit of the house"—a highly private entity whose relics of sentimental value will not tolerate the "pawing and sorting" of curious strangers:

Imagine the spirit of the house breaking out the windows and knocking down the doors, and all the neighbors astonished at the sovereign ease with which it burst its tomb, broke up its grave. Bang! and the clay that had held the shape of the Chinese jar was shattered, and the jar was a whirl in the air, ascending . . . bang! and the bureau mirror fell in shivers the shape of flame and had nothing to show but fire. Every last thing would turn to flame and ascend, so cleanly would the soul of the house escape. (209, 211–12)

Here, violence would maintain human dignity, would shelter a family's privacy—its coils of hair, its purses, its clothing—from "the disinterested scrutiny" of Fingerbone. Although the fire does not take and the house is saved, Ruthie and Sylvie never return to it; their subsequent lives are thus continually affirming and re-affirming the choice they have made. Robinson's paradox is this: that only through the destruction or abandonment of its artifacts can a family's spirit survive. Casting off property, Ruth and Sylvie trade a now-useless icon of domesticity for an existence that is, whatever its degrees of eccentricity, nonetheless a family life.

Yet in a novel that so clearly removes itself from the realm of either/or, nothing can be that simple. *Housekeeping* ends not with a loving, though subdued, description of Ruth's life with Sylvie. Rather, the closing lines evoke the solitary—in one sense, the abandoned—Lucille, whose own abandonment of the Foster home preceded the house fire and Ruth and Sylvie's flight from Fingerbone. Because this is a book about the devastating combination of memory and loss, because it tells of a sorrowful remembrance so great that it re-creates, hugely and obsessively, the things and people it cannot forget, what Sylvie and Ruth do to Lucille is terrible. After Sylvie and Ruth vanish from Fingerbone one night, they never refute anyone's assumption (presumably, including Lucille's) that they have drowned in the lake. Once again, however, the power of Ruth's lyricism overcomes the violence of "breaking the family" and even of death; by the novel's end, Lucille, Sylvie, and Ruth herself are part of Ruth's dreamy, gentle visions of all their lost kin. In keeping with *Housekeeping*'s smoothed narrative, simultaneous absence and presence suffuse its depiction of human connectedness.

NOTES

1. Marilynne Robinson, *Housekeeping* (New York: Bantam Books, 1980) 90. Subsequent quotations from this work are cited in the text.

2. As Annette Kolodny notes, even America's pastoral impulse leads inevitably to "the single-minded cultivation and mastery of the virgin continent" (*Lay of the Land* 153).

3. Leo Marx observes that Crèvecoeur admires not "'Nature-sweet-and-pure,'" but rather, "improved nature, a landscape that is a made thing, a fusion of work and spontaneous process" (112).

4. I am indebted here to Susan S. Lanser's discussion of Charlotte Perkins Gilman's choice of yellow for her famous wallpaper. Lanser notes the contradictions between Gilman's socialism and her racist fears about immigration's contamination of the American "national character" (Gilman 118). In her examination of turn-of-the-century Anglo America, Lanser finds a "culture obsessively preoccupied with race as the foundation of character, a culture desperate to maintain Aryan superiority in the face of massive immigrations from Southern and Eastern Europe" (425). Lanser takes issue with Gilbert and Gubar's assertion that "The Yellow Wallpaper" is "*the* story that all literary women would tell if they could speak their 'speechless woe'" (Gilbert and Gubar 89).

5. I do not mean to say that Robinson's reevaluation of property ownership is flawed but rather that the social and economic conditions of *Housekeeping* deserve as much attention as do those of every other novel under discussion in my study.

6. Siân Mile writes that Robinson advocates a self "constructed in relation to other selves, and she ultimately favors a process we can best describe as 'merging,' where there are no divisions between subject and other and maybe no gendered subjects at all" (129).

7. Contrast Ruth's position with the brutalities experienced by *Beloved*'s Sethe and Amy Denver in other people's kitchens (see chapter 3).

8. Similarly, in Champagne's estimation the flooding of Fingerbone (chapter 4) and the Fosters' house fire (chapter 10) "destroy all barriers and frames and portray a world without horizons" (323).

9. As Hayden White has observed, narrative is based not only on occurrences but also on events that are "left out" (10).

10. For an excellent discussion of the former notion, see Kirkby 91–95; regarding the latter, see Kolodny (*Lay of the Land*) and Champagne, who writes that "nature, always 'she,' becomes that which must be conquered and raped in order to claim one's 'rightful place' within culture" (321). Also useful is Carolyn Merchant's *The Death of Nature*, especially "Nature as Disorder: Women and Witches" and "Dominion over Nature."

11. I must emphasize, however, the difference between submerging violence and eliminating it completely. To imply that a "feminine" tradition has no place for

violence is both shortsighted and historically inaccurate. See, for example, Merchant, and Harris, *Folklore*, especially 152–57.

12. However, I see the "passion" in this book as submerged, not non-existent.

13. See Champagne (especially 326) for a differently situated argument about Ruth's (postmodern) rejection of emotional articulation.

14. Gunilla Florby connects this notion of lethal technology with Marx's *Machine in the Garden,* noting that train and "car are agents of death, they are machines shattering the peace" (212).

15. See Meese (*Crossing the Double-Cross* 58–59); Aldrich 127–31, and Kirkby, who writes that Foster "bequeathed the rituals and ceremonies of sustenance that comprise the art of housekeeping . . . [until] man and machine are dispatched from the garden" (98).

16. Ravits writes that the novel "offers no directives" (665); Kirkby, that it is "finally ambiguous" (107).

17. Siân Mile, however, complains that Ruth is so vague "that she may end up like Lily Tomlin's character Chrissy, who says, 'I've always wanted to be somebody. But I see now I should have been more specific'" (129).

18. As a number of critics have noted, "My name is Ruth" feminizes *Moby-Dick*'s "Call me Ishmael." See Ravits 644, 652; Kirkby 91ff; Mallon 96–97; Aldrich 127; Heller 96; and Lassner 51–52.

19. Toni Morrison reads Melville's chapter as examining "whiteness" idealized" in nineteenth-century America ("Unspeakable Things" 16–18).

20. See Marx 11–15.

21. Problematically, however, Edmund's "dark man" image evokes "the primitive," an association similar to the white culture's embrace of African and African American art in the Modernist period. See, for example, Baker and Ammons (*Conflicting Stories*).

22. Interestingly enough, however, while Edmund took a train one day from his underground sod house and ended up in Fingerbone, Ruth's grandmother was born there and never left. Ruth's statement that Edmund brought the family to Fingerbone Lake (149), therefore, is open to dispute.

23. In turning a cloak of invisibility to her advantage, Ruth invokes Emily Dickinson, whose other influences upon *Housekeeping* are discussed by Kirkby (94–95, 106), Aldrich (132), and Ravits (645–46, 650–51). For further discussion of privilege and invisibility, see Martin and Mohantry 208.

24. See Mile 132; Aldrich 129.

Chapter 6

How to Say It: Art and the Holocaust in Cynthia Ozick's *The Shawl*

Beloved (1987) begins as it does—bewilderingly, abruptly—because Toni Morrison wanted her readers to experience "the compelling confusion of being there as they [the characters] are; suddenly, without comfort or succor from the 'author,' with only imagination, intelligence, and necessity available for the journey" ("Unspeakable Things" 33). One could say the same about Cynthia Ozick's *The Shawl* (1989), which directly positions the reader alongside Rosa Lublin during her march to a Nazi death camp. As with *Beloved*, the reader is thrown into a painful journey, ending in the concentration camp where Rosa's baby, Magda, will be killed by a Nazi soldier.

Although Ozick unbalances her reader through the devices of fragmentedness, inversion, paradox, and surprise, *The Shawl* is simultaneously imbued with tradition. Her work employs what Elisabeth Rose calls liturgical postmodernism, combining the qualities of tradition and mysticism with the postmodern elements of "meaning-subversion and self-referentialism" (93). Liturgically committed in a nontraditional text, Ozick poses an Old Testament question: "How is it possible to live after a destruction?" (Ezek. 33:10) *The Shawl* responds to this question by exploring another: how is it possible to bear witness to such a destruction?

Ozick writes the unwritable by creating what she calls "liturgical literature." Like Judaism itself, her art is historically informed, yet paradoxically it is not "religious in any explicit sense." What makes it liturgical is its primary, communal concern: the *Yavneh* (the Yiddish term for a Jewish community in exile), and specifically, the American Jewish community. Eschewing what Ozick calls a private voice (created mainly to gratify the author) for a "choral" one, liturgical literature takes on "a public rather than a coterie form." This communal emphasis embraces artistic innovation but precludes experimentation for its own sake; for Ozick, all creative techniques must branch out of history and tradition. Favoring fluidity, surprise, and flexibility over "the didactic or prescriptive," "the liturgical mode will itself induce new forms, will in fact be a new form" (Ozick, *Art* 174, 175).[1]

The *Shawl*'s liturgical impulse emerges in four ways. First, its experimental narrative works against easy genre classification, thus avoiding the potentially desensitized category of "Holocaust literature." Second, it includes a pivotal gesture of enormous risk: the transfiguring, lyrical, and problematic depiction of Magda's brutal murder. Third, the figure of Magda meets Ozick's requirement of a communal purpose for her fiction; she resurfaces to become the sole, albeit imagined, audience for Rosa's written testimony about the *Shoah*.[2] Finally, Magda's metamorphosis at death reverberates throughout Ozick's textual framework, offering a scheme of ever-shifting meanings as a guide to surviving a destruction.

The *Shawl*'s form is a literary anomaly. In meeting the demands of Ozick's liturgical literature, its unclassifiable structure responds to the intellectual and religious context in which she works. One of the strongest injunctions in Judaism is to bear witness: "To be a Jew is to hear stories and claim them as one's own . . . to keep telling them to someone else" (Greenberg, qtd. in Berger 36).[3] Yet one such story, that of the Nazi Holocaust, strikes at the very bedrock of Judaism: the assurance of Jewish continuity on earth.[4] In the telling of it, post-Holocaustal Jews have the "obligation, self-imposed and self-accepted (however ineluctably), to describe a meaning and wrest instruction from the historical" (Cohen 2, qtd. in Berger 11). As secular nationalist Simon Dubnow shouted just before he was shot by Nazis: "*Yidn—Fahrschreibt! Fahrschreibt!* [Jews, record! record!]" (Fein xvii). But recording is not the same as creating. Elie Wiesel has elucidated the distinction, arguing that "Holocaust literature" is a contradiction because "Auschwitz negates all literature as it negates all theories and doctrines; to lock it into a philosophy means to restrict it" (*A Jew Today* 197).[5] Similarly, Michael Wyschogrod contends that art falsifies the *Shoah* by taking "the sting out of suffering" (Berger 30).

Ozick herself has long been concerned with the differences between recorded history and art, stating in 1969 that Jewish writers must "retrieve the Holocaust freight car by freight car, town by town, road by road, document by document. *The task is to save it from becoming literature*" (*Art* 19). Ozick warned then against what might be called "mere" literature: fiction that exists primarily for its own creativity and plays itself out against the Holocaust's horrific backdrop for dramatic effect. Such fiction, she has argued, is devoid of its "corona of moral purpose" and so is a form of idolatry, a violation of the Second Commandment ("Literature" 296).[6] Today, however, she cannot dismiss literature as unequivocally as she did almost twenty-five years ago, admitting in a recent interview that the Holocaust comes forth "unbidden, unsummoned" in her own literary work (Kremer 218).[7]

Although the precept of silence espoused by writers such as Wiesel, Trilling, and Steiner has long been discarded, the issues surrounding Holocaust literature are still fraught nearly to the stifling point. There is, as Walter Benn Michaels writes, still "a certain hostility to the idea that the Holocaust is the sort of thing that can be known" (8).[8] How can a twentieth-century Jewish writer bear witness to this history without reducing it to "a theme for [her] poems and stories" (S. Niger, qtd. in Alexander xiv)?

The Holocaust is always indescribable, incapable of representation, yet that sense of the ineffable must nevertheless be manifested. Through the eccentricity of *The Shawl*'s make-up, it is. Consistent with her censure of experimentalism for its own sake, Ozick acknowledges the need for a new way of telling her story. *The Shawl* comprises two connected yet separate narratives ("The Shawl" and "Rosa") that constitute neither a collection of short fiction nor a novella. Allotting only sixty-five pages to the Holocaust, the murder of a baby, and a mother's ensuing attempts to bear witness, this text's brevity and unique structure are informed by Ozick's particular liturgical gesture. Alan Berger writes that after the Holocaust, "there are no answers, only questions. Authentic post-Holocaust responses are, therefore, fragmentary rather than comprehensive in nature" (194–95). Ozick's response to the Holocaust combines fragmentation *and* completion into an experimental narrative shape, one that "utilizes every innovative device" while insisting on an organic "verbal experiment and permutation" (Ozick, *Art* 175).

The text's first tale, "The Shawl," begins by announcing a piecemeal journey of paradox, contradiction, and inversion. Ozick's first two lines are fragmented and urgent: "Stella, cold, cold, the coldness of hell. How they walked on the roads together, Rosa with Magda curled up between sore breasts, Magda wound up in the shawl."[9] The cold-hearted Stella becomes a star from hell, not heaven; in a world turned upside down, she reflects the chaos and contradiction of Nazi Europe. In re-creating the world of Auschwitz and Belsen in her fiction, Ozick must confront the most frightening aspect of the imagination: "the power to penetrate evil, to take on evil, to become evil" ("Literature" 296). Because entering that world is, on one level, impossible for both Ozick and the reader, her narrative doubles back upon itself in a whirl of assertions, denials, and, finally, inversion in a strenuous attempt to imagine the ghostly reality of it all. Rosa walks as though in a trance but simultaneously feels intensely alert: "someone who is already a floating angel . . . seeing everything, but in the air, not there, not touching the road. As if teetering on the tips of her fingernails" (3–4). The image ends with Rosa literally upside down. Magda too is marked by contradiction, as her innocence alternates with Nazi-like predation. First a "squirrel in a nest," she is then able to pass for "one of *their* babies": "eyes blue as air, smooth feathers of hair nearly as yellow as the Star sewn into Rosa's coat" (4). Traditional associations with life and nurturing become signposts of death. Rosa is described as a "walking cradle" but seems more like a walking grave when her milk dries up, her breast likened to a "dead volcano, blind eye, chill hole." Even Magda's first tooth is elegized as "an elfin tombstone of white marble" (4).

Like Ozick's definition of the imagination, "The Shawl" "seeks out the unsayable and the undoable, and says and does them" with a string of paradox ("Literature" 296). "Rosa was ravenous, but also not," while Magda's belly is "fat with air, full and round," and she drinks what cannot be drunk—"the shawl's good flavor, milk of linen." Rosa learns from Magda how to find sustenance where there is none—"how to drink the taste of a finger in one's mouth" (5–6). Magda, thinks Rosa, "should have been dead already, but she had been buried away deep inside the magic shawl": what sustains Magda is her own burial (6). Ozick's prose is full of reversals and contradictions, her sentences turning back upon themselves: "She was afraid to fall asleep; she slept with the weight of her thigh on Magda's body; she was afraid she would smother Magda under her thigh," yet the "weight of Rosa was becoming less and less; Rosa and Stella were slowly turning into air." Magda's shawl is a site for further contradictions: "No one could touch it; only Rosa could touch it" (6).

Ozick's argument that what "literature means is meaning" finds praxis in an image like "ash-stippled wind," which is literary *and* literal in its allusion to the burned flesh of the dead ("Literature" 296; *Shawl* 7). The wind is full of "bitter fatty floating smoke that greased Rosa's skin"—the mark of the dead that Rosa carries (albeit internally) for the rest of her life. That this description appears precisely when Magda is discovered by the guards has further historic resonance; "to save the S.S. difficulties all mothers who accompanied young children went to the gas chambers, irrespective of their age" (Reitlinger 118, qtd. in Heinemann 15). If discovered by Nazi guards, pregnant women were forced to undergo induced labor, after which their babies were killed. Pregnancy could also result in additional tortures, beatings, or even live cremation in the ovens. Giving birth in the camps was punishable by death, but a mother might survive by secretly killing or having someone else kill her baby. One survivor, Olga Lengyel, noted that although "the Germans succeeded in making murderers of even us," still "we saved the mothers" (Lengyel 100, qtd. in Heinemann 26).

A similar juxtaposition of murder and survival provides *The Shawl* with its defining paradox of history and art. The depiction of Magda's murder through a sequence of lyrical images constitutes Ozick's greatest ideological risk in writing about the Holocaust. The rhetorical move creates a place for multiple readings, one problematic, as I will shortly discuss. Ozick's artistry seemingly contradicts her opposition to transforming the *Shoah* to "literature," yet also fashions a startlingly graceful scene of liberation. For the author, redemption is born in possibility, the act of "turning away from, or turning toward, deliverance." Insisting on "the freedom to change one's life," entailing "amazement, marveling, suspense," redemption means, "above all, that we can surprise ourselves" ("Literature" 295). Through its implication of choice, the plurality of readings is itself significant in *The Shawl*'s redemptive enterprise. Still, in choosing to beautify a child's electrocution, Ozick risks glossing over the horror of the Holocaust in favor of aesthetics. Simultaneously, she grants the most powerless of victims a final moment of transcendence and, as I will argue later, centers her text on a transformative motif that responds directly to a historical crisis.

In Magda, "the idol upon whom Rosa has bestowed her life's meaning," Ozick creates a most unexpected meshing of beauty and power (Kauvar, "Dread of Moloch" 117). Described lovingly, the baby has eyes like "blue tigers"; her breath smells of sweet spices; her roundness provides respite from an angular, starved world of "elbows like chicken bones" and knees like "tumors on sticks" (4, 5). Magda's Aryan appearance is aesthetically pleasing, even as it evokes the Nazi ideal, even as it is starved on air, even as a guard hurls it at an electric fence:

All at once Magda was swimming in the air. The whole of Magda traveled through loftiness. She looked like a butterfly touching a silver vine. . . . Magda's feathered round head and her pencil legs and balloonish belly and zigzag arms splashed against the fence. (9–10)

As the story's horror culminates in this stunningly poetic image, the artistic challenge Ozick faces becomes obvious. To a far greater extent than the phrase "ash-stippled wind," the passage verges on sheer aesthetics.

Not surprisingly, Margot Martin concludes that "the soldier has freed [Magda] from her bondage to enjoy immortality, to join with the humming voices, and possibly to cross into that beautiful world beyond the fence" (35). That the text can, in part, bear this reading points to the explicit danger in beautifying a violent history. Seduced by one of the few lyrical moments in "The Shawl," a reader might conceptualize a Nazi soldier as an agent of freedom. Yet the focus here is not the soldier but the child. The Nazi appears only in a series of impersonal and finally inhuman fragments: first a disembodied shoulder, then a glinting helmet, a body like a "domino and a pair of black boots" (9). Ozick opposes the objectified, mechanical soldier (never even a *he*) with the living butterfly that Magda becomes, thus emphasizing their lack of connection.

Nonetheless, the issue of a beautiful murder gives rise to a number of questions. Has Ozick gotten carried away with her own prose? Has she, in fact, betrayed her purpose *not* to idolize art? Or is Magda's metaphoric transformation into a butterfly a gift of redemption for those who suffered in the Holocaust? Without dismissing the first interpretation, I must finally lean toward the latter. The element that makes this death problematic—its beauty—also makes it singular. If, as Ozick argues, the "moral purpose" of literature is "to distinguish one life from another," "to tell, in all the marvel of its singularity, the separate holiness of the least grain," then Magda's killing may be seen as particularized, not euphemized ("Literature" 297). In an otherwise bleak landscape, this graceful death signifies an instant of transcendence. In that instant Ozick does not deny the brutality of the Holocaust. Rather, she denies the Nazis' intention to wipe out Jewish resiliency, a motive explained by Adolph Eichmann's belief that

if he could succeed in destroying the biological basis of Jewry in the East . . . then Jewry as a whole would never recover. . . . The assimilated Jews of the West, including America, would . . . be in no position (and would have no desire) to make up this enormous loss of blood and there would therefore be no future generation worth mentioning. (Hess 242, qtd. in Berger 12)

Concerned with "the destruction of Jewish identity by the forces of deracination" from the *Shoah* to contemporary assimilation, Ozick creates a character who refuses to be "assimilated" into the role of Holocaust victim, turning butterfly instead (Pifer 92).[10]

Finally, there is the matter of *The Shawl*'s insistence on a painful memorial. Ozick's narrative relates the violent death of one victim out of the six million, an infant daughter whose loss dictates the plot for the rest of the text. In retrieving such an agonized history, *The Shawl* parallels *Beloved*, which, Toni Morrison has said, "is about something that the characters don't want to remember, I don't want to remember, black people don't want to remember, white people don't want to remember" (Angelo 120). Yet the injunction to remember is central to the strong sense of Jewish identity so imperative for Jewish survival. For so many readers the impulse to turn away from the picture of a murdered child remains strong, if not irresistible. *The Shawl* tempers this harrowing commemoration with a vision of a dead child transfigured.

Rosa's insistence on finding grace where none is expected grants her a final vision of Magda that reappears in her later life. She writes Magda endless letters and recognizes beauty only in remembrances and dreams of her lost daughter, whose later incarnations are imagined over and over: now a sixteen-year-old girl in a blue dress, now a successful married doctor, now a lioness who clenches and unclenches her "furry toes in all their power. Whoever steals you steals her own death" (15). In writing to Magda, Rosa's voice too is beautiful, describing the past not in her bitterly rough English but in elegant "literary Polish" (14). Lyrical passages describe Rosa's mother, a poet of infinite delicacy and complexity; her childhood house with its attic window from which "you could touch the top of the house by sticking [out] your arm . . . ; it was like pulling the whole green ribbon of summer indoors"; her family's collection of ink sketches, "the black so black and miraculous, how it measured out a hand and then the shadow of the hand" (42, 66, 68).

The text's only lyrical moments emerge through Magda, making a significant equation linking memory and loss with the sublime and the present with abhorrence. In memory, Rosa finds beauty, despite the fact that her daily existence in 1980s Florida is relentlessly ugly. This contrast can be read alongside Ozick's examination of diasporic existence; dispraising the values "of the surrounding culture itself," Ozick has "a revulsion against Greek and pagan modes, whether in their Christian or post-Christian vessels . . . against what is called, strangely, Western Civilization" (*Art* 156). This "Western civilization," Rosa believes, is determined to hollow out the meaning of historic horror. In America she cannot escape physical reminders of her wartime experience. Confronted by blue stripes on clothing and barbed wire around private beaches, she notes that "whatever was dangerous and repugnant they made prevalent, frivolous" (53). The sickening ugliness that we encounter in "Rosa" may be seen as a deliberate move against the frivolity that results from forgetting. Bent on remembering at all costs, Rosa is furious when Stella sends her a blue-striped dress, disregarding the stripes they both wore in the concentration camp: "As if innocent, as if ignorant, as if *not there*" (33).[11]

Rosa's own appearance and surroundings are nearly always marked by a grim physicality bordering on revulsion,[12] an ugliness that illuminates the link between Jewish present and past. Ozick's characters are permanently scarred by the Holocaust, even Stella, who tries to deny it; thus, a wholehearted redemption, a healing that binds all wounds, is impossible in what Berger has called an "Auschwitz planet" (194). Playing off the ever-pleasing figure of Magda is a series of hideous images: the rope of Rosa's apartment's dumbwaiter is blackened with "squads of dying flies"; her bedclothes are equally filthy and malodorous. The sun over her is an "executioner," the streets a "furnace"—images not to be taken lightly from the perspective of a woman who has survived the Holocaust. Looking around a cafeteria, she cruelly catalogues the effects of age: "mottled skin, ferocious clavicles, the wrinkled foundations of wasted breasts" (24). She worries that if she shifts in her chair, "an odor would fly up: urine, salt, old woman's fatigue" (24). Her persistent suitor, Simon Persky, removes an eggplant seed from under his lower plate of dentures and examines it closely at the table. She sees the women in her boardinghouse as pathetic, with their bulging fat at the nape of the neck and their smeared lipstick over "drawstring mouths" (28). The desk clerk maneuvers "clayey sweat balls up from" her cleavage (29). All human contact in this hellish world is revolting: walking on a beach crowded with couples, Rosa almost steps on the sweaty "faces of two lovers plugged into a kiss. A pair of water animals in suction" (48). Defined by such blasted visions, Rosa's present is endlessly mocked by her last glimpse of beauty: the image of her murdered daughter.

That image heralds the final moment of "The Shawl," which turns from Magda's electrocution to Rosa's paralyzed silence. Knowing that she will be killed should she move or scream, Rosa stands motionless and stuffs her mouth with Magda's shawl "until she was swallowing up the wolf's screech and tasting the cinnamon and almond depth of Magda's saliva; and Rosa drank Magda's shawl until it dried" (10).   An impossibility phrased in grammatically logical terms, the last clause seems to embody Elie Wiesel's comment about the Holocaust: "To substitute words, any words, for it is to distort it" (*A Jew Today* 197).

Yet words are all we have to work with in narrative, and Ozick deliberately turns a suppressed howl in "The Shawl" to an outpouring of writing in "Rosa," the text breaking cleanly into two stories along this faultline of voice. In doing so, she works against the image of Rosa's being "reduced to a wild animal" by introducing a Judaically informed emphasis upon written narrative (Scrafford 14–15).[13]   This second tale moves from fragmentation to a more conventional form, opening with a straightforward, declarative sentence from what seems to be an omniscient narrator: "Rosa Lublin, a madwoman and a scavenger, gave up her store—she smashed it up herself—and moved to Miami. It was a mad thing to do" (13). Like "The Shawl," however, this narrative inverts the terms of reality and sanity, turning its world upside down. "It was a mad thing to do," but as Berger notes, one might actually read Rosa's havoc as a sane form of protest against her customers' indifference to her Holocaust memories. He observes that in the perspective of survivors like Rosa, "if the world is Auschwitz, moral madness is preferable to 'sanity'" (122).

In trying to testify, Rosa is ignored by those around her, so she records her history in long letters to Magda.   These letters thus posit, by necessity, a communal and liturgical audience of her "significant dead."[14]   Through them, Ozick heeds Irving Greenberg's charge that "no statement [about the *Shoah*] should be made that would not be credible in the presence of the burning children" (qtd. in Berger 25).   Magda-as-audience fulfills Ozick's requirements of a "reciprocal moral imagination"; because of her, Rosa's voice is, in a fashion, no longer only "private" (Ozick, *Art* 169). The letters constitute both a historical *and* a religious ritual, despite Rosa's elitist attitude toward her fellow Jews in the Warsaw Ghetto (she calls them "old Jew peasants worn out from their rituals and superstitions, phylacteries on their foreheads sticking up so stupidly").[15]

Certainly her unmailed letters to Magda do not constitute a conventional public forum for Rosa's history.   Yet, as Ozick makes clear, they are the only option left to her.   Rosa has already made a fruitless search for a communal audience in her customers, who are as willfully ignorant as the villagers outside the steel fences in "The Shawl":

When I had my store I used to "meet the public," and I wanted to tell everybody—not only our story, but other stories as well.   Nobody knew anything. . . . Nobody remembered what happened only a little while ago.   They didn't remember because they didn't know. . . . I didn't tell [everything] to everyone; who would have the patience to hear it all out?   So I used to pick out one little thing here, one little thing there, for each customer. (66–69)

But the little things—such as the trolleys running directly through the Warsaw ghetto, carrying "witnesses" who refused to acknowledge what lay outside their windows—are too much for her patrons, who refuse to listen. Even Stella, her only surviving relative, "wants to wipe out memory" (58). Still, to some, wiping out memory can be a mode of survival itself, as Stella writes: "My God! It's thirty years, forty, who knows, give it a rest . . . . Rosa, by now, believe me, it's time you have to have a life" (31, 32). Persky too tells her, "Sometimes a little forgetting is necessary. . . . It's finished. Long ago it's finished" (58).

Implicit in the equation of forgetting with survival, however, is a kind of murder. How does one forget the past without again killing off one's significant dead? More important, to forget means to risk the permissiveness of oblivion, and hence disregard the reigning injunction of late twentieth-century Judaism: "Never Again." What both Stella and Persky forget is the figure of Magda herself, who in this novel represents not only all the significant dead of the Holocaust but the fragility of memory itself. Rather than lose sight of the ethereal butterfly Magda becomes, Rosa persists in bearing witness to the conditions that necessitated such a transformation.

When she shifts from oral to written testimony, the images of Rosa's writing are informed equally by the Judaic tradition of written history and Holocaustal elements. Rosa finds herself "inside a blazing flying current, a terrible beak of light bleeding out a kind of cuneiform on the underside of her brain" (69). The cuneiform signifies Judaism's emphasis on recorded history, as well as Rosa's own intellectual heritage, while the beak is for Ozick a suggestive image of violent imaginative transport. Her novel *The Messiah of Stockholm* (1987) depicts Lars Andemening, an intellectual book reviewer who fancies himself the son of the Polish writer Bruno Schulz, murdered by Nazis; when his writing is at its most inspired, his pen seems to emit "haloes of hot grease," and a "greased beak tore him off his accustomed ledge and brought him to a high place beyond his control" (*Stockholm* 8). Mixing metaphors of writing with "hot grease" and blood, Ozick creates a visceral reminder of the Holocaustal history surrounding these two characters: a woman who imagines her murdered baby into a grown woman and a man who imagines a father out of a murdered intellectual.

These images also reveal the influx of imagination into any recorded history. As shown by the troubling depiction of Magda's murder, while this influence renders the telling of history flexible, it also risks a denial of meaning. Informed by its pivotal image of a dying child turned butterfly, this text weaves back and forth, crossing and re-crossing between memory and forgetting, between the living and the dead, between the demands of history and the risks of art. Ozick has written that imagination is not only "the flesh and blood of literature" but also "something deeply perilous," something that

always has the lust to tear down meaning, to smash interpretation, to wear out the rational, to mock the surprise of redemption, to replace the fluid force of suspense with an image of stasis; to transfix and stun rather than to urge; to spill out, with so much quicksilver wonder, idol after idol. . . . The imagination, like Moloch, can take you nowhere except back to its own maw. ("Literature" 296)

As current literary and historical theories such as New Historicism and materialist feminism have amply shown, separating art from history can be not only misleading but dangerous.[16] *The Shawl* never resolves the tension between fluidity and "mere literature" but moves perpetually between both.

This movement whirls out of Rosa's violent history, which redefines the terms of her reality by creating a field of constantly changing meanings. *The Shawl* voices an epistemological crisis made at once personal and historical and exemplified by the changing nature of objects throughout the text: Rosa's telephone becomes her dead daughter at age sixteen, the concentration camp's electric wires are humming voices, a private beach turns into an Auschwitz by means of its barbed wire fence. The most significant transformation occurs to the shawl itself. It is something magical, holy, and life sustaining in the first tale; symbolic of a *tallit* (a prayer shawl), it also lends Magda's breath a scent of cinnamon and almonds, an aroma that "evokes a quasimystical image of the *besamim* [a spice box] which Jews sniff at the end of the Sabbath to prepare for the rigors of the profane week to follow" (Berger 54).[17] In "Rosa," however, it loses its religious significance and becomes a "colorless cloth"; "an old bandage; a discarded sling. For some reason it did not instantly restore Magda, as usually happened" (62). No longer a *tallit*, no longer evocative of Magda's holy breath of cinnamon and almonds, the shawl now has an ordinariness akin to Simon Persky's profession as a button salesman.

Magda herself is marked by a fluctuating paternity, as her mother does and does not agree with Stella's insistence that Magda's father is a Nazi rapist:

[Rosa] was always a little suspicious of Magda, because of the other strain, whatever it was, that ran in her. Rosa herself was not truly suspicious, but Stella was, and that induced perplexity in Rosa. The other strain was ghostly, even dangerous. It was as if the peril hummed out from the filaments of Magda's hair, those narrow bright wires. (65–66)

Earlier, Rosa denies sharing Stella's suspicion, writing that Magda's "father was not a German. I was forced by a German, it's true, and more than once, but I was too sick to conceive" (43). Gathered around the issue of Magda's uncertain paternity, and thus her identity, the first tale's pattern of assertion and denial resurfaces to acknowledge Ozick's finally impossible imaginative task in saying the unsayable. Rosa is a Jewish character; Ozick, a Jewish writer. Yet what does a Jewish identity mean in a post-Holocaustal world, if the defining tenet of Judaism is the covenant that Jews, the "chosen people," will thrive? What does "thriving" signify in the context of Nazi genocide and the conditions of increasing assimilation? Ozick is deeply concerned with

> maintaining a cohesive Jewish life in Dispersion, the challenge of combining Jewish
> commitment with the enormous impact Western culture has had on the Jews since the
> era of Emancipation. In a world of Exile and of cultural displacements multiplied
> many times over, questions of what Jews can and cannot meaningfully share as a
> people take on paramount importance. (Sokoloff 202)

Those questions are explored in "Rosa" through the medium of private, unmailed letters, whose imagined reader must perforce substitute for the living audience that Rosa lacks.

It is because this audience is supplied "perforce" that the issue of bearing witness remains problematic in *The Shawl*. Rosa is still alienated from her community and still deeply connected to her dead daughter. Ozick's text closes not in a lucid place of redemption but rather in a gray zone between healing and a gesture of madness. Rosa has her telephone reconnected and agrees to see Simon Persky, yet *The Shawl* finishes with these lines: "Magda was not there. Shy, she ran from Persky. Magda was away" (70). *Away* does not mean *dead*; Ozick refuses to tie up her tale neatly. As a writer, she prefers possibility over the determinedly positive outcome—what she calls a "moral mandate":

> I too recoil from all that: the so-called "affirmative" is simpleminded, single-minded,
> crudely explicit; it belongs either to journalism or to piety or to "uplift." It is the
> enemy of literature and the friend of coercion. ("Literature" 295)

An "affirmative" ending to *The Shawl* might offer a Rosa made whole and cheerful, might insist on her finding a niche in a bright, clean community and moving beyond her violent past. But such an ending would deny the realities of that past and the Judaic injunction of remembrance. These two requirements merge in the text's simultaneous acknowledgment of both Persky's charge that Rosa go on with her life and Magda's role as reminder of her mother's horrific past.

The flexibility informing *The Shawl*'s relationship to violence proves doubly vital to the reclaiming of a painful history: it expands the boundaries of historical narrative and allows for a position beyond victimization. Like *Beloved*, *Housekeeping*, and *Corregidora*, *The Shawl* tells a somewhat different story from that of earlier works (for example, Saul Bellow's *Mr. Sammler's Planet* or Elie Wiesel's *Night*). Marlene Heinemann writes that many Holocaust writers find no difference between male and female experiences in the death camps, thus ignoring the "biological roles by which patriarchal society has generally defined women: fertility and sexuality" (14). Yet the Nazis formulated a racially hypocritical definition of womanhood to support a sexual ideology of justified rape and murder. Mothers of "inferior races" were killed as quickly and efficiently as possible, but "the maternal role for other [read: Aryan] women was idealized and encouraged through extensive legislation to increase the German birth rate" (Heinemann 17).[18] In specifically depicting a woman's death camp experience and survival *as a mother*, *The Shawl* works against that supposition of no difference.

Conversely, this text also explores the limits of maternity in the face of history. For European Jews, the Holocaust created an insanely paradoxical situation: simply by giving birth, a mother could consign her Jewish child to the death camps, and possibly murder. The issue here is not of Rosa's responsibility; rather, as with *Beloved* and *Corregidora* both, I am concerned with the ways in which historical persecution can make a parent's position intolerable. Inevitably Rosa passes on a dangerous legacy of identity to Magda, who is born a Jew in Nazi-ruled Poland. Ozick has grappled with the irrational side of maternal accountability before. Her essay "The Hole/Birth Catalogue" attacks Freud's statement that anatomy is destiny: if this is the case, writes Ozick, then "all the truth any philosophy can really tell us about human life is that each new birth supplies another corpse" (*Art* 255). Following this line of reasoning, she argues, a woman—when seen *solely* as a childbearer—becomes the primary agent of death, a "disgorger of corpses. What is a baby-machine if not also a corpse-maker?" (*Art* 255).[19]

Through the figure of Magda, ironically marked by "Aryan" features, *The Shawl* addresses the "terrible logic" that "places the whole burden of humankind's failings on the woman's uterus": "Whoever destroys, whoever is aggressive, has first to be born; the childbearer becomes Shiva the Destroyer. . . . The uterus destines the woman to spew destruction" (*Art* 258). Obviously, Rosa is no more responsible for the emergence of the Nazis than Magda is representative of them. Yet Rosa's maternity gives shape and historic weight to Ozick's entire text, recognizing as it does both the Nazis' political machinations and her liturgically informed need to remember the dead.

It is also through Rosa that *The Shawl* defies the reinscription of victimization. Ozick repeatedly acknowledges the strengths of Jewish identity: its humor, its written tradition, its sense of community, its tenacity. Rosa's final line is a resonant example of such toughness and sharp wit. When Persky (whose wife has been institutionalized for years) appears in her rooming house lobby, she tells the receptionist: "He's used to crazy women, so let him come up" (65). Her words bring to mind the unnamed waiter in Hemingway's "A Clean, Well-Lighted Place." After his long meditation upon existential bleakness, characterized by the ceaselessly recurring word *nada* ("nothing"), the waiter finds himself standing in front of a bar. Asked what he will have, he responds, "Nada"—a bitter joke, but like Rosa's, a mark of resiliency. Through its shifting focus on Rosa Lublin's identity as mother, thwarted intellectual, and writer for her liturgical community of the dead, *The Shawl* reveals the disturbing nature of those roles. In describing the separation of mother and child,[20] Ozick also grapples with the issues of legacy and survival, to create a simultaneously redemptive and bleak vision of an Auschwitz planet.

NOTES

1. Obviously Ozick's use of the term *liturgical* for something so free of prescription merits explanation. As I will discuss later, "liturgical literature" meshes with Ozick's definition of redemption, which "insists on the freedom to change one's life" ("Literature" 295). Alan Berger discusses this open-endedness in Ozick's *The Cannibal Galaxy*, particularly in connection with the Judaic tradition of *midrash* (a series of complex rabbinical parables that explore the relationship between human beings and God without lapsing into the prescriptive). See Berger 24, 31–39, 130–36.

2. See Rose 93–94, for a clear discussion of Ozick's "perspective of literature as theology." As do Berger and several other scholars, I use the terms *Holocaust* and *Shoah* interchangeably and acknowledge the problematic nature of *Holocaust* itself, which although readily identifiable for a twentieth-century audience, also signifies a sacrificial burned offering. See also Kremer 8.

3. See also Kauvar, "Courier" 130.

4. As Alan Berger writes, "The long-range impact of [the Holocaust] puts into question the survivability of Judaism itself. There is no covenant without a covenant people" (12). See also Berger 130.

5. Lionel Trilling's *The Liberal Imagination* (1950) and George Steiner's *Language and Silence: Essays on Language, Literature, and the Inhuman* (1967) voice similar beliefs.

6. See also Ozick's "Preface" to *Bloodshed and Three Novellas*. Ruth Wisse sums up Ozick's position nicely; for her, fiction writing is "by nature an idolatrous activity. Art—in the Western tradition of truth to fiction as its own end—is against the Second Commandment, she says, and anti-Jewish in its very impulse" (40).

7. The contradictory tensions between Ozick's fiction and nonfiction have been well documented. See, for example, Katha Pollitt's "The Three Selves of Cynthia Ozick"; Leslie Epstein's "Stories and Something Else"; Ruth Rosenberg's "Covenanted to the Law"; Sanford Pinsker's "Jewish Tradition and the Individual Talent"; Ellen Pifer's "Invention and Orthodoxy"; Louis Harap's "The Religious Art of Cynthia Ozick"; and Janet Handler Burstein's "Cynthia Ozick and the Transgressions of Art." I must add, however, that I see such contradictions as related to the simple right to change one's opinion, particularly when a writer has been active for over three decades, as Ozick has been.

8. The maker of the film *Shoah*, Claude Lanzmann, has written that any attempt to explain or understand the Holocaust is an "absolute obscenity" ("Seminar" 85, qtd. in Michaels 8. See also Michaels 9–11). That obscenity appears in *The Shawl* in the letter sent to Rosa by Dr. Joshua Tree, a professor of social pathology who wants her to participate in his study of "survivors"; as Rosa notes, he never calls her a human being (36–37).

9. Cynthia Ozick, *The Shawl* (New York: Arthur A. Knopf, 1987) 3. Subsequent quotations from this work are cited in the text.

10. An interesting variation on this transformative notion of death may be found in Marilynne Robinson's *Housekeeping*, wherein Ruthie imagines the dead turned into flowers and shards of the moon (150–60).

11. The tremendous argument against forgetting the Holocaust is made clear by Lionel Rubinoff, who writes that Jews who neglect their religious and cultural heritage, who do not live fully as Jews, "destroy . . . Judaism by themselves co-operating in that destruction . . . [and] respond to Hitler by doing his work" (150, qtd. in Michaels 13).

12.   Earl Rovit complains, perhaps rather simplistically, that Ozick's work has "relatively little direct presentation of love, hope, growth, pity, or faith. . . . This is a fictional world peopled, for the most part, by unlikeable and unattractive characters." He adds that those who "merit not only our pity, but our most generous sympathy, repel it" (43).

13.   Rosa's endless writing in this second tale evokes the textual histories and doctrines upon which Judaism is founded. Jewish law and history are contained in a series of books: the Old Testament, the Talmud, the Torah (which chiefly contains the previous two texts), and the *midrash*.

14.   Sanford Pinsker's term *significant dead* refers to Bruno Schulz in *The Messiah of Stockholm*, but it might also apply to Magda ("Lost-and-Found" 234).

15.   "Rosa" 67.   Edward Alexander calls Rosa Lublin one of the "Jewish apostates . . . who had always showed their hatred for the Jews, being dragged, literally and metaphysically, back into the ghetto" (200).

16.   Ozick connects imagination with spirituality as well as with history, arguing that a Jewish writer's art must be "Biblically indebted." Removed from history, both imagination and spirituality can veer into the idolatrous: "the Holocaust, according to Ozick, was the product of crazed, misplaced spirituality; in her words, 'It is only what is called Spirit—i.e., Idolatry—that produces this kind of butchery'" (*Art & Ardor* 234, qtd. in Lyons 17).

17.   See Berger, who writes, "Wrapping oneself in a prayer shawl [a *tallit*] is tantamount to being surrounded by the holiness and protection of the commandments; as well as conforming to the will of God" (53).   Ozick calls the shawl "magic"; "it could nourish an infant for three days and three nights" ("Shawl" 5).

18.   This ideology extended to Jewish men as well.   In *Mein Kampf*, Hitler sees the Jewish male as a rapist of Aryan women and argues for the "need to protect pure womanhood from Jewish sexual vice" (Heinemann 17–18).   It is not difficult to trace connections between this "protective need" and that which inspired the lynchings of black men during the United States' Reconstruction Period.

19.   As Lawrence Friedman notes, however, Ozick has also found Judaism guilty of sexism, although she does not compare it to Freudianism (see 27–28).

20.   Heinemann discusses the separation of mothers and daughters in Holocaust literature, particularly those works in which mothers and daughters "transcend their separation . . . by struggling to remain together, through a later reunion, or symbolically through memory or friendship" (23–24).

Chapter 7

Comedic Violence and the Art of Survival: Leslie Marmon Silko's *Almanac of the Dead*

In *Reading National Geographic* (1993), Catherine A. Lutz and Jane L. Collins discover a connection between "friendly natives" and colonialism through the recurrence of smiling, "exotic" people in that magazine's photography. Such images help to disguise colonialism's violent invasiveness by celebrating the basic human sameness between American readers and people of other cultures. However, as Stephen Greenblatt writes in his review of the book, many cheerful portraits of tribal people have also formed a sense of global hospitality, convincing the viewer that "American imperial power would manifest itself not in territorial possession but in near-universal cultural and economic penetration" (113). Particularly after World War II, he adds, Americans who "traveled abroad with images from the *National Geographic* in their heads" went "not as colonial administrators but as tourists" (113).

Similarly, Leslie Marmon Silko identifies white North Americans as tourists—not abroad, but in the United States. In 1976 she wrote that much of American history has evaded "facts which are hard to swallow: namely, that at best, the Anglo-American is a guest on this continent; and at the worst, the United States of America is founded upon stolen land" ("Indian Attack" 84). Coming out fifteen years after Silko noted this intersection of tourism and colonialism in the Americas, *Almanac of the Dead* (1991) depicts an over-crowded, nearly depleted North America festering with murder and torture, and questions the notion of the Euro-American as even a welcome guest. As Silko has explained, the work's title refers to the now-fragmented Mayan almanacs[1] that were used as both planting guides and records of "famine and death, revolution and conquest"; in her book, Silko has created her own "missing pages" to this almanac, detailing visions and rituals and prophesying the "hundreds of years of exploitation of the Native American people here" (Coltelli 151, 52). With over fifty characters, nearly as many interconnected narratives, and a remarkable merging of violence and comedy, Silko's modern epic forces its readers to confront the consequences of the United States' own history of conquest and genocide.

In such a brutal book, it is not surprising that brutality serves as a truth teller in Silko's explorations of art, history, and survival. Like Ozick she is concerned with the consequences of art divorced from history and community, as well as from a connectedness with the earth. She critiques the empty uses of violence for artistic purposes by making a stunning link between the "clinical detachment" valued in high art[2] and the rationale behind the making and viewing of torture films. But brutality also functions more positively for Silko; by recognizing Native Americans' own capacity for ferocity and ruthlessness—and equally important, for humor and resilience—she undermines the dominant culture's romantic (and politically useful) view of Indians as dying and pathetic. Silko unbalances the non-Indian members of her audience by sounding jointly the notes of comedy and violence, a counterpoint that underscores a cultural vitality. This startling combination hints at the unpredictable, elusive presence of the trickster.[3] My point here is not to provide evidence that the work is or is not a kind of trickster narrative; since the trickster promises ambiguity and deception, we might do well not to expect its explicit appearance in Silko's book. What interests me is how *Almanac of the Dead*, through its moments of violence fused with humor and resiliency and its depiction of Indian life as complex, resourceful, and vital, works against the sentimental myth of the dying, silent Indian. By investing her contemporary story with elements of trickster tales—multiple meanings, inversion, profanity—Silko illustrates how the workings of Native American cultures are not static or fixed in history but are alive and well—are, in fact, undeniable participants in American literary tradition.

Like Silko's earlier work, *Ceremony* (1977), *Almanac of the Dead* relates the origin and subsequent history of Destroyers or Gunadeeyahs, who appear in Mexico centuries before the Europeans' arrival and whose sexually charged bloodthirstiness drives the Indians north.[4] Identified in Silko's Almanac notebooks by their "complete indifference about the life or death of other human beings" (534), the contemporary, Euro-American Gunadeeyahs thrive in the United States and Mexico as government officials, members of the military, well-connected assassins, police interrogators—even real estate developers, entrepreneurs, and artists. Their violence is relentless, abundant, repugnant: a police chief trafficking in torture videotapes castrates a man who is fully awake; a businessman ritually drains homeless men of blood and then harvests their usable organs for his "bio-materials" center. In exposing those who profit from exploiting human life, *Almanac of the Dead* strips their wealth and power of its seductive glamour—of its "art"; thus, the brutality of these modern-day destroyers also surfaces in Silko's depiction of a hollow, ugly art whose medium is violence and death, and for whose creators, as for the earliest destroyers, "the world is a dead thing" instead of a living planet (Silko, *Ceremony* 135).

In portraying a realm of contemporary art infused with violence for its own sake, *Almanac of the Dead* connects that art to films of vicious police interrogations and bloody operations, sold as erotica by characters like the aristocratic Beaufrey, and bought by judges, police chiefs, and governors. Commodified art turns brutal specifically through language as Silko repeats, verbatim, a description of the book's only instance of beautified violence. When David, a young artist involved with Beaufrey, finds and photographs the body of Eric, a former lover who has shot himself in the head, the picture is described from two different points of view, but each time in precisely the same way.   As I will explain, Silko's repetitious phrasing illustrates a variation on Mikhail Bakhtin's notion of heteroglossia, meaning the locus of historical and social conditions that give a word its various meanings and associations. Seese, David's lover and Eric's best friend, first sees pictured not a corpse but simply a human figure lying in a "field of peonies and poppies—cherry, ruby, deep purple, black," a "nude nearly buried in blossoms of bright reds and purples" (106). For Seese, the words *blossoms*, *peonies*, and *poppies* are meant in the strictest representational sense: that is, she believes she is looking at a picture of a nude lying in a field of flowers, until her second glance reveals what those blossoms really are. Then she no longer sees flowers, finding instead an ugly image of a thick black pool suffusing this photograph of "brains, bone, and blood" (107).

For Seese, flowers signify only flowers, and a corpse, only death. Yet though her language differs from that of the destroyers in David and Beaufrey's decadent art world, Seese's initial interpretation of the photograph is repeated, word for word, by an art critic when an exclusive gallery exhibits David's work. In praising the "pictorial irony of a field of red shapes which might be peonies—cherry, ruby, deep purple, black—and the nude human figure nearly buried in these 'blossoms' of bright red" (108), the critic meets Seese in a heteroglossia where meanings diverge at the point of violence. While Seese cannot reduce a corpse to artistic pleasure, the destroyer culture admires the use of blood as medium and extols the artist who has at last "found a subject to fit his style of clinical detachment and relentless exposure of what lies hidden in flesh" (108). Such obvious pleasure in destruction echoes in the perspective of another destroyer-artist, a hired assassin who imagines himself choreographing and designing commissioned executions. Max Blue recalls the "subjects" of these orchestrated murders as if remembering a favorite painting:

The paloverdes had been thick with bright yellow blossoms when they had hung the
"motorcyclist" upside down in a paloverde and left the bike appropriately skidded and
smashed lying at the bottom of the exit ramp. (354–55)[5]

This violent conjunction of thick yellow blossoms and shattered body
conjures up the photographs of Eric's body sprawled in its own nest of
flowers, evoking once again an inverted world where murder is art and
cadavers are objects in a still life.

Max's remembrance of the flowers is double-edged; though a destroyer,
he has a peculiar appreciation for natural beauty. Obsessed with the light of
the Tucson sky, he reflects on his memories of the great European cathedrals
"where light was celebrated as the presence of God" (356), and even before
coming to Tucson, he admires rural New Jersey's narrow back roads
bordering dairy farms, orchards, and fields. In Max, Silko has created a
profiteer of murder with a bizarre sense of natural aesthetics, a cold-blooded
killer who likes to look at clouds and dairy cows. But she does so not merely
for ironic effect. In a text so concerned with a ravaged planet, especially the
drought-ridden southwest United States, Max's distorted perspective on
nature reveals the hypocritical shallowness of those who claim empathy with
Indians' harmonious relationship with the earth while willfully ignoring the
plight of both Indians and their lands. As Linda Hogan has noted, many non-
Indians want to be "white shamans," trying to appropriate Native American
rituals while "forgetting that enlightenment can't be found in a weekend
workshop, forgetting that most Indian people are living the crisis of American
life" (75).

Max's wife, Leah, a real estate agent and developer, contributes to the
crisis that stems from the appropriation and decimation of Native American
lands. Building in the Arizona desert a city named "Venice" with a series of
lakes, fountains, and waterways running between custom-built neighborhoods,
Leah is unconcerned about the drought, as she elliptically argues that "science
will solve the water problem of the West. New Technology. They'll *have* to"
(374). Like David, Beaufrey, Max, and her lover Trigg (who uses the
homeless for his blood and organ banks),[6] Leah is a vampire-like figure who,
in ordering canals and lakes to be "scraped out" and deep wells to be dug,
sucks the earth dry (375). Her deadly vision violates the southwestern
landscape; when her nephew looks at the New Mexican terrain, he sees it
brutalized, with a sunset the color of dried blood, a breeze "slashing" the
yuccas and ricegrass, and the purple of twilight "bruising the flanks of the
low, sandy hills" (370–71).

The image of a violated landscape, especially in New Mexico, is finally
overcome by the powerful properties of Mount Taylor, which stands west of
Albuquerque; central to both *Ceremony* and *Almanac of the Dead*, this
mountain is sacred to the Laguna Pueblo Indians, who call it T'se-pi'na or
"The Woman Veiled in Clouds." Sterling, an exiled Pueblo, remembers how

T'se-pi'na is profaned by the construction of a nearby uranium mine, which has sprawled over whole mesas: "'Leave our Mother Earth alone,' the old folks had tried to warn, 'otherwise terrible things will happen to us all'" (759).[7] In *Almanac of the Dead*, the thirty-foot mountains of radioactive tailings are seen as new evidence of the Destroyers, yet they are finally shadowed by a giant sandstone snake that appears out of the sacred mountain overnight, a year before plunging uranium prices close the mine, its raised head and open jaws pointed at a basalt mesa left intact.

Functioning as an ancient spirit messenger who heralds the recovery of Indian lands, this snake was first imagined by Silko as the subject of a mural she painted on a Tucson building to proclaim "her ardent affiliation with the forces of benign spirits" (Maranto 18). Silko has said that before painting the mural, seven years into the novel, she became disheartened: "The novel took me over and put me through the ringer. I couldn't see any redemption, and I didn't think I could go on without that." The salvation Silko felt lacking in this novel about so many "suicidal, self-destructive" characters emerges not through moments of lyrical violence, as might occur in many dominant culture narratives, but instead through her vision of the giant snake, a spiritual messenger of the forces who will fight the destroyers (Silko, qtd. in Maranto 18).[8] This particular mode of redemption, stemming as it does from Native American kinship with the natural world, works in tandem with Silko's efforts to shatter the disabling myth of the Indians as "the Vanishing Americans" (Ramsey 194).

However, while not vanished, Native Americans are in crisis; as Silko wrote on the dust jacket of *Ceremony*'s first edition, contemporary Indians are plagued with "the despair which accounts for the suicide, the alcoholism, and the violence which occur in so many Indian communities today" (qtd. in Seyersted 26). Yet she notes in her foreword to Aaron Yiva's *Border Towns of the Navajo Nation* (which contains several sketches of drunken Native Americans on the streets of Gallup, New Mexico) that "despite these tremendous odds against us for two hundred years—the racism, the poverty, the alcoholism—we go on living" (qtd. in Seyersted 24–25). Notwithstanding the assertion of that final clause, much of mainstream United States culture conceives of the Native American as a dying breed whose spiritual wisdom can be sustained through "white shamanism" (the recycling of Indian tales and beliefs by white artists),[9] a perspective fusing indulgent sentimentalism with callous appropriation, as Linda Hogan explains: "My friend Shelly, a Grand Portage Indian, said that in a lot of ways [white shamanism] was like looking at Jews in concentration camps and saying, 'Oh, aren't they beautiful people and isn't Jewish mysticism wonderful'" (76). Simultaneously vapid and opportunistic, this response to contemporary Native Americans is the sentimental underside of colonialism, a superficial regret that "civilization, for all its greatness and goodness, inevitably destroyed the fabric of savage nobility" (Pearce 214). Roy Harvey Pearce adds that this reiterated motif in nineteenth-century American novels marks "a deep need in the collective

[European-]American imagination" to see the Indian as the doomed figure who "theoretically embodied all that good men should be" but could not survive the rigors of civilization (215–16, 136).[10]   The objectification of Indian-as-victim neatly follows Euro-America's genocidal practices (from 1500 to 1600, seventy-two million North and South American Indians were reduced to ten million).[11]   Persisting as a kind of epistemological genocide, this objectification constructs the Indians as a people who "don't exist" (Hogan 72).[12]

   Almanac of the Dead subverts this victimization from the very beginning, with a trickster-like combination of violence and comedy that is rich in anomaly, inversion, and multiple meanings.   Rather than weaving a tale around a trickster figure, Silko posits trickster traits in dialogue with each other, thereby exemplifying Gerald Vizenor's characterization of the trickster as "a comic sign, neither a real person nor a character with [what Paul Radin calls] 'aesthetic presence'" (207).   (The mortality of the various figures in the book who share some of these characteristics also precludes their being tricksters themselves.) [13]   The disarming combination of violence and comedy with which Silko creates her variation on trickster discourse opens the book. On a ranch in Tucson, Arizona, two Mexican-Indian sisters tease each other about witchery and old age in a kitchen filled not with food but with guns, ammunition, and drugs.   Sixty-year-old Lecha (who holds the missing pages of the Almanac) looks around the room and laughingly compares it to the Devil's kitchen.   At the stove, her twin sister, Zeta, is dyeing all her clothing dark brown, either in preparation for old age or because she wishes to be invisible at nighttime.   After calling her sister a witch, Lecha notes that *she* prefers using the black dye on her hair, not her clothes.   The need for ammunition and nighttime invisibility is not explained until nearly seven hundred pages later, when we learn of the indigenous people's revolution aimed at taking back the North American continent; yet Silko's encapsulation of extremes—violence and comedy—combined with multiple levels of meaning (Zeta could be a witch, a gun runner, or both; this is a home, a supply depot for an army, or both) plunges the reader into a realm of trickster-like inversion, where "what is bottom becomes top" and "a place of safety [can become] a place of danger and back again" (Hynes and Doty 37).[14]

   Like tricksters, the "notorious border breakers" who pull together the extremes of sacred and profane, life and death, order and chaos, Silko's novel also works "on the edge . . . [of] existing borders, classifications, and categories" by playing on the cultural expectations of a largely non-Indian audience (Hynes and Doty 33, 34).   Lecha and Zeta are not the "good Indians" of mainstream perception, speaking of harmonious wholeness between all living beings.   Lecha has grown wealthy from her spiritual gifts; first, people consult her to exact revenge on ex-lovers, relations, and business partners, and later, to locate the missing, which she does for a high price, and on national television, profiting from the "fascination the United States [has] for the 'other'" with exotic high Indian cheekbones (142). Zeta, on the other hand, is a successful drug and gun smuggler who has also sold Indian antiquities for cash and will eventually murder her weapons supplier. In one of the novel's most startling scenes, Lecha jubilantly digs up the graves of her family, all of whom (except for Zeta and her grandmother) she "had endured," now feeling that "she damn sure didn't have to lie there for eternity with them" (583). Here, in what I read as a deliberate move to confuse an audience who might expect its unexamined beliefs about Indian culture to be confirmed, Silko turns upside down the Native American emphasis on respect for ancestors and the dead.

The powerful Mexican-Indian revolutionary Angelita also evokes the trickster through her constant, irreverent humor—joking with El Feo, her lover, that Marx and Engels are his sexual rivals—and through her sexual vitality, which is matched by her oratorical abilities.[15] Like Coyote, whose "two-sidedness" enables him to survive despair with humor (Hogan 77), Angelita lies to the so-called friends of the Indians like Cuba, Germany, and Japan in order to obtain weapons and supplies necessary for her revolution, even using the image of the victimized Native American as a warrior's disguise: "Always they were poor, struggling Indians fighting for their way of life. If Angelita was talking to the Germans or Hollywood activists, she said the Indians were fighting multinational corporations who killed rain forests" (513–14). Silko's merging of violence and humor is evident in the nickname Angelita adopts—La Escapia (Meat Hook), which amuses her highly—and the video Angelita sends to Mexican television stations, in which she laughs while promising war and calls, "Adios, white man," as the screen shows the severed heads of the U.S. ambassador to Mexico and his aide (590). And when Bartolomeo, the Cuban Marxist who first taught her about communism and then sex, denies the Native Americans' history of genocide, she rouses her tribal army to convict him of "crimes against tribal histories" and has him hanged (531).

This scene of Bartolomeo's public execution is remarkable not only for its linking of violence and comedy but also as the book's only moment of organized violence on the part of indigenous people to reclaim a suppressed, denied history—a history Bartolomeo has devalued—and thus ensure their survival. Beginning with a trickster-like scatological reference to the jerry-built gallows, which resemble "an elevated outdoor privy . . . with only a simple hole in the boards for the shit to drop through" (532), the execution continues:

"Next time *don't lie* about our history!" shouted an old woman standing near the gallows as Bartolomeo fell through the hole and dangled.
    "So, sadly, they have been forced to terminate their relationship with dear comrade Bartolomeo," as a wisecracker at the graveyard had put it. (532)[16]

The absurdity of shouting a warning about "next time" to a corpse may be disingenuous, since from an Indian perspective, people's spirits do not disappear at death; thus, comic absurdity can also signify advice. Here, Silko reminds her readers, if only subliminally, that violence untempered by humor and unredeemed by the imperative of survival is indistinguishable from the violence perpetrated by the destroyers.

No matter how tempered, though, the most prominent aspect of *Almanac of the Dead* remains its relentless representation of brutal sex, drug addiction, torture, and murder. So many pages describe the despair of people like Seese, whose baby is stolen (and unknown to her, dissected for a film Beaufrey will market), or the depravity of people like the federal judge Arne, who sexually tortures prostitutes and has sex with his basset hounds, or Lecha and Zeta's incestuous Uncle Federico, who molests them when they are girls, that the reader finally wonders: what end does all this violence and revulsion serve? One answer is to look at this landscape of brutality through the prism of the trickster—specifically, through his sense of immoderation, which, as Laura Makarius observes, is

the lot of the being who knows neither laws nor checks nor limits. . . . The diverse forms of *impurity*—blood, menstruations, childbirths, excrements, corpses, organs of sexuality and excretion—are the favored domain of the one who is not constrained by taboo. (85)

The immoderation of *Almanac of the Dead* stems from the same rage that initiates its humor—rage that "the United States is built on the void left by destroying Indian cultures" (Octavio Paz, qtd. in Chapman 8).

Although many cultures have learned to combine humor and rage, this conjunction is peculiarly Native American in that it recognizes "a sustained genocidal drive to obliterate the American Indian as a distinct historical and cultural entity" and also "the ultimate failure of these genocidal drives" (Chapman 9).[17] Balancing a tradition of humor and survival with a "history of death," Paula Gunn Allen distinguishes between the humor of old Indian tales and that of contemporary Indian literature, which is "not defensive so much as it's bitter" (Coltelli 22).[18] The cultural appropriations of white shamanism also inspire this bitter wit, as Linda Hogan points out: "after the first twenty times somebody tells you that they were reincarnated Indians, you have to have a humorous perspective or you are going to put somebody up against the wall" (77).

Making fun of the sacred is part of the survival motif of Silko's novel, whose running theme of adaptability also emerges through Old Yoeme, Lecha and Zeta's grandmother. Claiming that her old age stems from her curiosity, Yoeme is coyote-like in her capacity for humor and survival—and so is the perfect candidate for sustaining a communal history.[19] It is she who holds a missing fragment of the Almanac of the Dead, which she later entrusts to Lecha for transcribing. Old Yoeme actually inserts a story of her own into this ancient history, as Lecha discovers:

That old woman! Years after her death, Lecha still could not top her. The story of Yoeme's deliverance [from both execution and the 1918 influenza epidemic] had been carefully inserted among the pages of the old almanac manuscript. Why had Yoeme called the story "Day of Deliverance"? What good was the story of one woman's unlikely escape from the hangman? Had old Yoeme known or cared that 20 to 40 million perished around the world while she had been saved? Probably not. (580)

Old Yoeme's mischievous ability to ridicule almost everything, to find humor in the most unlikely sources, helps to redeem the terrible bleakness of *Almanac of the Dead* by putting it in a more cosmic, if not comic, perspective. As Silko herself wrote in her foreword to Yiva's book, "The world remains for us as it has always been. One with itself and us, death and laughter existing side by side" (qtd. in Seyersted 24–25).

After writing *Ceremony* and before beginning *Almanac of the Dead*, Silko said that her next book would "be about the function of humor" and would involve a series of interrelated "funny stories": "Whatever just happened, it would be related to other things that had happened; that is, people . . . would tell of similar or even worse occurrences so that pretty soon, after the whole thing is over with, things are back in perspective" (Silko, qtd. in Fisher 23). Silko's rapid movement from funny stories to an accumulation of "worse occurrences" relates not only to a native history of comic violence but also to trickster's unbridled excess, at which she herself seems to laugh by the end of *Almanac of the Dead*. Perhaps the biggest joke of Silko's book is the ambiguity of its close, embodied in the observation of Sterling, who finally returns home from his exiled life as the gardener at Zeta's Tucson ranch. At the end of a book saturated with human brutalities, Sterling eyes the great stone snake near Mt. Taylor and reflects: "Burned and radioactive, with all humans dead, the earth would still be sacred. Man was too insignificant to desecrate her" (762). The joke, grim as it is, appears to be on the readers, who have followed "insignificant" human stories throughout an epic-length book. But readers—humans—are necessary to Silko's vision; as she points out in a recent interview, "humor is sacred. The world would become sterile and cold and die if there wasn't the clowning and the joking and the laughter" (qtd. in Perry 336). Yet even now there is a final twist, for the last words of the novel suggest that still more human violence will be required to restore the age-old balance of "death and laughter . . . side by side": "The snake was looking south, in the direction from which . . . the people would come" (763). These are Angelita's Poor People's Army, which is spilling over the Mexican border and will soon overrun the United States.

By simultaneously affirming and denying the value of human endurance, Silko's final, trickster-like note of ambiguity reinforces her work's apocalyptic uncertainty, calling attention to just how high the stakes are now for all humans, not just Native Americans. Her readers are left mulling over two choices—or perhaps *directions* is a better word. The first direction is homeward: Sterling's quiet retreat back to his family's sheep camp, where he reenacts the old people's ritual of giving food to the ants, who transport the prayers of the Indians to the earth.   The second direction leads to the clamorous world Sterling leaves behind when he gets out of Lecha's white Lincoln: the world of armies, blood, and Angelita's revolution. It is difficult not to read *Almanac of the Dead* as prophesy; even if one chooses the direction of home, the other still remains, insistent and threatening. Perhaps the least comforting yet most striking quality of Silko's work is its uncompromising vision—its representation of racial genocide spiraling into a warning about human extinction. Yet even in that warning, she demonstrates Native American cultural vitality, as she renews the traditions she has been heir to.

NOTES

1. Perhaps the best known of these surviving almanacs is the Quiche Mayan *Popul Voh: The Mayan Book of the Dawn of Life*, translated by Dennis Tedlock. See also Donna Perry's interview with Silko, especially 326–28.

2. Leslie Marmon Silko, *Almanac of the Dead* (New York: Penguin Books, 1992) 108. Subsequent quotations from this work are cited in the text.

3. See also Holland 342–43.

4. It is worth noting here that Silko creates the story of the Destroyers.

5. Telling also is that a passerby who sees the body reports finding "strange fruit" in the trees; here Silko evokes the Billie Holiday song, of the same title, that is about lynching.

6. Like many other destroyers, Trigg is sexually aroused by blood and death; as a homeless "donor" is unknowingly bled to death, Trigg performs fellatio on him. He also profits from death on a larger scale, harvesting hearts and skin from the hundreds of Mexicans killed weekly in civil uprisings (400).

7. As Laguna historian Joe Sando points out, the New Mexico mine supplied the Pueblos with jobs and matching funds for Laguna Industries, a company that has been awarded several government military contracts (153). Although Sando praises Laguna Industries' "practice of keeping politics out of the firm's operations" (153), there are alarmingly high instances of cancer and birth defects on Laguna land, and mining tailings retain 85 percent of the uranium's original radioactivity. In addition, the Environmental Protection Agency has found drinking water samples to contain radiation levels up to two hundred times the allowed amount (see Seyersted 12).

8. Tellingly mordant is Silko's observation that *Almanac of the Dead* is "my 763-page indictment for five hundred years of theft, murder, pillage, and rape. So is *Almanac* long? Sure, but federal indictments are long . . . [a]nd mine is a little more interesting reading" (qtd. in Perry 327).

9. See Coltelli 3, for example.

10. Pearce gives as examples of these works Lydia Maria Child's *Hobomok* (1824); the anonymous *The Christian Indian; or, Times of the First Settlers* (1825); Catherine Maria Sedgwick's *Hope Leslie; or, Early Times in Massachusetts* (1827); and Robert Strange's *Eoneguski; or, the Cherokee Chief* (1839). One might add Cooper's Leatherstocking Tales to the list.

11. These are the figures used in *Almanac of the Dead*. See also Chapman 12.

12. Hogan notes that not only whites have accepted this myth; she too once "thought of Indian people as vanishing," believing that "our stories and histories

were disappearing. . . . I got that idea from public education" (72). See also Allen, *Sacred Hoop* 267–68.

13. See Velie 133.

14. See also Holland 343.

15. El Feo and his twin brother, Tacho, represent the twin warrior gods, Maseway and Sheoyeway, whose guardianship the Pueblos were promised during "those times of conflict and danger that were to come" (Sando 24–25).

16. It might also be argued that Silko's use of *as* in this passage also indicates a trickster presence; the narrative suddenly seems to comment on itself both through this two-letter preposition, as well as by shifting its action from the simple past tense ("shouted an old woman") to the past perfect ("as a wisecracker . . . had put it"). Equally significant is that the shift in the text occurs precisely when a "wisecracker" *enters* the story.

17. I am reminded here of the bitter joke that closes Ozick's *The Shawl*, a joke that points to the madness caused by the Nazis' attempts at genocide.

18. See also, for example, Deloria.

19. See Bright and Babcock.

Chapter 8

Love, Sabotage, and the Missing Father: Exploring the Future

"We had all wanted the simplest thing, to love and be loved and be safe together," says Ruth Anne ("Bone") Boatwright in Dorothy Allison's powerful coming-of-age novel, *Bastard Out of Carolina*.[1] In a sense, she could be speaking for most of the characters in every work I have discussed. Yet it is what follows this realization—a moment of simultaneous maternal love and abandonment, reinforced with a legitimizing gesture of authorization for the protagonist-narrator—that offers an apt closing for my discussion. This maternally bestowed affirmation of identity recurs throughout the books examined in this study. *Bastard Out of Carolina* differs from the preceding texts in that it does not strictly revolve around a suppressed history. I have chosen to conclude with a brief look at Allison's novel, however, because it brings to the foreground at least two issues that all the other works share: the fraught relationships between mothers and children (primarily daughters), as well as the notable scarcity of fathers. While analyses of mothers in contemporary writing (including many of the works I have discussed) are far too numerous and exhaustive to detail here, the predominance of motherhood in literature that seeks to retrieve particularly violent histories is worth some attention. Taken together, these works imagine a paternal absence emphasized by a strong maternal presence, a peculiar imbalance that deliberately realigns narrative authority in the recuperation and retelling of suppressed stories. Equally important, they all acknowledge the necessity of abandoning—with however minute or grand a gesture, with an eye to either redemptive possibilities or irretrievable losses, or sometimes both—the usual role of victim.

In *Bastard Out of Carolina*, Anney Boatwright leaves her twelve-year-old daughter, Bone, for the husband who loves his wife "more than his soul" but who has just raped and beaten this child (37). Although she realizes that Anney is unable to live without her crazed husband, Bone nonetheless attains a peculiar state of peace and a confirmed sense of her own identity by leaning against her strong Aunt Raylene, "trusting her arm and her love. I was who I was going to be, someone like her, like Mama, a Boatwright woman" (309). In the book's closing words, the contours of her identity are shaped by the members of her tightly knit family and (particularly telling in this book) a legitimacy conferred by family name.

Boatwright is her mother's last name; her biological father vanished eight days after her birth, leaving her mother to do yearly battle with the courthouse officials who insist on stamping "illegitimate" on her daughter's birth certificate. Anney's last gift to her daughter is a clean slate: she hands her an unmarked birth certificate. Bone's mother is thus the agent who officially legitimizes her in the eyes of the outside world, just before leaving her with the reminder that "you're my baby girl, and I love you" (308). Love, abandonment, and authority: if Bone, instead of her mother, were setting out from her aunt's porch, she might, like Ruth Stone in *Housekeeping*, serve as a contemporary female version of the nineteenth- and twentieth-century questing hero. Her rootedness in familial identity is, of course, the point of Allison's closing image of Bone leaning against Raylene. But what of the mother who leaves her daughter for her terrifying husband? For the moment, I would like to move away from these particular characters, and instead look at the wrenching nature of Anney's *choice*—its uncompromising either-or quality. Such a decision emphasizes the price of relocating an authoritative historical voice.

In her 1985 study, *Gynesis*, Alice Jardine writes that within "traditional categories of thought, women can exist only as opposed to men" (63). At the risk of oversimplifying, these categories posit males as the ultimate arbiters of history and truth. The authorized father figure has "given the Western world its contours" and has been, at least until this century, its master storyteller (Jardine 80). Such an argument is by now commonplace in current feminism, as is the observation that recent women's writing can be said to recenter the authority of storytelling from the father to the mother. All of my selected books rely heavily, if not wholly, on mothers' (or daughters') narratives. Even the encyclopedic *Almanac of the Dead* returns sporadically to Seese's ongoing search for her kidnapped baby and depicts the powerful maternal influence of Lecha and Zeta's grandmother. Simultaneously, Ursa Corregidora, Denver and Beloved Suggs, Ruthie and Lucille Stone, and Bone Boatwright have no memory of their fathers, while Lecha and Zeta understand as very young girls that their largely absent father is spiritually empty and virtually dead.

Yet though mothers and their children hold center stage when telling their recovered histories, this restructuring of authority is neither smooth nor painless. Each novel contains a vacuum in place of a father, a space whose very hollowness draws attention to itself; no father or husband is left unmentioned or wholly unmourned. Ursa needs to learn about her father in order to cope with the endless chanting of her "mothers." And Zeta discovers a peculiar kinship to her pathologically detached father, a white mining engineer who, according to Zeta's grandmother, has been cursed with a deadening, hollow sensation from heart to throat as retribution for violating the earth. This might be the reason for *his* hollowness, but not for that of Zeta, who also feels "an empty space inside her rib cage, an absence" (Silko, *Almanac* 121). Halle Suggs's madness and subsequent disappearance are a significant part of the past Sethe tries to keep at bay. Ruthie's want of a father melts into her other wants, a loss that distances her still further from the world of warm kitchens and lighted windows. As Sylvie and Ruthie demonstrate, families need not be conventionally nuclear, but the families in much of current women's writing seem to be in flux. They are determinedly linked by female-to-female ties, while still glancing beyond the circle to the shadowy male figure who is cast out or removes himself. Despite its terrible stepfather, *Bastard Out of Carolina* best illustrates that the father's exclusion can be painful and also incomplete, as Dorothy Allison problematizes the refiguring of maternal and paternal authorities through a love story.

The shock of this text's conclusion is not that Anney Boatwright cannot choose between her husband and her child but that she can, despite what Aunt Raylene tells Bone: "No woman can stand to choose between her baby and her lover, between her child and her husband" (300). Daddy Glen Waddell, who cannot fathom his concurrent attraction to and repulsion for his stepdaughter, is at the same time deeply in love with his wife. And after her initial furious response to discovering him hunched over her daughter, Anney shows herself to love him just as much. Only moments later she cradles him, not her maimed daughter; Bone sees "his head pressed to her belly. His bloody hairline was visible past the angle of her hip. . . . I could see her fingers on Glen's shoulder, see the white knuckles holding him tight" (291). This oddly maternal image, bracketed by sexual violence, blood, and the anguished grip of white knuckles, reveals the difficulty of choosing between lover and child in a way that no other work discussed in this study does. Here, unlike every other mother I have discussed, Anney surrenders her maternal authority because she is unable to sever ties with her husband. To make a similar choice, notwithstanding her far less brutal circumstances, "just about killed" Raylene, the violence of whose words, as they are applied to Anney, seems especially apt by the novel's end. The visceral suffering of Anney's choice bespeaks the inherent agonies of not only telling these histories but also claiming the authority to do so.

Bone's authorization, a pivotal part of her coming of age as well as of the narrative as a whole, still celebrates the unity of kinship. Watching her mother disappear down the road, Bone turns to her obvious role model, a strong woman who lives by herself yet remains a central part of her family. She lets Raylene "touch my shoulder, let my head tilt to lean against her . . . I wrapped my fingers in Raylene's and watched the night close in around us" (309). *Beloved* and *Housekeeping* both end with forgotten ghosts; *Corregidora*, with a vehement shake; *The Shawl*, with what might be madness; *Almanac of the Dead*, with what might be an apocalyptic vision. Only *Bastard Out of Carolina* ends with an explicit maternal abandonment that nevertheless gives way to community and safety.

One could claim that, like the Boatwrights' story, the works discussed here all revolve around a wish for the "simplest thing, to love and be loved and be safe together" (307). But just how simple is that wish, and, more important, at what cost is it achieved, particularly in women's writing? By now, the association of women with a safe harbor of unconditional, maternal love has been so deeply challenged that it seems more mythic than actual. From the tragic reverberations of *Beloved*'s maternal protectiveness to the drugged stupor during which Seese's infant son is stolen from her in *Almanac of the Dead*, recent women's writing offers plenty of examples of *un*safe mothers. The complex bonds of motherhood itself are, in fact, just as likely to be made of barbed wire as heartstrings. Toni Morrison has said that *Beloved* illuminates a "persistent struggle" by black women to negotiate the equally imperious demands of survival and mothering: "The whole problem was trying to do two things: to love something bigger than yourself, to nurture something; and also not to sabotage yourself, not to murder yourself" ("Realm" 6). The distance between nurturing love and sabotage or murder, of oneself or one's child, can be collapsed in seconds, as in Sethe's case. It can also be navigated warily or half-unknowingly for years, as the mothers in *Corregidora* and *Bastard Out of Carolina* come to realize. But only two works deal with explicit, incomprehensible abandonment. Even Sethe's act of "too-thick" mother love discloses a kind of ferocious commitment that the mothers in *Housekeeping* and *Bastard Out of Carolina* are finally unable to make. And both these mothers disappear—one through suicide, the other down a dark road with a tortured man. In doing so, these mothers effectively remove themselves from historical time by dismissing the future, as represented by the lives of their children, and relinquishing the narrative authority to recuperate the past.

That authority, entangled as it is with the American theme of shedding old selves, has undergone rapid transformation in the last twenty years. Bharati Mukherjee has written that the

American protagonist as a pained, privileged, male Anglo-Saxon has been pushed to the periphery by the American as a mournful yuppie or a beer-drinking dead-ender, and these men in turn have had to make room for the American hero as aggrieved member of a minority group pressing a class action suit against the Founding Fathers. (12)

I am fully aware that many contemporary American women's novels might be classified as a series of such class action suits. For what other reason are these histories retrieved, if not to right an old wrong?   The danger of victimization politics is that they can be divisive and, finally, offputting to their potential audience. As Rose Kernochan notes in a 1996 review of Nina Vida's *Between Sisters*, a novel about repressed memory and child abuse: "A long line of suffering . . . forms a kind of Wailing Wall that threads through our culture, splitting us into factions: soft-eyed humanists and tough-minded conservatives." Kernochan closes her review by praising Vida's novel for its apparent message to survivors: "Get over it" (24). The impatience Kernochan displays in this review is by no means an isolated case and points to the urgency of finding new ways to remember and relate abusive, brutal histories. It is, I believe, the violence of such retrievals that transforms the potentially whining tone of aggrieved protagonists to a powerful, dangerous voice. The problematic relationship between grievances, victimhood, and art is certainly worthy of future exploration, not only in the fiction of Morrison, Jones, Robinson, Ozick, and Silko but also in Carolivia Herron's *Thereafter Johnnie* (1991) and the work of Sigrid Nunez (*A Feather on the Breath of God*) and Nina Vida, to give a very few examples. But for now I am more interested in the troubling crucible of violence within which contemporary North American women writers are attempting to purge their emerging artistry of those grievances.

When I first thought about this study, I kept returning to Audre Lorde's oft-quoted warning about not using the master's tools to dismantle the master's house. How could violence as wielded by women authors differ substantially from that wielded by men, beyond the generalized differences in power that male and female writers experience, and beyond the clear endeavor to undo the shopworn plot of female victim and male abuser? Much of the readers' uncertainty, and even discomfort, aroused by these books may stem in large part from the fact that this is, after all, *women*'s writing—and women are supposed to have a better alternative than violence, aren't they? So much feminist scholarship, particularly that which hinges upon the politics of linguistics, asserts this. Do women, then, have a different way of speaking and writing? Do they have a better method of resolving conflict? Is the wielding of violence in women's writing justified sheerly on the basis of need?   Such questions hover on the periphery of my previous readings, particularly regarding the discovery of beauty in the midst of violence. Furthermore, what are we to make of the incipient aesthetic pleasures provoked and imparted by these works?

Dorothy Allison takes that question beyond aesthetics and into the physical realm when she has her narrator masturbate to fantasies of sexual violence.   Like Gayl Jones, Allison uses sexuality as a basis for her explorations of the seductiveness of violence, as is clear in Bone's masturbatory fantasies:

> I imagined people watching while Daddy Glen beat me, though only when it was not happening. . . . Sometimes a whole group of them would be trapped into watching. They couldn't help or get away. . . . Those who watched admired me and hated him. I pictured it that way and put my hands between my legs. It was scary, but it was thrilling too. Those who watched me, loved me. It was as if I was being beaten for them. I was wonderful in their eyes. (112)

Bone carefully distinguishes her fantasies, which grow "more violent and more complicated" as her stepfather continues to beat her, from the actual abuse, which allows for "no heroism . . . just being beaten until I was covered with snot and misery" (112, 113). It is not difficult to identify the reader with those whose forced watching gives the "victim" pleasure. Perhaps at this moment in reading these works, it is this experience of discomfiture that matters most rather than one's attempts to analyze (and thereby on some level dispose of) it.

In *Bastard Out of Carolina*, Allison creates a brutal *kunstlerroman*, but ironically Bone never becomes the artist, the gospel singer, she longs to be. Not only is she a terrible singer, but she is merely trying on Christianity for size. It finally fails her, and she turns instead to family and her own strong self. Forsaking the futile dreams of performing musically, Bone instead fastens on "who I was going to be"—a woman who, like her mother, is strong, "desperate, determined, and ashamed" (309). Still, her calm, authoritative voice as narrator (or writer) firmly establishes her as a different kind of artist, since the book is generally read as autobiography. Of course, one can trace this motif of artistry most obviously in *Corregidora* and *The Shawl*, but what of *Beloved*? Sethe's domestic arts, Baby Suggs's search for color, and the consuming need to tell, to find a way to bear witness, can all be read as a search for art form. *Housekeeping* has the peculiar art of Edmund Foster, whose own way of seeing is passed on and embodied in Ruthie's bizarre visions. And certainly *Almanac of the Dead* explores the greater implications of art and violence.

Rage and abuse color more than Bone's explorations of her own sexuality. They also fuel her creativity (the gruesome and fascinating stories she tells her cousins) and fix the rules of the friendship she forges with the unfortunate Shannon Pearl, who "simply and completely hated everyone who had ever hurt her, and spent most of her time brooding on punishments either she or God would visit on them" (157–58). The closest Bone feels to Shannon is when the obese albino child reacts to those who show their disgust at her ugliness: "The hate in her face was terrible. For a moment I loved her with all my heart" (166). Such a passionate union of hatred and love underpins the urgency of all the works examined here.

The novels are linked by what they juxtapose: treatments of race and ethnicity, explorations of maternal authority, and reclamations of brutal history. In examining them, I have asked, What is it in *Beloved*, *Corregidora*,

Housekeeping, The Shawl, and *Almanac of the Dead* that maps out new territory for American women's writing? Like the works themselves, the answers are various: Toni Morrison locates a space for community as she probes the brutal rupturing of African American families in nineteenth-century America; Gayl Jones reclaims the possibility for desire in light of a history of sexual and racial abuse; Marilynne Robinson revises Western opposition to nature while exploring intersections of race, privilege, and homelessness; Cynthia Ozick grapples with an American Jew's injunction to remember the dead of the Holocaust, even in the face of public denial; and Leslie Marmon Silko traces the spiraling effects of greed, bloodthirstiness, and alienation on the living planet in a stark depiction of contemporary America. In giving a voice to the illiterate, the outcast, and the disenfranchised, each author exposes previously submerged layers of American history. That those layers also reveal a stunning foundation of violence says much about the cost of suppression and repression; violence not only constitutes these histories but also catalyzes their emergence.

By re-creating violence in their art, contemporary women writers acknowledge the force necessary to move between two frequently separate realms, the personal and the public, which are linked in the texts I discuss. The personal and the political weave across divisions between interior spaces of "myth, spirituality, and the transformation of subjective consciousness," and exterior spaces of national, racial, and political histories (Felski 128). The public and the private do not merge in these novels, but they meet—generally explosively. Morrison, Jones, Robinson, Ozick, and Silko create prisms through which to examine the inescapable violence in the personal and national histories they reclaim, ranging from lyricism to political empowerment, from subdued acceptance to a totalizing immersion that simultaneously represents a culture's suffering and foreshadows its possible future.

Strikingly, each book ends in an uncertain space between resolution and continued violence, asserting an ambiguity that refuses to downplay the brutality of the history revisited and revised. To call back the dead and to see the current repercussions of their lives and histories is to renounce a neat conclusion; nowhere is this more apparent than in *Almanac of the Dead,* the most recently published—and perhaps most daunting—of these works. *Almanac of the Dead* most strongly emphasizes the volatility of the present and the uncertainty of the future. Yet all the authors I have discussed share a conviction that inclusion of the historically dispossessed demands a violent undoing of their equally violent exclusion.

NOTE

1. Dorothy Allison, *Bastard Out of Carolina* (New York: Penguin Books, 1992) 307. Subsequent quotations from this work are cited in the text.

Works Cited

Accardo, Annalucia, and Alessandro Portelli. "A Spy in the Enemy's Country: Domestic Slaves as Internal Foes." Sollors and Diedrich 77–87.

Aldrich, Marcia. "The Poetics of Transience: Marilynne Robinson's *Housekeeping.*" *Essays in Literature* 16.1 (Spring 1989): 127–40.

Alexander, Edward. *The Resonance of Dust: Essays on Holocaust Literature and Jewish Fate.* Columbus: Ohio State UP, 1979.

Allen, Paula Gunn. Interview in Coltelli 11–39.

———. *The Sacred Hoop: Recovering the Feminine in American Indian Traditions.* Boston: Beacon, 1986.

Allison, Dorothy. *Bastard Out of Carolina.* New York: Dutton (Penguin Books USA Inc.), 1992.

Alvarez, A. "Flushed with Ideas." Bloom 52–56.

Ammons, Elizabeth. *Conflicting Stories: American Women Writers at the Turn into the Twentieth Century.* New York: Oxford UP, 1991.

———. "Stowe's Dream of the Mother-Savior: *Uncle Tom's Cabin* and American Women Writers Before the 1920s." Sundquist 181–86.

Anderson, Linda. "The Re-Imagining of History in Contemporary Women's Fiction." *Plotting Change: Contemporary Women's Fiction.* Ed. Linda Anderson. London: Edward Arnold, 1990. 129–41.

Andrews, William. *To Tell a Free Story: Toward a Poetics of Afro-American Autobiography, 1760–1785.* Urbana: U of Illinois P, 1986.

Angelo, Bonnie. "The Pain of Being Black." *Time* 22 May 1989: 120–22.

Armstrong, Nancy. "Why Daughters Die: The Racial Logic of American Sentimentalism." *Yale Journal of Criticism* 7.2 (Fall 1994): 1–24.

Armstrong, Nancy, and Leonard Tennenhouse. *The Imaginary Puritan: Literature, Intellectual Labor, and the Origins of Personal Life.* Berkeley: U of California P, 1992.

Babcock, Barbara. "'A Tolerated Margin of Mess': The Trickster and His Tales Reconsidered." *Critical Essays on Native American Literature.* Ed. Andrew Wiget. Boston: G. K. Hall & Co., 1985. 147–85.

Baker, Houston A., Jr. *Blues, Ideology and Afro-American Literature: A Vernacular Theory.* Chicago: U of Chicago P, 1984.

———. *Modernism and the Harlem Renaissance.* Chicago: U of Chicago P, 1987.

Bakhtin, Mikhail. *The Dialogic Imagination: Four Essays.* "Discourse in the Novel." Trans. Caryl Emerson and Michael Holquist. Ed. Michael Holquist. Austin: U of Texas P, 1981.

Baldwin, James. "Everybody's Protest Novel." *Notes of a Native Son.* Boston: Beacon, 1955. Rpt. in *Uncle Tom's Cabin.* By Harriet Beecher Stowe. Ed. Elizabeth Ammons. New York: Norton, 1994. 495–501.

Baym, Nina. *Woman's Fiction: A Guide to Novels by and about Women in America, 1820–1870.* Ithaca: Cornell UP, 1978.

Bellin, Joshua. "Up to Heaven's Gate, Down in Earth's Dust: The Politics of Judgment in *Uncle Tom's Cabin.*" *American Literature* 65.2 (June 1993): 275–95.

Bellow, Saul. *Mr. Sammler's Planet.* New York: Viking Press, 1970.

Bercovitch, Sacvan. *The American Jeremiad.* Madison: U of Wisconsin P, 1978.

———. *The Puritan Origins of the American Self.* New Haven: Yale UP, 1973.

Berger, Alan L. *Crisis and Covenant: The Holocaust in American Jewish Fiction.* Albany: State U of New York P, 1985.

Bernard, Jessie. *The Sex Game.* Englewood Cliffs, NJ: Prentice-Hall, 1968.

Berry, Wendell. *The Hidden Wound.* San Francisco: North Point P, 1989.

Bloom, Harold, ed. *Cynthia Ozick: Modern Critical Views.* New York: Chelsea, 1986.

Boelhower, William Q. *Through a Glass Darkly: Ethnic Semiosis in American Literature.* Venice: Edizioni Helvetia, 1984. New York: Oxford UP, 1987.

Booth, Alison. *Famous Last Words: Changes in Gender and Narrative Closure.* Charlottesville: UP of Virginia, 1993.

Bourne, Jenny. "Homelands of the Mind: Jewish Feminism and Identity Politics." *Race and Class* 29.1 (1987): 1–24.

Bowers, Susan. "*Beloved* and the New Apocalypse." *Journal of Ethnic Studies* 18.1 (Spring 1990): 62–64.

Bradstreet, Anne. *The Works of Anne Bradstreet.* Ed. Jeannine Hensley. Cambridge: Harvard UP, 1967.

Brandt, Ellen. "Anne Bradstreet: The Erotic Component in Puritan Poetry." *Women's Studies* 7 (1980): 39–53.

Braxton, Joanne M. "Ancestral Presence: The Outraged Mother Figure in Contemporary Afra-American Writing." *Wild Women in the Whirlwind: Afra-American Culture and the Contemporary Literary Renaissance.* Ed. Joanne M. Braxton and Andrée Nicola McLaughlin. New Brunswick: Rutgers UP, 1990. 300–315.

Breitweiser, Mitchell Robert. *American Puritanism and the Defense of Mourning: Religion, Grief, and Ethnology in Mary White Rowlandson's Captivity Narrative.* Madison: U of Wisconsin P, 1990.

Brenkman, John. "Multiculturalism and Criticism." *English Inside and Out.* Ed. Susan Gubar and Jonathan Kamholtz. New York: Routledge, 1993. 87–101.

Bright, William. "The Natural History of Old Man Coyote." *Recovering the Word: Essays on Native American Literature.* Ed. Brian Swann and Arnold Krupat. Berkeley: U of California P, 1987. 339–87.

Brooke-Rose, Christine. "Woman as Semiotic Object." Suleiman 305–16.

Burstein, Janet Handler. "Cynthia Ozick and the Transgressions of Art." *American Literature* 59.1 (March 1987): 85–101.

Byerman, Keith. *Fingering the Jagged Grain: Tradition and Form in Recent Black Fiction.* Athens: U of Georgia P, 1985.

Caldwell, Patricia. "Why Our First Poet Was a Woman: Bradstreet and the Birth of an American Poetic Voice." *Prospects: An Annual Journal of American Cultural Studies* 13 (1988): 1–35.

Carby, Hazel. *Reconstructing Womanhood: The Emergence of the Afro-American Woman Novelist.* New York: Oxford UP, 1987.

———. "White Women Listen! Black Feminism and the Boundaries of Sisterhood." *The Empire Strikes Back: Race and Racism in 70's Britain.* Educational Center for Contemporary Cultural Studies. London: Hutchinson, 1982. 212–35.

Carlin, Deborah. *Cather, Canon, and the Politics of Reading.* Amherst: U of Massachusetts P, 1992.

Castiglia, Christopher. *Bound and Determined: Captivity, Culture-Crossing, and White Womanhood from Mary Rowlandson to Patty Hearst.* Chicago: U of Chicago P, 1996.

Cather, Willa. "Books and Magazines." *Leader* April 8, 1898: 11.

———. *My Ántonia.* 1918. New York: Dover, 1994.

———. *Not Under Forty.* New York: Knopf, 1936.

———. *O Pioneers!* 1913. New York: Dover, 1993.

Champagne, Rosaria. "Women's History and *Housekeeping*: Memory, Representation and Reinscription." *Women's Studies* 20.3–4 (1992): 321–29.

Chapman, Abraham, ed. *Literature of the American Indians: Views and Interpretations: A Gathering of Indian Memories, Symbolic Contexts, and Literary Criticism.* New York: New American Library, 1975.

Christian, Barbara. *Black Feminist Criticism: Perspectives on Black Women Writers.* New York: Pergamon, 1985.

———. "The Race for Theory." *Gender and Theory: Dialogues on Feminist Criticism.* Ed. Linda Kauffman. New York: Basil Blackwell, 1989. 225–37.

Cixous, Hélène. "The Laugh of the Medusa." *Signs* 1.4 (Summer 1976): 875–93. Rpt. in *Critical Theory Since 1965.* Ed. Hazard Adams and Leroy Searle. Tallahassee: Florida State UP, 1986. 309–20.

Clarke, Cheryl. "The Failure to Transform: Homophobia in the Black Community." *Home Girls: A Black Feminist Anthology.* Ed. Barbara Smith. New York: Kitchen Table, 1983. 197–208.

Clément, Catherine, and Hélène Cixous. *La Jeune Née (The Newly Born Woman).* Trans. Betsy Wing. Minneapolis: U of Minnesota P, 1986.

Cohen, Arthur. *The Tremendum: A Theological Interpretation of the Holocaust.* New York: Crossroad, 1981.

Collins, Patricia Hill. *Black Feminist Thought: Knowledge, Consciousness and the Politics of Empowerment.* Boston: Unwin Hyman, 1990.

Coltelli, Laura. *Winged Words: American Indian Writers Speak.* Lincoln: U of Nebraska P, 1990.

Combahee River Collective. "A Black Feminist Statement." *This Bridge Called My Back: Writings of Radical Women of Color.* Ed. Gloria Anzaldúa and Cherríe Moraga. New York: Kitchen Table, 1983. 210–18.

Cooke, Michael G. *Afro-American Literature in the Twentieth Century: The Achievement of Intimacy.* New Haven: Yale UP, 1984.

Cott, Nancy F. *The Bonds of Womanhood: "Woman's Sphere" in New England, 1780–1835.* New Haven: Yale UP, 1977.

Courier, 28 September 1895: 8. Rpt. in Slote 281–82.

Cox, Oliver Cromwell. *Caste, Class, and Race: A Study in Social Dynamics.* 1976. Garden City, NY: Doubleday, 1948.

Davis, Cynthia. "Speaking the Body's Pain: Harriet Wilson's *Our Nig.*" *African American Review* 27.3 (1993): 391–403.

Davis, Margaret H. "Mary White Rowlandson's Self-Fashioning as Puritan Goodwife." *Early American Literature* 27.1 (1992): 49–60.

de Crèvecoeur, J. Hector St. John. *Letters from an American Farmer.* London, 1782. New York: Albert Boni and Charles Boni, 1925.

Dehler, Kathleen. "The Need to Tell All: A Comparison of Historical and Modern Feminist 'Confessional' Writing." *Feminist Criticism: Essays on Theory, Poetry, and Prose.* Ed. Cheryl L. Brown and Karen Olson. Metuchen, NJ: Scarecrow, 1978. 339–52.

de Lauretis, Teresa, ed. *Feminist Studies/Critical Studies.* Bloomington: Indiana UP, 1986.

Deloria, Vine. "Indian Humor." Chapman 152–69.

Derounian, Kathryn Zabelle. "The Publication, Promotion, and Distribution of Mary Rowlandson's Indian Captivity Narrative in the Seventeenth Century." *Early American Literature* 23.3 (1988): 239–61.

Dickinson, Emily. Poem # 1129: "Tell All the Truth but tell it slant—" *The Poems of Emily Dickinson.* Ed. Thomas H. Johnson. Cambridge: Belknap P of Harvard UP, 1983.

Dietrich, Deborah J. "Mary Rowlandson's Great Declension." *Women's Studies* 24.5 (1995): 427–39.

Dillard, Annie. *Pilgrim at Tinker Creek.* 1974. New York: Bantam, 1981.

Dixon, Melvin. "Singing a Deep Song: Language as Evidence in the Novels of Gayl Jones." Evans 236–48.

Doriani, Beth Maclay. "Black Womanhood in Nineteenth-Century America: Subversion and Self-Construction in Two Women's Autobiographies." *American Quarterly* 43.2 (June 1991): 199–222.

Doueihi, Anne. "Inhabiting the Space between Discourse and Story in Trickster Narratives." Hynes and Doty 193–201.

Douglas, Ann. *The Feminization of American Culture.* New York: Knopf, 1977.

Drinnon, Richard. *Facing West: The Metaphysics of Indian-Hating and Empire-Building.* Minneapolis: U of Minnesota P, 1980.

Eberwein, Jane D. "Civil War and Bradstreet's 'Monarchies.'" *Early American Literature* 26.2 (1991): 119–44.

Elias, Amy J. "Puttermesser and Pygmalion." *Studies in American Jewish Literature* 6 (Fall 1987): 64–74.

Epstein, Leslie. "Stories and Something Else." Bloom 47–51.

Erickson, Darlene E. "Toni Morrison: The Black Search for Place in America." *Dolphin* 20 (Spring 1991): 45–54.

Evans, Mari, ed. *Black Women Writers (1950–1980): A Critical Evaluation.* Garden City, NY: Anchor/Doubleday, 1984.

Fackenheim, Emil. *The Jewish Return into History.* New York: Schocken Books, 1978.

Fein, Helen. *Accounting for Genocide: National Responses and Jewish Victimization During the Holocaust.* New York: The Free Press, 1979.

Felman, Shoshona, and Dori Laub. *Testimony: Crises of Witnessing in Literature, Psychoanalysis, and History.* New York: Routledge, 1992.

Felski, Rita. *Beyond Feminist Aesthetics: Feminist Literature and Social Change.* Cambridge: Harvard UP, 1989.

Fetterley, Judith. "*My Ántonia,* Jim Burden, and the Dilemma of the Lesbian Writer." *Lesbian Texts and Contexts:Radical Revisions.* Ed. Karla Jay, Joanne Glasgow, and Catherine R. Stimpson. New York: New York UP, 1990.

Fields, Karen E. "To Embrace Dead Strangers: Toni Morrison's *Beloved.*" Pearlman 159–69.

Finney, Brian. "Temporal Defamiliarization in Toni Morrison's *Beloved.*" *Obsidian II* 5.1 (Spring 1990): 20–36.

Fischer, Mike. "Pastoralism and Its Discontents: Willa Cather and the Burden of Imperialism." *Mosaic* 23.1 (Winter 1990): 31–44.

Fisher, Dexter. "Stories and Their Tellers: A Conversation with Leslie Marmon Silko." *Third Woman: Minority Women Writers of the United States.* Ed. Dexter Fisher. Boston: Houghton Mifflin, 1980. 18–23.

Fitzgerald, Jennifer. "Selfhood and Community: Psychoanalysis and Discourse in *Beloved.*" *Modern Fiction Studies* 39.3, 4 (Fall/Winter 1993): 669–87.

Fitzpatrick, Tara. "The Figure of Captivity: The Cultural Work of the Puritan Captivity Narrative." *American Literary History* 3 (1991): 1–26.

Fleenor, Juliann Evans. "The Gothic Prism: Charlotte Perkins Gilman's Gothic Stories and Her Autobiography." *The Female Gothic.* Ed. Juliann Evans Fleenor. Montreal: Eden, 1983. 227–41.

Florby, Gunilla. "Escaping This World: Marilynne Robinson's Variation on an Old American Motif." *Moderna Sprak* 78.3 (1984): 211–16.

Foster, Frances. "Adding Color and Contour to Early American Self-Portraitures: Autobiographical Writings of Afro-American Women." Pryse and Spillers 25–38.

Foster, Thomas. "History, Critical Theory, and Women's Social Practices: 'Women's Time' and *Housekeeping.*" *Signs* 14.1 (Autumn 1988): 73–99.

Fox-Genovese, Elizabeth. *Feminism Without Illusions: A Critique of Individualism.* Chapel Hill: U of North Carolina P, 1991.

———. "To Write My Self: The Autobiographies of Afro-American Women." *Feminist Issues in Literary Scholarship.* Ed. Shari Benstock. Bloomington: Indiana UP, 1987.

———. *Within the Plantation Household: Black and White Women of the Old South.* Chapel Hill: U of North Carolina P, 1988.

Frankenberg, Ruth. *White Women, Race Matters: The Social Construction of Whiteness.* Minneapolis: U of Minnesota P, 1993.

Friedman, Lawrence S. *Understanding Cynthia Ozick.* Columbia: U of South Carolina P, 1991.

Fryer, Judith. *Felicitous Space: The Imaginative Structures of Edith Wharton and Willa Cather.* Chapel Hill: U of North Carolina P, 1986.

Fuss, Diana. *Essentially Speaking: Feminism, Nature, and Difference.* New York: Routledge, 1989.

Fussell, Paul. *The Great War and Modern Memory.* New York: Oxford UP, 1975.

Garraty, John A., and Peter Gay. *The Columbia History of the World.* 1972. New York: Harper & Row, 1987.

Gates, Henry Louis, Jr. "Beyond the Culture Wars: Identities in Dialogue." *Profession* (1993): 6–11.

———, ed. *Black Literature and Literary Theory.* New York: Methuen, 1984.

———. "The Blackness of Blackness: A Critique on the Sign and the Signifying Monkey." *Figures in Black: Words, Signs, and the "Racial" Self.* Ed. Henry Louis Gates, Jr. New York: Oxford UP, 1987. 235–76.

———. "Foreword: In Her Own Write." *The Collected Works of Phillis Wheatley.* The Schomburg Library of Nineteenth-Century Black Women Writers. New York: Oxford UP, 1988.

———, ed. *"Race," Writing, and Difference.* Chicago: U of Chicago P, 1986.

———, ed. *Reading Black, Reading Feminist: A Critical Anthology.* New York: Meridian, 1990.

———. *The Signifying Monkey: A Theory of African-American Literary Criticism.* New York: Oxford UP, 1988.

Gelfant, Blanche. "The Forgotten Reaping-Hook: Sex in *My Ántonia.*" *American Literature* 43 (March 1971): 60–72. Rpt. in *Critical Essays on Willa Cather.* Ed. John J. Murphy. Boston: G. K. Hall, 1984. 147–64.

Giddings, Paula. *When and Where I Enter: The Impact of Black Women on Race and Sex in America.* New York: William Morrow, 1984.

Gilbert, Sandra, and Susan Gubar. *The Madwoman in the Attic: The Woman Writer and the Nineteenth Century Literary Imagination.* New Haven: Yale UP, 1979.

———, eds. *The Norton Anthology of Literature by Women: The Tradition in English.* New York: Norton, 1985.

Gilman, Charlotte Perkins. 1915. *Herland.* New York: Pantheon Books, 1979.

———. *The Home: Its Work and Influence.* New York: McClure, Phillips, 1903.

———. "Immigration, Importation, and Our Fathers." *Forerunner* 5 (May 1914).

———. *The Living of Charlotte Perkins Gilman: An Autobiography.* New York: D. Appleton-Century, Co., 1935.

———. *Women and Economics: A Study of the Economic Relation Between Men and Women.* 1898. Amherst, N.Y.: Prometheus Books, 1994.

———. "The Yellow Wallpaper." 1892. New York: The Feminist Press, 1973.

Gilroy, Paul. "Living Memory: Meeting Toni Morrison." *The Black Atlantic: Modernity and Double Consciousness.* London: Verso, 1993.

Goldman, Anne E. "'I Made the Ink': (Literary) Production and Reproduction in *Dessa Rose* and *Beloved.*" *Feminist Studies* 16.2 (Summer 1990): 313–30.

Gordon, Linda. "What's New in Women's History." de Lauretis 20–30.

Greenblatt, Stephen. "Kindly Visions." *New Yorker* 11 October 1993: 112–20.

Greene, Gayle, and Coppelia Kahn, eds. *Making a Difference: Feminist Literary Theory.* New York: Methuen, 1985.

Greenstein, Michael. "The Muse and the Messiah: Cynthia Ozick's Aesthetics." *Studies in American Jewish Literature* 8.1 (Spring 1989): 50–65.

———. "Ozick, Roth, and Postmodernism." *Studies in American Jewish Literature* 10.1 (Spring 1991): 54–64.

Gwin, Minrose. "Green-Eyed Monsters of the Slavocracy: Jealous Mistresses in Two Slave Narratives." Pryse and Spillers 39–52.

Halttunen, Karen. "Gothic Imagination and Social Reform: The Haunted House of Lyman Beecher, Henry Ward Beecher, and Harriet Beecher Stowe." Sundquist 107–34.

Hammond, Jeffrey. *Sinful Self, Saintly Self: The Puritan Experience of Poetry.* Athens: U of Georgia P, 1993.

Handlin, Oscar. *The Uprooted: The Epic Story of the Great Migrations that Made the American People.* Boston: Little, Brown, 1951.

Harap, Louis. "The Religious Art of Cynthia Ozick." *Judaism* 33.1 (Summer 1984): 353–63.

Harding, Sandra. *Whose Science? Whose Knowledge? Thinking From Women's Lives*. Ithaca: Cornell UP, 1991.

Harper, Michael S. "Gayl Jones: An Interview." *Massachusetts Review* 18.4 (Winter 1977): 692–715.

Harper, Michael S., and Robert B. Stepto, eds. *Chant of Saints: A Gathering of Afro-American Literature, Art, and Scholarship*. Urbana: U of Illinois P, 1979.

Harris, Janice. "Gayl Jones's *Corregidora*." *Frontiers* 5.3 (Fall 1981): 1–5.

Harris, Trudier. *Fiction and Folklore: The Novels of Toni Morrison*. Knoxville: U of Tennessee P, 1991.

Hedges, Elaine R. Afterword. "The Yellow Wallpaper." By Charlotte Perkins Gilman. 1899. New York: The Feminist Press, 1973. 37–63.

Heinemann, Marlene E. *Gender and Destiny: Women Writers and the Holocaust*. Contributions in Women's Studies. 72. Westport, CT: Greenwood, 1986.

Heller, Dana A. *The Feminization of Quest Romance*. Austin: U of Texas P, 1990.

Henderson, Mae Gwendolyn. "Speaking in Tongues: Dialogics, Dialectics, and the Black Woman Writer's Literary Tradition." Gates, *Reading Black* 116–42.

———. "Toni Morrison's *Beloved*: Re-Membering the Body as Historical Text." Spillers, *Comparative American Identities* 62–86.

Hennessy, C. Margot. "Earning It: Black Women and White Women Coming Together at the Side of the River." American Women Writers of Color Conference. Salisbury State University, Maryland. October 1992.

Hennessy, Rosemary. *Materialist Feminism and the Politics of Discourse*. New York: Routledge, 1993.

Herron, Carolivia. *Thereafter Johnnie*. New York: Random House, 1991.

Hess, Rudolf. *Commandant of Auschwitz*. Trans. C. FitzGibbon. Cleveland: World Publishing Co., 1960.

Hills, L. Rust. *Writing in General and the Short Story in Particular: An Informal Textbook*. Boston: Houghton Mifflin, 1987.

Hirsch, Marianne. "Maternal Narratives: 'Cruel Enough to Stop the Blood.'" Gates, *Reading Black* 415–30.

Hogan, Linda. Interview in Coltelli 71–86.

Holland, Sharon. "'If You Know I Have a History, You Will Respect Me': A Perspective on Afro-Native American Literature." *Callaloo* 17.1 (Winter 1994): 334–50.

Holloway, Karla C. "*Beloved*: A Spiritual." *Callaloo* 13.3 (Summer 1990): 516–25.

———. *Moorings and Metaphors: Figures of Culture and Gender in Black Women's Literature*. New Brunswick: Rutgers UP, 1992.

Horvitz, Deborah. "Nameless Ghosts: Possession and Dispossession in *Beloved*." *Studies in American Fiction* 17.2 (Autumn 1989): 157–67.

House, Elizabeth B. "Toni Morrison's Ghost: The Beloved Who Is Not Beloved." *Studies in American Fiction* 18.1 (Spring 1990): 17–26.

Howe, Susan. *The Birth-mark: Unsettling the Wilderness in American Literary History*. Hanover: UP of New England for Wesleyan UP, 1991.

Hubbard, Susan. "Sexing the Writer: Gender Stereotypes in the Writing Workshop." Conference of the Organization for the Study of Communication, Language and Gender. Monterey, California. October 1996.

Hurston, Zora Neale. *Their Eyes Were Watching God.* 1937. Urbana: U of
   Illinois P, 1978.
Hyman, Rebecca. "Women as Figures of Exchange in Gayl Jones's *Corregidora.*"
   Xanadu 14 (1991): 40–51.
Hynes, William J., and William G. Doty, eds. *Mythical Trickster Figures:
   Contours, Contexts, and Criticisms.* Tuscaloosa: U of Alabama P, 1993.
Irigaray, Luce. *Ce sexe qui n'en est pas un.* Trans. Catherine Porter with Carolyn
   Burke. Ithaca, New York: Cornell UP, 1985.
———. *Speculum de l'autre femme.* Trans. Gillian C. Gill. Ithaca, New York:
   Cornell UP, 1985.
Jackson, Shirley. *The Lottery.* New York: Farrar, Straus, & Giroux, 1949.
Jacobs, Harriet. *Incidents in the Life of a Slave Girl.* 1861. The Schomburg
   Library of Nineteenth-Century Black Women Writers. New York: Oxford UP,
   1988.
———. *Incidents in the Life of a Slave Girl Written by Herself.* 1861. Ed. Jean
   Fagan Yellin. Cambridge: Harvard UP, 1987.
Jaggar, Alison M., and Susan R. Bordo, eds. *Gender/Body/Knowledge: Feminist
   Reconstructions of Being and Knowing.* New Brunswick, NJ: Rutgers UP,
   1989.
Jardine, Alice. *Gynesis: Configurations of Woman and Modernity.* Ithaca: Cornell
   UP, 1985.
Jenkins, Jennifer. "Failed Mothers and Fallen Houses: The Crisis of Domesticity
   in *Uncle Tom's Cabin.*" *ESQ* 38.2 (1992): 161–87.
Jones, Gayl. "About My Work." Evans 233–35.
———. *Corregidora.* Boston: Beacon, 1975.
———. *Liberating Voices: Oral Tradition in African American Literature.*
   Cambridge: Harvard UP, 1991.
Jones, Jacqueline. *Labor of Love, Labor of Sorrow: Black Women, Work and the
   Family from Slavery to the Present.* New York: Vintage Books, 1985.
Kaplan, Carla. "Narrative Contracts and Emancipatory Readers: *Incidents in the
   Life of a Slave Girl.*" *Yale Journal of Criticism* 6.1 (Spring 1993): 93–120.
Kauvar, Elaine. "Courier for the Past: Cynthia Ozick and Photography." *Studies
   in American Jewish Literature* 6 (Fall 1987): 129–44.
———. *Cynthia Ozick's Fiction: Tradition and Invention.* Bloomington: Indiana
   UP, 1993.
———. "The Dread of Moloch: Idolatry as Metaphor in Cynthia Ozick's
   Fiction." *Studies in American Jewish Literature* 6 (Fall 1987): 111–28.
———. "Ozick's Book of Creation." Bloom 145–57.
Kaye, Frances W. *Isolation and Masquerade: Willa Cather's Women.* New
   York: Peter Lang, 1992.
Keenan, Sally. "'Four Hundred Years of Silence': Myth, History, and
   Motherhood in Toni Morrison's *Beloved.*" J. White 45–81.
Kelly, Joan. *Women, History, and Theory: The Essays of Joan Kelly.* Chicago: U
   of Chicago P, 1984.
Kennard, Jean E. "Convention Coverage or How to Read Your Own Life." *New
   Literary History* 13 (Autumn 1981): 69–88. Rpt. in *Charlotte Perkins Gilman:
   The Woman and Her Work.* Ed. Sheryl L. Meyering. Ann Arbor: University
   Microfilms International Research, 1989. 75–93.
Kernochan, Rose. "Repressed Memory: Review of Nina Vida's *Between Sisters.*"
   New York Times Book Review 12 May 1996: 24.

Kibbey, Ann. *The Interpretation of Material Shapes in Puritanism: A Study of Rhetoric, Prejudice, and Violence.* Cambridge: Cambridge UP, 1986.

Kincaid, James. "Who Gets to Tell Their Stories?" *New York Times Book Review* 3 May 1992: 1+.

Kirkby, Joan. "Is There Life After Art? The Metaphysics of Marilynne Robinson's *Housekeeping.*" *Tulsa Studies in Women's Literature* 5.1 (Spring 1986): 91–109.

Kolodny, Annette. *The Land Before Her: Fantasy and Experience of the American Frontiers, 1630–1860.* Chapel Hill: U of North Carolina P, 1984.

———. *The Lay of the Land: Metaphor as Experience and History in American Life and Letters.* Chapel Hill: U of North Carolina P, 1975.

———. "A Map for Rereading: Or, Gender and the Interpretation of Literary Texts." *New Literary History* 11.3 (Spring 1980): 451–67.

Kopacz, Paula. "'To Finish What's Begun': Anne Bradstreet's Last Words." *Early American Literature* 23.2 (1988): 175–87.

Kremer, S. Lillian. *Witness Through the Imagination: Jewish American Holocaust Literature.* Detroit: Wayne State UP, 1989.

Kristeva, Julia. "Stabat Mater." Suleiman 99–118.

Krupat, Arnold. *The Voice in the Margin: Native American Literature and the Canon.* Berkeley: U of California P, 1989.

Kubitschek, Missy Dehn. *Claiming the Heritage: African American Women Novelists and History.* Jackson: U of Mississippi P, 1991.

Lakoff, Robin. *Language and Woman's Place.* New York: Harper & Row, 1975.

Lang, Amy Schrager. *Prophetic Woman: Anne Hutchinson and the Problem of Dissent in the Literature of New England.* Berkeley, U of California P, 1987.

Lanser, Susan S. "Feminist Criticism, 'The Yellow Wallpaper,' and the Politics of Color in America." *Feminist Studies* 15.3 (Fall 1989): 415–41.

Lanzmann, Claude. "Seminar on *Shoah.*" *Yale French Studies* 79 (1991): 82–99.

Larsen, Nella. *Passing.* 1929. New Brunswick: Rutgers UP, 1986.

———. *Quicksand.* 1928. New Brunswick: Rutgers UP, 1986.

Lassner, Phyliss. "Escaping the Mirror of Sameness: Marilynne Robinson's *Housekeeping.*" Pearlman 49–58.

Lindemann, Marilee. "'This Woman Can Cross Any Line': Power and Authority in Contemporary Women's Fiction." *Engendering the Word: Feminist Essays in Psychosexual Poetics.* Ed. Temma F. Berg et al. Urbana: U of Illinois P, 1989. 105–21.

Logan, Lisa. "Mary Rowlandson's Captivity and the 'Place' of the Woman Subject." *Early American Literature* 28.3 (1993): 255–77.

Lorde, Audre. "Coal." *Undersong: Chosen Poems Old and New.* New York: Norton, 1973.

Lutz, Catherine A. and Jane L. Collins. *Reading National Geographic.* Chicago: U of Chicago P, 1993.

Lyons, Bonnie. "Cynthia Ozick as a Jewish Writer." *Studies in American Jewish Literature* 6 (Fall 1987): 13–25.

Makarius, Laura. "The Myth of the Trickster: The Necessary Breaker of Taboos." Hynes and Doty 66–86.

Mallon, Anne-Marie. "Sojourning Women: Homelessness and Transcendence in *Housekeeping.*" *Critique* 30.2 (Winter 1989): 95–105.

Maranto, Gina. "Storyteller: Leslie Marmon Silko Writes Stories of the Land." *Amicus Journal* (Winter 1993): 16–18.

Martin, Biddy, and Chandra Talpade Mohanty. "Feminist Politics: What's Home

Got to Do with It?" de Lauretis 191–212.

Martin, Jacky. "From Division to Sacrificial Reconciliation in Toni Morrison's Novels." *Obsidian II* 5.2 (Summer 1990): 80–99.

Martin, Margot. "The Theme of Survival in Cynthia Ozick's 'The Shawl.'" *RE: Artes Liberales* 14.1 (Fall/Spring 1988): 31–36.

Marx, Leo. *The Machine in the Garden*. New York: Oxford UP, 1964.

Mather, Increase. *Brief History of the WARR With the INDIANS in New England*, in *So Dreadfull a Judgment: Puritan Responses to King Philip's War, 1676–1677*. Ed. Richard Slotkin and James K. Folsom. Middletown, CT: Wesleyan UP, 1978.

Mathieson, Barbara Offutt. "Memory and Mother Love in Morrison's *Beloved*." *American Imago* 47.1 (Spring 1990): 1–21.

McConnell-Ginet, Sally, Ruth Borker, and Nelly Furman. *Women and Language in Literature and Society*. New York: Praeger, 1980.

McCullough, Kate. "Slavery, Sexuality, and Genre: Pauline Hopkins and the Representation of Female Desire." *The Unruly Voice: Rediscovering Pauline Elizabeth Hopkins*. Ed. John Cullen Gruesser. Urbana: U of Illinois P, 1996. 21–49.

McDowell, Deborah. "New Directions for Black Feminist Criticism." *The New Feminist Literary Criticism: Essays on Women, Literature, Theory*. Ed. Elaine Showalter. New York: Pantheon, 1985. 186–99.

McKay, Nellie. "The Girls Who Became the Women: Childhood Memories in the Autobiographies of Harriet Jacobs, Mary Church Terrell, and Anne Moody." *Tradition and the Talents of Women*. Ed. Florence Howe. Urbana: U of Illinois P, 1991. 105–24.

Meese, Elizabeth A. *Crossing the Double-Cross: The Practice of Feminist Criticism*. Chapel Hill: U of North Carolina P, 1986.

———. *(Ex)tensions: Refiguring Feminist Criticism*. Urbana: U of Illinois P, 1990.

Merchant, Carolyn. *The Death of Nature: Women, Ecology and the Scientific Revolution*. London: Wildwood House, 1980.

Michaels, Walter Benn. "'You who never was there': Slavery and the New Historicism, Deconstruction and the Holocaust." *Narrative* 4.1 (January 1996): 1–16.

Mile, Siân. "Femme Foetal: The Construction/Destruction of Female Subjectivity in *Housekeeping*, or Nothing Gained." *Genders* 8 (Summer 1990): 129–36.

Miller, Perry. *Errand into the Wilderness*. Cambridge: Belknap P of Harvard UP, 1956.

———. *The New England Mind: The Seventeenth Century*. Cambridge: Harvard UP, 1954.

Moi, Toril. *Sexual/Textual Politics: Feminist Literary Theory*. New York: Methuen, 1985.

Moraga, Cherríe. "From a Long Line of Vendidas: Chicanas and Feminism." de Lauretis. 173–90.

Morgan, Edmund S. *Visible Saints: The History of a Puritan Idea*. 1963. Ithaca: Cornell UP, 1965.

Morgan, Winifred. "Gender-Related Difference in the Slave Narratives of Harriet Jacobs and Frederick Douglass." *American Studies* 35.2 (Fall 1994): 73–94.

Morrison, Toni. *Beloved*. New York: Penguin, 1988.

———. "In the Realm of Responsibility: A Conversation with Toni Morrison." With Marsha Darling. *Women's Review of Books* 5. 6 (March 1988): 5–6.

———. "'Intimate Things in Place': A Conversation with Toni Morrison." *Chant of*

Saints: A Gathering of Afro-American Literature, Art and Scholarship. Ed.
Michael S. Harper and Robert B. Stepto. Urbana: U of Illinois P, 1979. 213–
29.

———. "Unspeakable Things Unspoken: The Afro-American Presence in
American Literature." *Michigan Quarterly Review* 28.1 (Winter 1989):
1–34.

Mukherjee, Bharati. "A Buddha Among the Hummels: Review of Sigrid Nunez's
A Feather on the Breath of God." *New York Times Book Review* 8 January
1995: 12.

Newton, Judith L., and Deborah Rosenfelt, eds. *Feminist Criticism and Social
Change: Sex, Class and Race in Literature and Culture.* New York: Methuen,
1985.

Nielsen, Aldon L. *Writing Between the Lines: Race and Intertextuality.* Athens: U of
Georgia P, 1994.

Nudelman, Fanny. "Harriet Jacobs and the Sentimental Politics of Female Suffering."
English Literary History 59.4 (1992): 939–64.

Nunez, Sigrid. *A Feather on the Breath of God.* New York: HarperCollins, 1995.

O'Brien, Mary. *Reproducing the World: Essays in Feminist Theory.* Boulder:
Westview, 1989.

O'Brien, Sharon. *Willa Cather: The Emerging Voice.* New York: Oxford UP,
1987.

Omolade, Barbara. "Hearts of Darkness." *Desire: the Politics of Sexuality.* Ed.
Ann Snitow, Christine Stansell, and Sharon Thompson. New York:
Monthly Review Press, 1983. 350–67.

Otten, Terry. *The Crime of Innocence in the Fiction of Toni Morrison.* Literary
Frontiers Edition. 33. Columbia: U of Missouri P, 1989.

Ozick, Cynthia. *Art & Ardor: Essays.* New York: Knopf, 1983.

———. *Bloodshed and Three Novellas.* New York: Knopf, 1976.

———. *The Messiah of Stockholm.* New York: Knopf, 1987.

———. *The Shawl.* New York: Knopf, 1989.

———. "What Literature Means." *Partisan Review* 49.2 (1982): 294–97.

Pearce, Roy Harvey. *Savagism and Civilization: A Study of the Indian and the
American Mind.* 1953. Baltimore: Johns Hopkins UP, 1965.

———. "The Significances of the Captivity Narrative." *American Literature* 19
(1947): 1–20.

Pearlman, Mickey, ed. *Mother Puzzles: Daughters and Mothers in Contemporary
American Literature.* Westport, CT: Greenwood, 1989.

Pérez-Torres, Rafael. "Knitting and Knotting the Narrative Thread—*Beloved* as
Postmodern Novel." *Modern Fiction Studies* 39.3, 4 (Fall/Winter 1993): 689–
707.

Perry, Donna. *Backtalk: Women Writers Speak Out.* New Brunswick: Rutgers
UP, 1993.

Peterman, Michael. "Kindling the Imagination: The Inset Stories of *My Ántonia.*"
Rosowski, *Approaches to Teaching* 156–62.

Phelan, James. "Toward a Rhetorical Reader-Response Criticism: The Difficult, the
Stubborn, and the Ending of *Beloved.*" *Modern Fiction Studies* 39.3, 4
(Fall/Winter 1993): 709–28.

Pifer, Ellen. "Invention and Orthodoxy." Rainwater and Scheick 89–106.

Pinsker, Sanford. "Jewish-American Literature's Lost-and-Found Department: How
Philip Roth and Cynthia Ozick Reimagine Their Significant Dead." *Modern
Fiction Studies* 35.2 (Summer 1989): 223–35.

————. "Jewish Tradition and the Individual Talent." Bloom 121–25.

Pollitt, Katha. "The Three Selves of Cynthia Ozick." Bloom 63–67.

Poovey, Mary. "Feminism and Deconstruction." *Feminist Studies* 14.1 (Spring 1988): 51–65.

Pryse, Marjorie, and Hortense J. Spillers, eds. *Conjuring: Black Women, Fiction, and Literary Tradition.* Bloomington: Indiana UP, 1985.

Rainwater, Catherine, and William J. Scheick, eds. *Contemporary American Women Writers: Narrative Strategies.* Lexington: U of Kentucky P, 1985.

Ramsey, Jarold. *Reading the Fire: Essays in the Traditional Indian Literatures of the Far West.* Lincoln: U of Nebraska P, 1983.

Ravits, Martha. "Extending the American Range: Marilynne Robinson's *Housekeeping.*" *American Literature* 61.4 (December 1989): 644–66.

Reitlinger, Gerald. *Final Solution.* 2nd rev. and augm. ed. South Brunswick: T. Yoseloff, 1961.

Reynolds, Guy. *Willa Cather in Context: Progress, Race, Empire.* New York: St. Martin's, 1996.

Ricoeur, Paul. *Time and Narrative.* Chicago: U of Chicago P, 1985.

Rigney, Barbara Hill. *The Voices of Toni Morrison.* Columbus: Ohio State UP, 1991.

Rimmon-Kenan, Shlomith. "Narration, Doubt, Retrieval: Toni Morrison's *Beloved.*" *Narrative* 4.2 (May 1996): 109–23.

Robinson, Douglas. *American Apocalypses: The Image of the End of the World in American Literature.* Baltimore: Johns Hopkins UP, 1985.

Robinson, Marilynne. *Housekeeping.* New York: Bantam, 1980.

Robinson, Sally. *Engendering the Subject: Gender and Self-Representation in Contemporary Women's Fiction.* Albany: State U of New York P, 1991.

Roediger, David. *The Wages of Whiteness: Race and the Making of the American Working Class.* London and New York: Verso, 1991.

Rose, Elisabeth. "Cynthia Ozick's Liturgical Postmodernism: *The Messiah of Stockholm.*" *Studies in American Jewish Literature* 9.1 (Spring 1990): 93–107.

Rosenberg, Ruth. "Covenanted to the Law." Bloom 57–61.

Rosenmeier, Rosamond R. *Anne Bradstreet Revisited.* Boston: Twayne, 1991.

Rosowski, Susan J. *Approaches to Teaching Cather's My Ántonia.* New York: Modern Language Association of America, 1989.

————. "Willa Cather and the Fatality of Place: *O Pioneers! My Ántonia*, and *A Lost Lady.*" *Geography and Literature: A Meeting of the Disciplines.* Ed. William Mallory and Paul Simpson-Housley. Syracuse: Syracuse UP, 1987. 81–94.

Rovit, Earl. "The Two Languages of Cynthia Ozick." *Studies in American Jewish Literature* 8.1 (Spring 1989): 34–49.

Rowlandson, Mary White. *The Soveraignty and Goodness of God, together with the Faithfulness of His Promises Displayed; Being a Narrative of the Captivity and Restoration of Mrs. Mary Rowlandson, Commended by her to all that Desire to Know the Lord's Doings to, and Dealings with Her, Especially to her Dear Children and Relations* (Cambridge: Samuel Green, 1682), rpt. as *A Narrative of the Captivity and Removes of Mrs. Mary Rowlandson.* Fairfield, WA: Ye Galleon Press, 1974.

Rushdy, Ashraf H. A. "Rememory: Primal Scenes and Constructions in Toni Morrison's Novels." *Contemporary Literature* 31.3 (Fall 1990): 300–323.

Said, Edward. *Culture and Imperialism.* New York: Knopf, 1993.

Sanchez-Eppler, Karen. *Touching Liberty: Abolition, Feminism, and the Politics of the Body*. Berkeley: U of California P, 1993.

Sando, Joe S. *Pueblo Nations: Eight Centuries of Pueblo Indian History*. Santa Fe: Clear Light Publishers, 1992.

Sandoval, Cheyla. "U.S. Third World Feminism: The Theory and Method of Oppositional Consciousness in the Postmodern World." *Genders* 10 (Spring 1991): 1–24.

Scott, Joan W. *Gender and the Politics of History*. New York: Columbia UP, 1988.

Scrafford, Barbara. "Nature's Silent Scream: A Commentary on Cynthia Ozick's 'The Shawl.'" *Critique* (Fall 1989): 11–15.

Scruggs, Charles. *Sweet Home: Invisible Cities in the Afro-American Novel*. Baltimore: Johns Hopkins UP, 1993.

Seyersted, Per. *Leslie Marmon Silko*. Western Writers Series. Boise: Boise State UP, 1980.

Showalter, Elaine. "Feminist Criticism in the Wilderness." *Critical Inquiry* 8.2 (Winter 1981): 179–205.

Silko, Leslie Marmon. *Almanac of the Dead*. New York: Simon & Schuster, 1991; New York: Penguin Books, 1992.

———. *Ceremony*. 1977. New York: Viking Penguin, 1986.

———. Foreword. *Border Towns of the Navajo Nation*. Aaron Yiva. Alamo, CA: Holmganger, 1975. 1–5.

———. Interview in Coltelli 135–53.

———. Interview in Perry 313–40.

———. "An Old-Fashioned Indian Attack in Two Parts." *Yardbird Reader* 5 (1976): 77–84.

Simmons, William. *Cautantowwit's House: An Indian Burial Ground on the Island of Conanicut in Narragansett Bay*. Providence: Brown UP, 1970.

Sivanandan, A. "RAT and the Degradation of Black Struggle." *Race and Class* 24 (1985): 1–33.

Slote, Bernice, ed. *The Kingdom of Art: Willa Cather's First Principles and Critical Statements, 1893–1896*. Lincoln: U of Nebraska P, 1966.

Slotkin, Richard. *Regeneration Through Violence: The Mythology of the American Frontier, 1600–1860*. Middletown: Wesleyan UP, 1973.

Slotkin, Richard, and James K. Folsom, eds. *So Dreadfull a Judgment: Puritan Responses to King Philip's War, 1676–1677*. Middletown: Wesleyan UP, 1978.

Smith, Patricia. "Writer Toni Morrison Swings to 'Jazz.'" *Boston Globe* 28 April 1992: 60–63.

Smith, Valerie. *Self-Discovery and Authority in Afro-American Narrative*. Cambridge: Harvard UP, 1987.

———. "Split Affinities: The Case of Interracial Rape." *Conflicts in Feminism*. Ed. Marianne Hirsch and Evelyn Fox Keller. New York: Routledge, 1990. 271–87.

Sokoloff, Naomi. *Imagining the Child in Modern Jewish Fiction*. Baltimore: Johns Hopkins UP, 1992.

Sollors, Werner. "Foreword." Boelhower 1–4.

Sollors, Werner, and Maria Diedrich, eds. *The Black Columbiad: Defining Moments in African American Literature and Culture*. Cambridge: Harvard UP, 1994.

Spelman, Elizabeth V. *Inessential Woman: Problems of Exclusion in Feminist Thought*. Boston: Beacon, 1988.

Spender, Dale. *The Writing or the Sex? or, Why You Don't Have to Read Women's*

Writing to Know It's No Good. New York: Pergamon, 1989.

Spiller, Robert E., Willard Thorp, Thomas H. Johnson, Henry Seidel Canby, and Richard M. Ludwig, eds. *Literary History of the United States*. 1946. New York: Macmillan, 1963.

Spillers, Hortense. "Changing the Letter: The Yokes, the Jokes of Discourse, or, Mrs. Stowe, Mr. Reed." *Slavery and the Literary Imagination*. Ed. Deborah McDowell and Arnold Rampersad. Baltimore: Johns Hopkins UP, 1989. 25–61. Rpt. in *Uncle Tom's Cabin*. By Harriet Beecher Stowe. Ed. Elizabeth Ammons. New York: Norton, 1994. 542–68.

———, ed. *Comparative American Identities: Race, Sex, and Nationality in the Modern Text*. Essays from the English Institute. New York: Routledge, 1991.

———. "Mama's Baby, Papa's Maybe: An American Grammar Book." *diacritics* 17.2 (Summer 1987): 65–81.

Spivak, Gayatri Chakravorty. *In Other Worlds: Essays in Cultural Politics*. New York: Routledge, 1988.

Stanford, Ann. *Anne Bradstreet: The Worldly Puritan*. New York: Burt Franklin, 1974.

Steiner, George. *Language and Silence: Essays on Language, Literature, and the Inhuman*. New York: Atheneum, 1967.

Stern, Julia. "Excavating Genre in *Our Nig. American Literature* 67.3 (September 1995): 439–66.

Stimpson, Catherine R. *Where the Meanings Are: Feminism and Cultural Spaces*. New York: Methuen, 1988.

Stowe, Harriet Beecher. *Uncle Tom's Cabin*. 1852. Ed. Elizabeth Ammons. New York: Norton, 1994.

Suleiman, Susan Rubin, ed. *The Female Body in Western Culture: Contemporary Perspectives*. Cambridge: Harvard UP, 1986.

Sundquist, Eric J., ed. *New Essays on Uncle Tom's Cabin*. New York: Cambridge UP, 1986.

Tate, Claudia. *Black Women Writers at Work*. New York: Continuum, 1983.

Thoreau, Henry David. *Walden and "Civil Disobedience."* Ticknor and Fields, 1854; New York: Viking Penguin, 1983.

Todorov, Tzvetan. "'Race,' Writing, and Culture." Trans. Loulou Mack. Gates, *Race* 370–80.

Tompkins, Jane. "'Indians': Textualism, Morality, and the Problem of History." Gates, *Race* 59–77.

———. *Sensational Designs: The Cultural Work of American Fiction, 1790–1860*. New York: Oxford UP, 1985.

———. "Sentimental Power: *Uncle Tom's Cabin* and the Politics of Literary History." *Glyph 2*. 1978. Rpt. in *Uncle Tom's Cabin*. By Harriet Beecher Stowe. Ed. Elizabeth Ammons. New York: Norton, 1994. 501–22.

Toulouse, Teresa A. "'My Own Credit': Strategies of (E)Valuation in Mary Rowlandson's Captivity Narrative." *American Literature* 64.4 (December 1992): 655–76.

Trilling, Lionel. "Art and Fortune." *The Liberal Imagination*. New York: Viking, 1950.

Mrs. Nicholas Trist Papers, Southern Historical Collection, UNC Library, Chapel Hill.

Trumbull, John. *The Adventures of Daniel Boone . . . [and] A Narrative of the captivity, and extraordinary escape of Mrs. Francis Scott*. Norwich, CT: John

Trumbull, 1786.

TuSmith, Bonnie. *All My Relatives: Community in Contemporary Ethnic American Literatures*. Ann Arbor: U of Michigan P, 1993.

Uffen, Ellen Serlen. "The Levity of Cynthia Ozick." *Studies in American Jewish Literature* 6 (Fall 1987): 53–63.

VanDerBeets, Richard. *The Indian Captivity Narrative: An American Genre*. Lanham, MD: UP of America, 1984.

Velie, Alan. "The Trickster Novel." Vizenor 121–39.

Vida, Nina. *Between Sisters*. New York: Crown, 1996.

Vizenor, Gerald. "Trickster Discourse: Comic Holotropes and Language Games." *Narrative Chance: Postmodern Discourse on Native American Literatures*. Ed. Gerald Vizenor. Albuquerque: U of New Mexico P, 1989. 187–211.

Walker, Cheryl. *The Nightingale's Burden: Women Poets and American Culture before 1900*. Bloomington: Indiana UP, 1982.

Washington, Mary Helen. *Invented Lives: Narratives of Black Women, 1860–1960*. Garden City, NY: Doubleday, 1987.

Weed, Elizabeth, ed. *Coming to Terms: Feminism, Theory, Politics*. New York: Routledge, 1989.

Welter, Barbara. *Dimity Convictions: The American Woman in Nineteenth-Century Literature*. Athens: Ohio UP, 1976.

White, Deborah. *Ar'n't I a Woman? Female Slaves in the Plantation South*. New York: Norton, 1985.

White, Hayden. "The Value of Narrativity in the Representation of Reality." *On Narrative*. Ed. W. J. T. Mitchell. Chicago: U of Chicago P, 1980. 1–23.

White, Jonathan, ed. *Recasting the World: Writing after Colonialism*. Baltimore: Johns Hopkins UP, 1993.

Wiesel, Elie. *A Jew Today*. Trans. Marion Weisel. New York: Random House, 1978.

———. *Legends of Our Time*. Trans. Steven Donadio. New York: Holt, Rinehart & Winston, 1968.

———. *Night; Dawn; Day*. Northvale, NJ: Aronson, 1985.

Wilson, Christopher P. "Charlotte Perkins Gilman's Steady Burghers: The Terrain of *Herland*." *Women's Studies* 12 (1986): 271–92.

Wilson, Harriet. *Our Nig; or, Sketches from the Life of a Free Black, in a Two-Story White House, North. Showing That Slavery's Shadows Fall Even There*. 1859. New York: Random House, 1983.

Wilt, Judith. *Abortion, Choice, and Contemporary Fiction*. Chicago: U of Chicago P, 1989.

Winsbro, Bonnie. *Supernatural Forces: Belief, Difference, and Power in Contemporary Works by Ethnic Women*. Amherst: U of Massachusetts P, 1993.

Wisse, Ruth. "Ozick as American Jewish Writer." Bloom 35–45.

Wolff, Cynthia Griffin. "'Margaret Garner': A Cincinnati Story." *Discovering Difference: Contemporary Essays in American Culture*. Ed. Christoph K. Lohmann. Bloomington: Indiana UP, 1993. 105–22.

———. "'Masculinity' in *Uncle Tom's Cabin*." *American Quarterly* 47.4 (December 1995): 595–618.

Woolley, Paula. "Fire and Wit: Storytelling and the American Artist in Cather's *My Ántonia*." *Cather Studies*. 3. Ed. Susan J. Rosowski. Lincoln: U of Nebraska P, 1996. 149–81.

Yezierska, Anzia. *Arrogant Beggar*. 1927, 1954. Durham: Duke UP, 1996.

———. *Bread Givers: A Struggle Between a Father of the Old World and a Daughter of the New*. 1925. New York: Persea Books, 1975.

———. *Hungry Hearts and Other Stories.* 1920. New York: Persea Books, 1985.

Zaborowska, Magdalena. *How We Found America: Reading Gender Through East European Immigrant Narratives.* Chapel Hill: U of North Carolina P, 1995.

Zafar, Rafia. "Capturing the Captivity: African Americans Among the Puritans." *MELUS* 17.2 (Summer 1991–1992): 19–35.

Index

About the Author

AMY S. GOTTFRIED is Assistant Professor of Rhetoric at Boston University's College of General Studies. In the Fall of 1998 she is moving to Maryland where she will be an Assistant Professor at Hood College. She has contributed to such publications as *African American Review*, *Studies in American Jewish Literature*, the *Oxford Companion to Women's Writings in the United States*, and the *Oxford Companion to African American Literature*.

ISBN 0-313-30160-3

HARDCOVER BAR CODE